Class, Race, and Labor

Class, Race, and Labor

WORKING-CLASS CONSCIOUSNESS IN DETROIT

JOHN C. LEGGETT

New York OXFORD UNIVERSITY PRESS 1968

To the
Detroit auto workers and the
Delano strikers.
May their alliance
spark the rejuvenation of the
labor movement.

Preface

In the United States, we can now apply survey research techniques to study class, race, and consciousness within an insurrectionary context. Times have changed since we did our study of working-class consciousness eight years ago. As a result we did not observe these three phenomena as our restive cities entered an insurrectionary stage of politics halfway through this decade. But we did examine the class consciousness and electoral politics of people found in a large industrial community immediately prior to what has become the revolutionary present. Many working-class people are angry and militant because of contemporary and past problems, some of which we have examined in this study of Detroit.

Today, with all hell breaking loose in our larger cities, we can understand why social scientists might be interested in studying class consciousness in black and white working-class communities. But why did we initiate such a study of Detroit workers eight years ago? What motivated people like us, a group of graduate students at the University of Michigan? Perhaps the desire to declare irrelevant the pronouncements enunciated by the sociological establishment of the 1950's moved us as young social scientists to do something. Whatever the motivation, we decided to translate rejection into study, and in this respect, Karl Marx and C. Wright Mills inspired many of the leftist graduate students of the 1950's.

Our dependence on Marx and the young Mills led us to doubt a myth that had become quite widespread during that period. According to this formulation, working-class consciousness had disappeared in the United States, precisely because of the bountiful rewards made available to almost everyone within the affluent society. Because of the new prosperity, working-class persons had lost the capacity for identification with their class, although, as some would admit, a few old-timers from the 'thirties had clung to the categories of the past; certainly there were no outstanding groups opposed to mainstream thinking on the essential classlessness of the United States. Could we believe it?

To many of us, these analyses were unacceptable, only because the journalists and experts were stereotyping class attitudes and consequently depicting them as lacking variability. These alleged "class" attitudes purported to describe the views of almost all workmen. From our own observations, we knew that in Detroit (and in the United States as a whole) the working class was, and remains, a motley crew, individuals and sub-groups with quite different relations to the world of work, employment, unions, and landlords. These four considerations have traditionally been crucial in determining class attitudes. Where one works, whether one works, how one works, and how one lives have been historically very significant in deciding whether blue-collar people become militant or otherwise. As history has indicated and as social science has demonstrated, when blue-collar workers are industrial workmen, union men, unemployed, and tenants they tend to think differently from home-owning, manual service workers who are employed and not in unions. Indeed, these two diverse categories of workmen move in quite different worlds, although they may live in the same community.

If this has been the case historically, why shouldn't these differences appear in Detroit? Why should this industrial town, one with both a diverse working-class population as well as a long history of class and class-racial struggle, be an exception? Consequently, we decided to study the distribution of class attitudes within a large segment of Detroit's blue-collar world. We also observed the connection between class views and class votes. What we found has led us to believe that facile generalizations on the disappearance of class consciousness are false.

Sacramento   J.C.L.
January 1968

Acknowledgments

I would like to thank the many people who made this study possible. First, the blue-collar workers who consented to be interviewed and who tolerated our delving into their private thoughts and gave us their time.

I am also fortunate in having had the critical observations of many staff members of both the University of Michigan and the University of California. To David Aberle I am indebted for his comments on economy and outlook. Herbert Blumer discussed my ideas on class consciousness, union membership, and voting. Morris Janowitz offered provocative comments on the relationship of ethnic groups and downward mobility to working-class attitudes. I am also grateful to Daniel Katz for his penetrating suggestions on the content of class views. In addition, Werner Landecker's criticisms and suggestions conceptualizing the major sources of working-class consciousness helped enormously. Eugene Litwak was a source of numerous insights, especially in our discussion of block clubs. Guy Swanson alerted me to the sources, contents, and functions of variable experience—including consciousness. Harold Wilensky made me sensitive to the use of precise categorical distinctions for dealing with class consciousness, and he alerted me to the many forces which work against the formation and retention of consciousness. His analysis of the downwardly mobile was also helpful. David Street made many fruitful suggestions on working-class Negroes and their potential militancy.

The research was supported by the Social Science Research Council, the Department of Sociology of the University of Michigan, the Rackham School of Graduate Studies, Wayne State University, and Simon Fraser University. All are to be thanked for their support of an endeavor which must have appeared adventurous in the extreme at the time the project was conceived.

Many people have helped to conduct the study and gather information for this book, particularly Dr. Robert Mowitz and John Gilmore, both members of the Wayne State University Political Science Department. The core of the project labor force consisted of students enrolled in a public opinion and pressure groups course given at Wayne State University during the Spring semester of 1960. These students did the bulk of the interviewing and a great deal of clerical work as well. I would also like to thank the secretarial staff of the Wayne State University Political Science Department for their assistance.

Miss Florence Cassidy of the United Community Services of Metropolitan Detroit offered advice on the location of ethnic groups in the city, and her knowledge was instrumental in our selecting certain key areas for sampling purposes. Dozens of others helped me in one way or another. Karel and Marga Beth Cibulka co-ordinated field work in its final stages and were of great assistance in interviewing and coding. Karel's ability to speak Polish and German and Marga Beth's capacity to charm difficult Polish and Negro workers were invaluable aids.

The list of those who performed outstandingly in this study would not be complete without the names of Lloyd Douglas and John Magney. Mr. Douglas did an excellent job of interviewing unco-operative respondents. In addition, he performed much of the repetitive and in other ways unrewarding work. For the chapter on class consciousness and voting and that on block clubs

Mr. Magney's critical comments proved to be extremely helpful.

Valuable criticisms of the manuscript were made by Irving Louis Horowitz, Sheldon Meyer, and Phillip Lillienthal. They helped immeasurably in sharpening the focus of the book.

The study owes its completion in large measure to the editorial acumen and unfailing encouragement of my wife, Iris. She also typed the bulk of the text. For their fine typing, proofreading, and tabular work, I also wish to thank Shirley Anderson, Mary Balfry, Lynn Crescione, Carol Clymo, Lena Dominelli, Pat Ferguson, Norrine Gallisdorfer, and Jackie Smedley.

My greatest indebtedness is to Dr. Gerhard E. Lenski, who advised and encouraged me from the very beginning of the research, and whose ideas permeate this book. His suggestion concerning the utility of treating class consciousness in terms of degree is an entirely new tack in the empirical study of this subject.

Finally, I salute all of the study's workers, most of whom endured their subordinate and insecure positions without developing a high degree of class consciousness, a radical expression of which might have undermined our study of Detroit blue-collar workers.

Contents

Class, Race, and Labor

Introduction: Class, Thought, and Action

Our Times and Class Consciousness

With the rebirth of American radicalism during the 1960's in Detroit, Vicksburg, Watts, Chicago, and other communities, there is a renewed interest in working-class consciousness. Not that we expect workmen to emancipate mankind. Our hopes are limited: experience has tempered expectations. And workers are not heroic; nor do they share the mentality ascribed to them either by Marxist intellectuals or elitist cynics. In fact, workers are variegated: black and white; bright and dumb; those who belong to unions, those who do not; those who have known economic insecurity, and those who have not. Above all, most workers lead ordinary lives. They eat, drink, work, vacation, fornicate, and think. Yet class views do color the opinions of some workers more than of others. Consequently, it is foolish to generalize about the working class, treating it as a homogeneous lot.[1]

Professionals, however, have created a stereotype of the workman. Reformers have often assumed that working-class people are incapable of making rational decisions. Supposedly they require professional aid and leadership. This view must now be reconsidered at a time when some Americans are turning to an idea filled with explosive implications: namely, let the people themselves identify their problems and determine what they need to solve them. Let them run their own neighborhoods, their

3

own unions. Above all, let there be an alternative to the paternalism of welfare and union bureaucracies.[2]

In the light of this and other issues, a return to the subject of working-class consciousness should not entail using stereotypes to describe working-class people. Rather, it demands analysis that is both careful and detailed: What do we mean by working-class consciousness? What are its sources? What, if any, are its political consequences, and when do they occur?

The Negro Revolt: Its Class Content

These questions cannot fail to pique our imaginations now when many American Negroes have displayed class consciousness by expressing militant views and by taking aggressive political action. The militant Negro is particularly common among blue-collar workers found in large urban ghettoes. Almost a decade ago, unemployed Negroes living in Detroit expressed startling opinions on what might happen if America were to have another great depression. Here is what they said:

> There'd be widespread riots. People would be out after hunger and clothes. Those with money won't be very comfortable.

> There'd be destruction by the people, breaking into homes, they'd rob banks. Some guys with jobs would be scared to walk home. There would be a civil war between the rich and poor. They'd kick the shit out of some of those people.

> It may be called a revolution. If he gets hungry, he won't stand for it. The young people won't take it. They will steal. A lot of them steal now because they aren't working.

> I'm almost scared to say. So many things could happen . . . . The younger generation won't take it; a lot of bad things would happen. Couldn't hardly go out of their doors. In fact, they might have a war here in the U.S. People are used to a good way of living. Every time you pick up a paper, you hear about robbery and killing. Take me. I got kids, think I'm going to let them go hungry? Even the welfare won't

give you anything. This is the first time I've ever been out of a job. I've always worked. I don't know what I'll do when my compensation runs out. People got homes and cars now, and they aren't going to stand around and lose them. Take this place. I just bought it. I haven't got enough paint to paint it. Have to use my money to feed my kids.

Could not be nothing but a war. The people would start fighting because people have to have something to feed their family on. I know I would. If things don't pick up, God knows what will happen. If they don't stop this discrimination, there is going to a civil war. A man is a man; that's all I think about it.

The poor would be trying to get food and things and the rich would try to keep theirs.

Oh hot! Everybody would get a ball bat and start swinging.[3]

These attitudes are not unique. Today many Negroes express their anger over economic inequity even in times of prosperity. Watts and Detroit Negroes demonstrated how they felt toward the private property of businessmen. The Watts insurrection indicated not only contempt for the rule of law, but a commitment to the acquisition of commodities. Many Negroes looted in an attempt to redistribute the wealth. Yet more was involved. When they spoke of the insurrection, they talked about the positive aspects of their escapades; many were proud of their trophies. They gave strong indications of believing that their actions were legitimate. They seldom evinced regret, for they believed they had given the business community the kind of treatment it deserved.[4]

Many analysts dismiss the views of these Negro workers, labeling their opinions as petulant and regarding them as irrelevant for American politics. Others say these attitudes and actions represent a loss of faith in government and capitalism. This loss is bad, they add. That Negro workmen have unwisely abandoned their sense of respect for political authority and private property is, to these critics, the major concern. Thus, they regard the problem as one of restoration of loyalty and not redistribution of wealth.

Both these interpretations overlook the possibility of rational pursuit of working-class objectives. Furthermore, they create a stereotype that ignores the sources, content, and consequences of class consciousness. These are the concern of this book.

The Sources of Consciousness: A Static View Versus the Relevance of Change

The perspectives of blue-collar workers stem largely from the workplace and neighborhood structure. Both appear to be major determinants of outlook, but work ties seem to be especially relevant in casting class views.

Here we follow Marx, who viewed relations between working class and employing class as significant sources of class opinions. From his point of view, economic dislocations create friction between employers and workmen which engenders the development and reinforcement of working-class consciousness. This consciousness may in turn have political consequences, as it finds expression in the political process. Indeed, a modern industrial city such as Detroit, Akron, or South Bend may foster consciousness and provide outlets for its expression.

The city, however, includes not only workplace but neighborhood, and when workmen are concentrated in residential pockets, the neighborhood will give their lives a collective quality as they become dependent upon one another. Marx did not foresee the significance of neighborhood organization, for to him its destruction was predictably linked to an industrial division of labor. Marx saw only that industrialization shattered neighborhood structures in town and country and failed to create them in industrial settings. Today, however, social scientists would be foolish to avoid the significance of the neighborhood, for block and neighborhood groups concerned with self-help are springing up all over industrial America, especially in the Negro ghettoes.

These local groups may someday become as important as unions. Neighborhood conflicts would thereby take their place next to conflicting relations at work as important influences on how workmen think and act. Students of society need to be concerned with the development of contemporary relations between groups in order to assess the sources and direction of class consciousness.

In this sense, the past is important. Yesterday's class struggles created class consciousness in industrial America. Workers fought and criticized capitalism, and mental residues of these conflicts are still with us. An unusually large number of Depression generation workers continue to express militant opinions at a time when capitalism has already reached an advanced stage. But class conflicts are not unique to the past generations. Economic insecurity and class interests are common to the present age even though today's problems stem from relatively new factors—automation, plant relocations, and other structural considerations. These foster the formation of class views among many workmen, but especially among uprooted Negroes who belong to industrial unions. In other words, Negroes become more militant when they move from agrarian regions to industrial cities and when they subsequently join industrial unions.

Past observers have focused exclusively on white workmen. While it is true that the exclusion of Negroes simplifies class analysis, it is only when we include Negro workmen that we can hope to grasp the range of class views within the blue-collar world. In addition to noting the differential incidence of class consciousness among ethnic and racial groups, we wish to consider another aspect of the subject: the political importance of class consciousness.

Briefly, it is our contention that class perspectives have an impact on political choices, especially among those who belong to a politicized union; furthermore, that racial differences engender an uneven distribution of class consciousness within the working class; but that class consciousness *per se* has a predictable impact upon the political actions of workmen.

1

Sources and Consequences of
Working-Class Consciousness

Both economic insecurity and working-class organizational affiliation are the important sources of working-class consciousness in industrial societies, while class consciousness in turn helps to determine how people act politically.

Economic insecurity takes at least three forms—agrarian-industrial mobility (as in the case of uprooted workers), tenuous occupational position (as among the unemployed), and membership in a marginal racial or ethnic group (as in the case of Negro blue-collar workers). When one or more of these characteristics is shared by unionized workmen, the net result is an accentuation of class consciousness. Furthermore, regardless of the source, class consciousness becomes significant politically when there is widespread economic insecurity, progressive party organization, a pro-labor candidate, and a political labor union.

Three Labor Force Considerations

When a person or group is marginal to the labor force, it will seek ways to eliminate this insecurity. In so doing, it creates unions [1] and other organizations. As workers begin to deal with their economic problems, they develop a class frame of reference.

Class consciousness is significant not only in capitalist but in socialist countries as well, for governmental controls and ownership have not eliminated job insecurity and consequent worker organization. However, for the purposes of analysis, we will confine the scope of these general remarks to capitalist societies.

Industrial societies at all stages of development have multiple forms of economic insecurity and labor organization. In early industrialization, where the stress is on the development of primary (i.e., extractive) and secondary (i.e., manufacturing) industries, mining and factory organizations subject their new labor force to the vicissitudes that we associate with sharp dips in the business cycle. In an advanced industrial society, with its tendency to emphasize rapid automation and labor force reorganization, business subjects the labor force to structural and psychological insecurities by eliminating occupational positions, minimizing workers' control over pace and kind of work, and in some cases, by severely limiting entire regional economies.

Whatever the stage of industrialization, we observe that for many workers different forms of insecurity generally occur, and may overlap one another. Many workers, for example, experience a series of economic mishaps, several of which come at the same time. When we analyze these events as they occur *seriatim*, we obtain a more accurate basis for judging why many workmen become class conscious. For we can observe the impact of the events, and at the same time gauge their interrelatedness (such as the connection between uprootedness and subsequent tenuous job security in an industrial city), as they come to bear on the creation of class consciousness.

If we consider types of marginality that are associated with a society's labor force, three types appear to be crucial and interconnected. These are: agrarian-industrial mobility, tenuous occupational position, and working-class membership in a marginal racial or ethnic group.

Agrarian-industrial mobility occurs when people move from a low-prestige class position in an agrarian region to another low-status class position in an industrial area. Perhaps we can best understand the importance of agrarian-industrial mobility by showing its connection to agrarian-industrial and industrial (whether early or advanced) societies.

In an agrarian-industrial society, industrial organization plays a relatively unimportant part in the total economy, while the labor force derives its livelihood primarily from agricultural pursuits. Yet the society has been touched by industrialization, as evidenced by the beginnings of modern transportation networks, mining, and light industry. Also, trade has developed between it and industrial societies, as indicated by its dependence on markets in more developed countries. An example would be Canada prior to World War I, when the society was overwhelmingly agricultural, but nonetheless committed to the development of its lumber, mining, and other primary industries which were geared to the import needs of England and the United States. Another example would be Yugoslavia immediately before World War II. At that time, British and French firms played a leading role in developing the mining and railroad industries, while the country as a whole remained overwhelmingly agricultural.[2]

Theoretically, an industrial society exists when the population depends almost entirely upon industrial employment for its sustenance, and agriculture supplies only a fraction of the population with its livelihood. Most of the people are located within industrial regions, and the economic and social structure rests upon a modern technological base. Obvious examples would be contemporary United States and Great Britain.

In an industrial society, however, one may find areas where industry creates relatively little wealth, and where the population maintains agrarian forms of social organization and values. Such an enclave may be called an *agrarian region*. In many ways, the social organization and value system of an agrarian region are like those of an agrarian-industrial society. Our Appalachia would be a good illustration. Another example would be the Scottish highlands.

Agrarian regions should not be confused with rural areas in industrial regions. Industrial regions such as the Midwest may well contain rural areas like the corn belt, that is, clusters of agricultural (and/or mining) communities equipped with modern technological equipment and tightly integrated into the industrial economy. As such, these rural areas differ considerably from agrarian regions, such as Appalachia, which rest upon a less developed technology and an economy closer to subsistence level.

Movement from agrarian to industrial regions has been a common phenomenon in Europe and elsewhere for the last two centuries. Former peasants have frequently taken positions as industrial workers. Indeed, their movement and resettlement has constituted the human base for the industrialization of many societies. Without them, industrial societies would have been unable to work mines, to construct steel mills, and to operate mass industries. When peasants or other inhabitants of an agrarian area move to an industrial region and become part of the working class, the process may be called *agrarian-industrial mobility,* and those who make this transition may be labeled "the uprooted." [3]

The uprooted have difficulties in adapting readily to the needs of a modern industrial labor force. Their few saleable skills, their lack of formal education, their commitment to agrarian values, indeed, their initial gullibility, place them in positions where they may be exploited by employers. When uprooted employees are treated in this manner, and when they couple these experiences with similar circumstances that drove them out of agrarian regions, they acquire a propensity to express class opinions. This tendency finds its fullest expression when workmen move to an industrial town whose working class has effectively confronted employers on matters of pay and production and has consequently created a class frame of reference for the working class as a whole. The uprooted in industrial towns such as Detroit, Toledo, Montreal, and Cleveland thus express a high degree of class consciousness.

Industrial mobility refers to movement within or between industrial regions, when individuals move from one blue-collar position to another, or in some cases, from mechanized farming to industry. Such individuals may be called "prepared," because they have acquired skills that facilitate their adaptation to an industrial community. Consequently, the prepared should be less class conscious that the uprooted.

Tenuous occupational position refers to workers who are not employed, those who face the immediate probability of becoming unemployed, particularly due to a contraction in the labor force (not because of racial or ethnic discrimination), and those who have little control over the pace and kind of work they do. For example, during a recession, we would find the unemployed as well as the lesser skilled to be highly class conscious. Or if workmen face a company policy of speed-up of work (and hence a violation of contract) and if they protest, they might well lose their jobs. Here, economic insecurity stems from the workers' lack of authority to decide how goods are to be produced. Admittedly, control over production is less significant for workmen than unemployment, especially during times of economic recession or its immediate aftermath. Hence, the reader should not be surprised by our emphasis on unemployment, since this study was conducted shortly after the end of a recession.

Of course, many workers are involved in short-term unemployment of the kind seldom associated with insecure occupational position. For the purpose of analysis, it was necessary to include the short-term, i.e., frictional unemployed, since only by combining the long- and short-term unemployed were we able to obtain a sufficient number of cases for statistical analysis. However, the use of a broad category that includes both the frictional as well as the long-term (structural) unemployed does not help gain acceptance of the assumptions herein made on the significance of marginal occupational position, for it forces us to include among the insecure many who are only slightly less likely than the employed to keep their occupations.

Another conceptual problem might occur to the reader when he ponders what we except from inclusion within the rubric "tenuous occupational position." This category would fail to include the uprooted, for their problem is not only one of finding and retaining employment when unskilled, but of avoiding and resisting exploitation when employed. For these workers, avoidance of excessive exploitation would apply not only at a particular point in time but would have reference to their entire biography—experienced past, questionable present, and anticipated future. Hence, the uprooted worker is more than a person without ready employment or usable skill for a limited span in time.

Working-class membership in a marginal racial (or ethnic) group is another source of class consciousness. A racial (or ethnic) group is marginal when the cultural values of an industrial society and/or a dominant class move employers to engage in racial discrimination against marginal *workmen* both at work and elsewhere. Such discrimination contributes to their job insecurity, social isolation, sub-cultural homogeneity, intensive interaction within a proletarian-class minority sub-community, and organized protest and class (or class-racial) consciousness. Marginal workmen subject to this discrimination become an isolated substratum within the working class, a pocket of beleaguered blue-collar people who belong to the same race, a group quite distinct from working-class groups found within the dominant racial group (yet quite similar to workers found in other racial groups that are collectivities with little prestige, power, and wealth). Marginal workers (such as Negroes) may be uprooted or prepared, occupants of tenuous occupational positions or participants with high-seniority employment. In this respect, the proletarianized racial enclave is heterogeneous, but it nonetheless acquires unique characteristics, a point worthy of elaboration.

MARGINAL AND MAINSTREAM WORKING CLASS

Crucial to an understanding of the differing class perspectives of urban American workmen in an advanced industrial community is the distinction between the *marginal* and *mainstream* working class, for the marginal working class has many of the characteristics (described by Marx, and Kerr and Siegel) conducive to the formation of class consciousness.[4]

The *marginal* working class refers to a sub-community of workers who belong to a subordinate ethnic or racial group which is unusually proletarianized and highly segregated. Workmen of this type fill many manual roles in heavy industry and face an inordinate amount of economic insecurity. This is evidenced by their large concentration in marginal occupational positions, their lack of formal education, and finally and most obviously, their high rate of unemployment. These factors are related, the high unemployment rate stemming in large part from inadequate training and selective job hiring, which can be traced to racial prejudice and discrimination because of low prestige. In turn, their low prestige derives largely from their historic lack of power, i.e., an inability to manipulate society's political and economic institutions that allocate wealth, power, and hence prestige.

This particular working-class minority, this working-class racial group sharing the same sub-cultural traditions—is considerably isolated from the remainder of the community in general and from the middle class in particular. Its assimilation being thus limited, its homogeneity is accentuated. Most of these working-class people share values and norms based upon a common place of origin, similar levels of educational achievement, near-identical class backgrounds, and intermarriages and friendships among the group. When they join recreational, religious, and political organizations, they generally remain inside their community. However, some social relationships do cross racial or ethnic boundaries to link members of different groups within labor organizations. For example, industrial labor unions accept marginal group workmen.

In fact, a disproportionately large number of them belong to industrial unions. They develop reciprocal ties with mainstream workmen as they become experienced unionists.

Because of their successful involvement in industrial unions, marginal workmen cannot be characterized as completely isolated or desperately poor. By working-class standards, the majority earn medium and sometimes high incomes, although almost all of them are economically insecure, a consideration which accentuates their unrest and militancy.

The term *mainstream* working class denotes a category of workers who are culturally heterogeneous and who also belong to a dominant *racial* group, one whose occupational composition is disproportionately white-collar. Like marginal workmen, they are also found in an urban, advanced industrial setting. But unlike marginal workmen, they enjoy considerable economic security, in part because they predominate in the more educated and skilled categories of the labor force. These qualifications plus high racial or ethnic prestige enhance their relations with middle-class members of their own group and limit ties with members of the marginal working class. In fact, almost all their close relationships occur within their own racial or ethnic group, and familial, peer, and similar relationships often extend across class lines and promote discrimination in their favor. (See page 37 for a schematic specification of class structure in the modern industrial community.) In this sense, mainstream workmen differ considerably from marginal workers and express relatively less class consciousness.[5]

Working-Class Organization: An Additional Consideration

Economic insecurity contributes strongly to working-class consciousness but does not by itself create it. Organizations also help bring about class consciousness; hence, we must take them into account.

Working-class organizations committed to advancing the economic interests of blue-collar people are of two types. Work groups generally take the form of _unions_. In fact, for the United States, the key work group has been the union, of both the craft and industrial variety. In addition, there are *neighborhood organizations* which attempt to advance the material interests of the working class. Both groups are significant because they have the potential to interpret events for workmen in terms of class categories and to involve workers in confrontations or conflicts with business firms, the result of which creates consciousness.

Unions are the more important of these two types of organizations, for they have the most bearing on sustenance, an item of considerable interest to workmen when they contemplate maintenance and advancement of their personal and family interests. Because of this vital connection, unions provide the lead on matters conducive to the formation and reinforcement of class opinions. Although unions are significant sources of class consciousness in all stages of all industrial societies, they appear to be most important in communities where they have conducted successful economic and political struggles and won positive recognition among union people—cities such as Flint, Akron, and Detroit; Vancouver, Winnipeg, and Sudbury; Liverpool, Birmingham, and London; and Calais, Marseilles, and Lyons.

The Multi-Faceted Character of Working-Class Consciousness

Too often we treat class consciousness as a quality either present or absent, much as we would define a person as a Catholic or non-Catholic (using a nominal scale of measurement).[6] Actually, class orientation is seldom ordered in such terms; rather, it builds step-by-step (ordinal) as on a continuum.[7]

Whatever its degree, class consciousness may combine with racial or ethnic consciousness. Many class conflicts reflect this blending. In some situations, for example, employers are predominantly members of one race, and discriminate against a marginal segment of the working class. The net result is the creation of considerable class-racial consciousness among working-class people in the marginal racial group.

The Political Consequences of Working-Class Consciousness

In *early* stages of industrial society, class consciousness is frequently associated with revolutionary social movements. In *advanced* industrial societies and communities, however, class consciousness is seldom linked with calls for total reorganization of society. Instead, class consciousness finds political expression in reform or labor parties, unless a war paralyzes the economy for a prolonged period of time or threatens to destroy it. In that case, working-class consciousness becomes tied to radical movements committed to seizure of state power and property transformation.

Returning to the reformist context, the one most common in advanced industrial societies, class consciousness aids reform politics only when: (1) large sections of the working class face an economic crisis, and class issues (such as unemployment) loom as significant; (2) a political party presents a program in keeping with working-class interests and needs on relevant issues; (3) a pro-labor candidate supports this party program; and (4) a labor union takes advantage of the times and activates workmen, supports the pro-labor party, and embraces the pro-labor politician.

A Composite View of Consciousness and Action

A particular worker would in all likelihood become highly class conscious if he came from an agrarian region, settled in an industrial town, belonged to a marginal racial or ethnic group, joined a labor union, and lived in a neighborhood whose inhabitants were concerned with unemployment and housing, as well as with less controversial issues. With class consciousness emerging from this background, he would cast a class-conscious vote when the times demanded it, the party solicited it, the candidate sought it, and the union endorsed it.

2

Sources and Consequences of Working-Class Consciousness: Classical Arguments

Affluence and the Absence of Consciousness

It must be obvious to the reader by now that we question the view which holds that modern industrial capitalism has eliminated economic insecurity and tranquilized all levels of labor organization so that conditions no longer generate class consciousness and class politics. Specifically, we hold that agrarian-industrial mobility is not confined to early industrialization, although its relative incidence is greatest at this stage. Correlatively, we reject the view that the affluent society, the welfare state, the giant corporation, and union leaders have eradicated occupational insecurities. Although their importance may swell and dissipate in wave-like fashion, through time they nonetheless give rise to class consciousness, sometimes with racial overtones.

We also challenge the view that marginal racial group position creates race consciousness only and fails to produce class consciousness. Similarly, we feel that marginality to the labor force creates more than pockets of concern over obtaining and keeping a job. In maintaining that labor force marginality and trade unions engender class as well as job consciousness, we disagree with Selig Perlman [1] and others who have emphasized job consciousness. At the same time, we part company with those

Marxists who point to the presence of class consciousness, but who exclude the significance of the racial factor in accounting for the content and disposition of working-class consciousness. Although Perlman's and Marx's arguments are replete with weaknesses of this kind, both general positions contain elements of truth, a point we will now consider.

Job Consciousness Only?

The classical arguments over the relevance of economic relations to class consciousness have ignored the racial overtones of many class conflicts, preferring instead to focus on the significance of workplace and union membership. The school associated with the writings of Karl Marx and followers of the views of Selig Perlman have continued to shape the character of research on class and working-class consciousness. Both groups have uncovered information relevant for social sciences and have dwelt on topics pertaining to the question of job versus class consciousness.

THE IMPACT OF WORK RELATIONS AND
JOB-SEEKING ON WORKING-CLASS VALUES

Crucial in assessing Marx's contribution is an understanding of the difference between the formulations of Marx, the historical philosopher, interested in the general direction of historical development, and Marx, the sociologist, who dealt with the combination of forces and processes that generate conflict and consciousness within a community.[2]

As an historical philosopher, Marx held that work relationships between dominant and subordinate classes were never static but always in a state of flux simultaneously characterized by harmony and conflict, with one generally being more important than the other for prolonged periods. Applying his assumption to capitalist society, Marx portrayed the middle and working classes as involved simultaneously in symbiotic and antagonistic relations. At times, class relations would be relatively harmonious, as employers and workers co-operated at work and accepted the distributive pattern of goods, while the class struggle proceeded at an almost imperceptible pace, or perhaps receded in importance. But during other phases of a society's development—especially during what Marx saw as the inevitable period of capitalist decay—the bonds between classes would loosen and eventually give way, until relations became almost entirely negative in character.

Workers' strikes, company lock-outs, and pitched battles between militia and workmen, scabs and strikers, would climax two earlier phases of economic development: a long period of relative prosperity for the community and related peaceful ties between classes, succeeded by a short span of economic collapse and consequent questioning of the legitimacy of ruling-class authority. As this pattern was repeated, the resulting class strife would generate increased class awareness among workmen, who would move from tentative vocal support for their class to outright avowal of socialist equality. Further, once militant goals had become embedded in the minds of workmen, these ideas would become an important vehicle of revolutionary change, forces as powerful as the motor itself: the tools, ties, and antagonisms of the workplace which were associated with poverty at home and alienation from self, plant, product, and law. The progressive degradation and mental disengagement of the working class, processes induced largely by capitalism, would press the working class to alter even more its perceptions and evaluations of capitalism and to develop subsequently a revolutionary level of consciousness capable of contributing to the elimination of capitalism itself.[3]

Perlman was struck by the gulf between Marx's developmental prediction and the American reality of the 1920's. As a labor economist sensitive to (and sympathetic with) American trade unionism, he observed what he judged to be the pure and simple character of American labor in the early part of this century and commented on its sober moderation. Carpenters, plumbers, bricklayers, trainmen, and the like were not notably aggressive in their relations to capital. Rather, Perlman observed that American workers would organize unions and attempt to improve working conditions, wages, and job security, but that they would not support tactics such as the general strike. Interestingly, Perlman dismissed the possibility of a general strike in his discussion of workers' views, but in so doing implied that such a strike might well reflect or encourage the formation of consciousness.[4]

Moreover, unlike Marx, Perlman rejected the assumption that work relations were critical for understanding the thought of workmen. He insisted that workmen were "job-oriented," in the sense that they were primarily concerned with marketing their labor in a way that would maximize their personal gains. Originally, workers had been forced to market their labor individually on the basis of supply and demand. Given a surplus of labor as well as a concentration of power in the hands of business firms and their political allies, workmen's wages proved to be less than adequate. In addition, unfair recruitment practices, long work days, and dangerous working conditions forced workmen to defend themselves through the organization of unions. Designed to elevate wages, shorten work days, establish hiring halls, and improve work rules, unions were to make his job more palatable to the average workman and provide him with greater economic security.[5] These innovations did not appear on the American scene automatically, but were rather the outgrowth of struggle. Much later, governmental bodies and unions engaged in the specification, legislation, and enforcement of regulations to improve job conditions.

According to Perlman, unions proved to be successful largely because they monopolized the marketing of labor. Thus, when bosses failed to make concessions to unions, the latter would withdraw the scarce skills of workmen. Given their command over this supply, labor unions frequently extracted economic concessions from businessmen who had no choice but to compromise. On the basis of the success of craft unionists, Perlman forecast improved prospects for the entire blue-collar labor force.

Yet Perlman's logic and observations were faulty, as the evidence shows, for the position of workmen in the mass industries, even during the 1920's, was not comparable to that of members of craft and related unions.[6] Industrial workers had lower incomes and status, enjoyed less workplace safety, and commanded less power. They were not part of labor's aristocracy.

Perlman also assumed that as the conditions of trade unionists improved, the proportion of radical workmen would decrease noticeably. Perlman argued that workmen came to view extremist attitudes as antithetical to working-class interests. In Perlman's analysis, workers reasoned that if revolutionary action were to fail, the defeat would result in the destruction of all the material gains made by them. Consequently, even when American workmen were sympathetic to socialism, communism, and syndicalism, they would become increasingly unwilling to support revolutionary action which might jeopardize hard-won gains. In short, given the strategic pragmatism and limited goals of unions, plus their success in collective bargaining, these unions could not imbue their members with revolutionary zeal; as a result, Perlman believed, the working class would never rise above a trade union level of awareness. Strikes would focus on particular issues, while the pecuniary struggle would lead to greater equity within the capitalist system. Workers would not fight for the realization of equality through socialism or communism.[7] Perlman published these views during the 1920's, and he believed that events had confirmed his theory.

THE EFFECT OF IMPROVED LIVING STANDARDS
ON WORKERS' POLITICAL ATTITUDES

Marx and Perlman differed also on the impact of a higher standard of living on the political behavior of workmen. As a sociologist, Marx felt that the degree of worker consciousness was based upon economic fluctuations and the kind of social organization that existed at the workplace. He held that a higher standard of living increased workers' material wants, while at the same time the cyclical character of capitalist economy prevented their demands from being met on a continuous basis. When an economic depression followed a period of prosperity, workers would experience disappointment in a new standard of living that departed drastically from the old consumption levels, and in buying power that differed unfavorably from their recent expectations. Finding that normal political procedures proved useless in dealing with these problems, workers would turn to revolutionary ideas to bring about changes in society. However, these ideas would not appear in a vacuum. Most of them would occur to workmen who were simultaneously isolated from middle-class contact, accustomed to similar occupational hazards, jammed next to one another at work, and linked to each other through aggressive unions.[8]

Perlman viewed these sociological formulations as inapplicable to the American scene. The American working class held views peculiar to it, he thought, although manual laborers elsewhere in the world faced common problems. Perlman agreed that the economy might indeed fail to meet the heightened expectations of American workers, but, he answered, workmen were gifted with patience and intimidated by the power of employers to penalize workers by blacklisting or firing. Thus, in spite of company practices they judged unfair, almost all U.S. workmen viewed the capitalist system as essentially tolerable if not improvable. They were inveterate optimists; they believed that they could realize the good things in life by operating within the capitalist system, although, on occasion, serious setbacks might occur. Even during periods of economic malaise, Perlman claimed, workers were more concerned with keeping their jobs or getting back to work than giving credence to revolutionary formulas.[9] This stress on the essential pliancy of workmen differed considerably from Marx's appraisal, with its emphasis upon the relative militancy of workmen.

Climate of Inquiry and Direction of Evidence:
Marx Versus Perlman

Although the two schools have discussed approximately the same phenomena, they have drawn support for their respective positions from quite different historical periods. Most of the evidence for Marx's analysis was gathered during a period of either economic collapse or recession that followed a time of prosperity, while Perlman and his supporters have concentrated on a long span of good times.

Those influenced by Marxian sociology have documented the tendency of unionized workmen to use the sit-down strike and the picket line to recoup losses and make gains during periods of economic dislocation or the immediate period thereafter. Thus, in his study of Akron sit-down strikes during the mid-1930's, Alfred W. Jones observed a high level of worker consciousness; he noted that union members favored such forms of direct action as the reverse lock-out, a tactic devised by a group of Saginaw (Michigan) public utilities workers to force management out of a power plant which the workmen managed for several weeks before winning their crucial strike. The overwhelming majority of Akron C.I.O. workers favored such action. By contrast, the notorious "red apples"—workmen who belonged to a company union—were, in almost all cases, opposed to it.[10]

During the Great Depression, the Akron experience was not unique; all across the country workmen acted in ways that were not consistent with Perlman's thesis. In fact, the dramatic sit-down strikes and violent struggles of Akron rubber workers, San Francisco longshoremen, Detroit auto workers, Minneapolis truckers, New York maritime unionmen, and Chicago steel and packinghouse workers contradicted Perlman's blanket assertions on the supine character of American labor.[11] Presumably the passage of fifteen years and a combination of other factors accounted for the difference. Yet on at least one point Perlman's analysis seemed applicable, even to the 1930's and the mass industries. For Jones found that although Akron's unionized rubber workers were radical in a manner quite inconceivable in the 1920's, they still preferred the practical, reform politics of Roosevelt to the distant promises and programs of Socialist Norman Thomas and Communist Earl Browder. The Great Depression helped to advance aggressive class attitudes and organizations which subsequently generated a bloc working-class vote committed to a reform candidate.[12]

In another study, Liston Pope observed the mill workers of Gastonia, North Carolina. They had suffered wage cuts, organized a union, and used the strike as a means of rectifying their losses. Pope found that the violent conflict between mill owners and textile workers was accompanied by the creation, reinforcement, and persistence of aggressive attitudes among strikers. Unfortunately, Pope's study only touched upon the militant attitudes of the mill workers, but it did carefully document the chronology and character of a bloody strike that was led by outside activists and supported by workmen; leaders and followers alike dedicated themselves to organizing mill unions and bettering material conditions.[13]

Clearly, modified Marxian theory is helpful in explaining a high level of class consciousness in both Akron and Gastonia *during periods of economic depression.* Not only the poverty of the average person, but the vivid contrasts in wealth, the relative decline in workers' standards of living and the widening gap between what the worker expected and the middle class obtained were undoubtedly relevant. In addition, the social organization of the workplace helped to instill a class point of view. The fact that they worked closely together and shared the same backgrounds fostered communication among workers, the development and extension of close ties within the sub-group, and the formation of labor organizations dedicated to advancing working-class interests.

Marx had made explicit the importance of density of population and consequent ease of conversation among workmen. Contrasting workmen with farmers, he observed that poverty alone had not moved either French farmers or Indian peasants to develop class consciousness. They lacked high population density and a social organization such as the factory and mine which could bring workers together informally on a sustained basis.[14]

Marx's dual concern with both the sources and consequences of class consciousness influenced many social scientists who went on to relate class position and class consciousness to political views during prosperous periods immediately following a great depression. Richard Centers, who studied class opinions sampled from workmen throughout the United States during the mid-1940's, found that the majority identified with the working class. Among those who did, a disproportionately large number favored reform social legislation.[15]

Nonetheless, it is clear that the relationship between class identification and political behavior is not a simple one. For example, Mark Abrams surveyed England under historical circumstances similar to those encountered by Centers, and his observations led him to conclude that a sizable minority of workers both (1) identified with the working classes, and (2) preferred deferential relations with higher classes. These workmen voted for the Tories. They viewed themselves as rightfully subordinate within a class system essentially legitimate. Yet this lack of class consciousness should not surprise us, since most of these workers were found in industries, regions, and unions where class conflict was not widely known.[16]

Whom does this empirical evidence support—Marx or Perlman? During periods of economic crisis, as we have seen, workers often exhibit a high incidence of class consciousness which can be related to political affiliation (but *not* to revolutionary politics). Furthermore, social consciousness apparently remains with most workmen for some time following a depression, even after most have become relatively prosperous and secure. Perhaps some form of cultural lag not understood by social scientists operates under such circumstances. In any event, Centers's material testifies that it may be useful to revise and apply some of Marx's ideas. Yet few would deny that Perlman's views have great applicability during periods of prolonged economic prosperity, as during the late 1940's and early 1950's.

Many social scientists examining the American scene at that time found few militant workmen. These sociologists had assumed that if American workers were highly class conscious, they would agree among themselves on the nature of the class order. Conversely, they equated an incoherent perspective with a low level of class consciousness. The results of their studies were surprising. They showed that many manual workers were vague or inconsistent when asked to identify their class. They viewed themselves as middle class one moment and working class the next.[17] Furthermore, workmen were unable to agree among themselves on the number and structure of classes in their communities.[18] They also failed to use the same criteria for describing or determining their class.[19] These studies indicated a widespread lack of sophistication on class matters, as Perlman had maintained. They also lead one to doubt the pertinence of Marxian theory for understanding the attitudes of most workmen during periods of extended prosperity.[20]

CONDITIONS LIMITING CONSCIOUSNESS

During the 1950's, many social scientists accordingly abandoned their Marxian assumptions and turned to an examination of why U.S. workers lacked militant class attitudes. One of these analysts, Morris Rosenberg, outlined several important phenomena that tended to diminish working-class consciousness: the structure of large-scale industries, the system of political representation, membership in many groups, the contemporary "style of life," and the common goals of a society.[21]

Rosenberg maintained that the present organization of the mass industries, with the formal control net of management and the informal levels of skill specialization within the working class, creates confusion in the minds of workmen concerning who is responsible for problems at the workplace. According to Rosenberg, the stockholder wields power in ways unclear to workers. Therefore, it is easier for workmen to find fault with the man on the spot—the foreman—than with the owners or executives of the corporation. It is also easier to vent their hostility accordingly, if only because workmen tend to think in terms of direct experience. Workmen cannot readily hold the remote responsible or view it as reprehensible. Though at times workmen do, they are never quite sure who (or what) is the guilty party, and who should consequently receive blame. Criticism without clear focus is a poor source of class consciousness.

An equally important aspect of industrial structure is job differentiation, which hinders the formation of class solidarity. Blue-collar workers range from tool- and die-makers and other skilled workmen to floor-sweepers. This job differentiation prompts a sense of hierarchy among manual workers. Tool- and die-makers, for example, often consider themselves an elite group and demand special contracts and considerations. Those who define themselves as superior fail to develop amicable relations with less-skilled workmen. Status ranking makes it difficult for workmen to associate on a sustained basis, either within a labor union or labor party.

Rosenberg made another observation, one seldom cited even by astute analysts: the political structure of democratic society weakens class solidarity because it operates according to *territorial* representation. The elected are called upon to act in behalf of not one but several classes, with conflicting interests, all of which demand representation. The system thereby places the politician in a difficult position: forced to take positive action, he faces the conflicting demands of groups at odds with one another, plus the continuing need to rally the support of these groups to further his political career. The politician who chooses to compromise blunts the effect of proposals backed by militants. Since

2·30 – 3·30
3–30 – 5·30 SEMINA
7 – 9·30 – SYST

he seldom translates aggressive class views into legislation, class consciousness cannot find a political outlet, and thus declines, unable to sustain itself without action and success. A diminution of militant views presumably would *not* take place if political representatives were elected along syndicalist-occupational, rather than geographical, lines. For example, were union internationals or occupational categories to elect candidates for state legislatures or Congress, workers would wield direct control, and programs and consciousness would be less diluted.

A third element, simultaneous membership in groups composed of multiple classes with differing perspectives, also lessens consciousness. For example, workmen may belong to unions that create and guide their militancy, while at the same time participating in groups that promote conservative values. It is possible for workers to admire the views of both groups, despite the logical inconsistencies involved. In so doing, they may be caught between two definitions of problems and solutions, one proposed by the union, the other articulated by middle-class organizations such as church, veterans', and educational groups. Given contradictory appraisals of issues such as unemployment or automation, workers might very well compromise their views, or perhaps reject any solution, as is often the case when people face cross pressures. In turn, this rejection might lead to disengagement from all thought and action on class issues.

A fourth factor, "style of life," makes it difficult for the working class to see themselves as subordinate. Contemporary Americans have developed buying tastes that cut across class lines. For example, classes can no longer be told apart by the kind of clothes they wear, as was the case fifty years ago. Although changes in dress are partly due to the growth of working-class affluence resulting from a high degree of industrialization, they also reflect the commercialization of taste associated with mass advertising and the mass media. Today, the white shirt, striped tie, gray suit, and polished shoes—all within the average man's means—are worn by workers identifying with the general social norms.

Finally, when classes in a society share goals, they may reach agreement on many other matters as well, including the best way to obtain their goals. Thus, during the Second World War, all classes presumably agreed that defeating fascism was the first order of business. Workers agreed not to strike and management followed a policy of no lock-outs, mass firings, or speed-ups. Under such conditions, harmony is encouraged, conflict is dampened, and class consciousness thereby diminishes.

Rosenberg's observations certainly suggest a number of forces inhibiting the development and maintenance of militant class views. But Rosenberg did not present evidence to support his observations. Nor did he examine the origins, variability, and consequences of working-class consciousness. Assuming both a low level of class identification and solidarity among American workmen, he simply attempted to account for these. He did not measure the varying degrees of class consciousness among different types of workers or those with different levels of skills.

Status Politics Only?

Another influential current view has bearing on the issue of consciousness. This view holds that status politics has replaced class politics. Status politics is an admittedly vague term, but it essentially has come to represent the following position: Economic insecurity is no longer significant in the lives of workers, and class consciousness and class politics have consequently become irrelevant. Workers now deal with problems of consumption rather than security, and in so doing, they focus on competition for prestige derived from consumption of goods. When a person or group threatens this prestige, workers will be predisposed to support the politician or party willing to protect their acquisitions and status. Hence, status politics.

This point of view has applicability, especially in situations where workers are accustomed to a high level of consumption throughout a prolonged period of economic prosperity. For example, white workers who have known twenty years of almost continuous affluence, who have purchased consumer goods, such as houses, and used them for prestige competition, will not wish to lose this status. Should an influx of low-status minorities into their neighborhood seem to threaten their possessions or prestige, workmen will vote for the party and/or politician who promises to protect their prestige.

STATUS POLITICS AND STATUS-GROUP POLITICS: A DIFFERENCE

Status politics should not, however, be confused with status-group politics, the politics of a submerged racial, religious, or ethnic group attempting to release itself from the fetters of discrimination associated with lesser status. Status-group politics is often extremely important, especially when members of the marginal working class acquire class-racial consciousness. On the other hand, working-class minority group efforts may fail, for the acquisition of class-racial consciousness and its political expression may foster internal competition and conflict between the marginal and affluent sections of the working class.

THE EARLY SOCIALIST CRITICS

Commenting on the problem of status-group politics and status-group conflict, a number of writers—most of them socialists—have described the forces that militate in favor of the formation of class-racial consciousness and limit class solidarity—both in the plant and at the polls. Engels studied the American labor movement as it emerged after the Civil War and discussed the problem of ethnic divisions among workers. For example, he noted how nationality differences had split American workers into different language groups, thereby limiting communication among them.[22]

Engels did not spell out the implications of his observation for

Marxian theory, but they were obvious. (Marx, in his general theory of class consciousness, had assumed that workers were very much alike, and so able to communicate easily and thereby develop a kind of class consciousness that would permeate the entire working class,[23] although Marx was aware of exceptions, such as the Irish-English split in England and the Negro-white division in the United States.) If American workers were split into different language groups and thus semi-isolated from one another, class solidarity would develop only with considerable difficulty. For even though proletarianized ethnic groups were often sparked by class-ethnic consciousness during the 1870's and 1880's, when Engels made his observations, Engels recognized that it would be extremely hard for a socialist movement to weld such a fragmented class into a social unit marked by political solidarity.

Many Europeans took up the ethnic problem, although their focus was different from that of Engels. Whereas he had dwelt on ethnic divisions inside one class, they examined the ethnic quality of inter-class conflict. The problem was of particular concern to writers who lived in the Austro-Hungarian Empire at the turn of the century. Uneven concentrations of ethnic groups gave rise to numerous conflicts there. The Viennese Ludwig Gumplowicz, for instance, observed how the ethnic makeup of the Empire's ruling classes differed markedly from that of subordinate classes. For while the upper class was overwhelmingly German, the peasants and laborers were generally Slavs. The most prominent struggles thus involved groups that differed not only in terms of class, but nationality as well.[24] Another Viennese, Joseph Schumpeter, formulated a theory on the rise and fall of "whole classes" in which he referred to distinct nationalities as constituting entire ruling or subordinate classes.[25]

As one of the leaders of the Marxist wing of Austrian socialism in the Empire, Otto Bauer had to deal continuously with the problems and conflicts of different ethnic groups working together or against one another inside the socialist movement.

Bauer observed not only that the middle classes were disproportionately German and the working classes Slavic, but he focused
on the way in which class and ethnic stratification shaped class
conflict and working-class solidarity.[26]

Bauer studied what is today Czechoslovakia and observed how
ethnic groups differed in over-all occupational position. By using
statistical materials, he demonstrated a close relationship between ethnic character and class position. He observed that German residents found in predominantly Czech areas were largely
entrepreneurs, whereas the Czechs were primarily working-class
people who defined themselves as both workers and exploited
Czechs. Predictably enough, they viewed their employers as both
exploiting property owners and Germans.

The Germans, who viewed the Slavs as an inferior group, were
not especially offended by this attitude. Having unimpeded
access to strategic resources such as capital gave some ethnic
groups advantages in prestige over others, Bauer noted. And
clearly the Germans were on top in this regard. These status
differences often led to strife between German and Czech workers. For example, because Czech workmen had lower status and
consequently felt no sense of class affinity with their German
counterparts, they often became strike-breakers when German
workers went on strike. In turn, the Germans deprecated the
Bohemians, Moravians, and Slovakians for this and other reasons,
and reciprocated by acting as strike-breakers when Czech workmen went on strike.

Bauer's remarks have obvious implications for working-class
solidarity in the United States, for the American Negro today is
the historical counterpart to the Czech, while white manual
workers are comparable to those German workmen found in the
Sudetenland, Bohemia, and Moravia prior to World War I. Differences in group prestige, skill level, and income—and isolation—
exist in both settings. Negroes, like Czechs, have enjoyed less
prestige, held proportionately fewer skilled jobs, earned less income, and on occasion acted as strike-breakers. On their side,

white workmen have generally discouraged Negro participation
in labor unions; craft unionists, in particular, have isolated themselves and their economic benefits. Discrimination such as this
has helped to push Negroes to engage in status-group politics, as
will be shown in Chapter 7.

Class: The Use and Modification of Marx

Marx, in addition to specifying several of the interrelated sources
and consequences of class conscious, stressed also the importance
of objective measures of class and multiple degrees of class consciousness. But before we examine how Marx saw these measures
of class consciousness, we should understand what Marx meant
by "class."

Marx generally defined class by using objective criteria. His
indices of class position were readily discernible from one another and based on economic and occupational roles (see Table
2-1).[27]

A member of the *haute bourgeoisie*, for example, was defined
as a person who owned private property in large amounts, who
processed raw materials indirectly, and in some cases, managed
their manufacture and distribution. All of these things were done
for profit. As an indirect processor of raw materials, he never directly handled the semi-finished and finished goods; these tasks
were left to manual workers. The capitalists merely co-ordinated
the capital and the manpower. Included in this class were
wealthy manufacturers, important merchants, and financiers,
among others.

A second class was the *petite bourgeoisie*, subdivided into (1)
small-scale owners and investors and (2) non-propertied white-
collar workers who co-ordinated production, distribution, or
exchange, or who performed related services for the capitalists.

A member of the first group was generally a retailer or farmer
who might own property, but who earned his income through
business operations. For his efforts he received a profit, which

Table 2–1. Class Structure in Early Industrial Society (Capitalist)*

CLASS	OCCUPATION	PRIVATE PROPERTY OWNERSHIP	ECONOMIC ROLE PERFORMED	ECONOMIC REWARD RECEIVED
MIDDLE CLASS (*haute bourgeoisie*)	WHITE-COLLAR (1) Big Business Owners (2) High Financiers	Large amounts	Indirect Processors: (1) Control Investment (2) Manage (in most cases) operation of business	Profit
LESSER MIDDLE CLASS (*petite bourgeoisie*)	(1) Small Business Owners (2) Small Financiers	Small amounts	Indirect Processors: (1) Control Investment (2) Manage operation of business	Profit
	(3) Managers (4) Professionals (5) Clerks	None	Indirect Processors: (1) Co-ordinate activities at workplace (2) Develop scientific knowledge	Salary or wage
WORKING CLASS	BLUE-COLLAR (1) Skilled workers (2) Unskilled workers	None	Direct Processors: (1) Extract (2) Process (3) Transport	Wage
	Lumpen Proletariat	—	—	—

* This does not include reference to class structure in rural areas, partially because of its declining significance in industrial society.

was often meager and frequently doomed to shrink to the point where the small entrepreneur could not simultaneously replace worn-out capital, expand his business, and eke out a profit. Yet, he had to do all three if he was to survive.

Also among the *petite bourgeoisie* were white-collar workers who did not possess private property but who indirectly processed goods. These employees provided accounting, legal, architectural, scientific, and other semi- and fully professional services for the large and small owners of capital. For their efforts they generally earned a salary, but on occasion received a wage.

The working class consisted of those who did not own capital and could not therefore invest funds for profit. Workmen acted as direct processors and performed one of three types of roles: extracting raw materials from nature, as did miners, fishermen, and others in the primary industries; processing unfinished or semi-finished goods, as steel-makers and smelter workers in the secondary industries; or transporting either goods or people. Such workers received a wage.

Although Marx was well aware of the range of skills within the blue-collar sector, he chose not to comment analytically on the implications of job differentiation to the study of consciousness, except to make a distinction between employable workers and the dregs heaped permanently at the bottom of the class system. He defined this stratum as *lumpen proletariat,* a category of ragged and motley unskilled, generally unemployed and unemployable types, who were frequently derelict in character and not part of the progressive sections of the working class.

Whatever the merits of this typology for understanding early industrial society, Marx's framework is inadequate for portraying the contemporary scene. It fails to summarize the true outlines of the class structure of today's society. In particular, the growth of a new middle class renders Marx's model obsolete.

The writings of Lewis Corey and C. Wright Mills have helped to revise the framework so as to distinguish among old middle, new middle, and working classes.[28] As Table 2-2 indicates, the old

Table 2-2. Class Structure in Late Industrial Society (Capitalist) *

CLASS		OCCUPATION	PRIVATE PROPERTY OWNERSHIP	ECONOMIC ROLE PERFORMED	ECONOMIC REWARD RECEIVED
OLD MIDDLE CLASS	Affluent	WHITE-COLLAR (1) Big Business Owners (2) High Financiers	Large amounts	Indirect Processors: Manage and/or control capital	Profit, and in some cases salary
	Marginal	(3) Small Business Owners (4) Small Financiers	Small amounts	Indirect Processors: Manage and/or control capital	Profit
NEW MIDDLE CLASS		(1) Managers (2) Professionals (3) Clerks (4) Some foremen	(1) Large amounts (2) Small amounts (3) None	Indirect Processors: (1) Manage business enterprises (2) Perform other indirect functions	Salary, and in some cases profit
WORKING CLASS		BLUE-COLLAR (1) Some foremen (2) Craftsmen and other skilled workers (3) Factory, mine, and mill workers (4) Other workers (including *lumpen proletariat*)	(1) Small amounts (2) None	Direct Processors: (1) Extract (2) Process (3) Transport (4) Maintain	Wage, and in some cases profit, and/or salary

* This diagram does not make reference to rural classes in late industrial society, largely because of their political, social, and economic insignificance.

middle class consists of affluent and marginal elements. The affluent stratum includes big business owners and high financiers who own large investments, process goods as owners, managers, and the like, and receive a profit (and in some cases, a salary) for their efforts. The marginal element operates in a similar way, except that its proportion of total assets is less, its over-all share having decreased through time.

Marx did not foresee the importance of the new middle class. He was aware of its emergence, but he believed it would be small and insignificant in the long run. Corey and Mills, however, have shown that the new middle class, with three important strata—managers, professionals, and white-collar service workers —includes those found in the major growth sectors of the economy. For example, office supervisors, plant directors, store clerks, school teachers, social workers, and computer technicians would fall in this category. Primarily occupied in managerial and service fields, the members of this class sometimes own significant amounts of capital as well. From these investments they derive profits to augment their salaries.

The main source of income for the modern working class still consists of manual, i.e., blue-collar, labor performed with varying degrees of skill in the extraction, process, and transportation of goods. Although its members on occasion maintain investments, they are meager compared to those enjoyed by the new and old middle classes. However, despite the absence of significant income from investments, most workmen in advanced industrial societies receive incomes considerably greater than is the case in an early industrial society. Moreover, proportionately more workers are well above the poverty line, no matter how that line is measured. The working class subsumes a variety of occupational positions at the bottom of which remains the *lumpen proletariat*, who are in many ways similar to the poor of early industrial society. However, today a smaller proportion are found in this category. In part because of their decline, we have limited our analysis so as to say little about the very poor. We will emphasize the class views of the remainder.

There are a number of ways in which we can define working-class consciousness. We prefer to define it as the varying degrees to which workers acquire a perspective that emphasizes class terms and calls for the maximization of working-class interests through class struggle—whether at work or in the neighborhood.

This definition is consistent with Marx's, for implicit in Marx's formulations on class is a distinction between "cognitive" emphasis and "evaluative" demand. The cognitive aspect refers to whether workers utilize class terms, identify with their class, and display an awareness of the allocation of wealth within the community or society. The evaluative aspect refers to the extent to which workers think in terms of class struggle [29] in order to achieve *class goals*.

Marx argued that under certain circumstances, economic conditions generate an awareness of membership in a class and the ability to think and verbalize in class terms. For example, he noted how British workmen could develop an awareness of the class to which they belonged as a result of what he called "the underground civil war" between the middle and working classes.[30]

But class identification was not the only aspect of working-class consciousness. Perhaps as important was the ability of the workman to use class terms spontaneously—that is, for his language to reflect the most important considerations in his life, namely, how he relates to property, work, and wage structures. In *The German Ideology*, Marx argued that if a community contains social classes, its inhabitants would learn to use class symbols when circumstances were propitious. As Marx would say, class symbols reflect relationships, both present and past.[31]

Touching upon yet another facet of working-class consciousness, Marx proposed that in the long run the class struggle would generate not only a common sense of class identity, but a high degree of class solidarity and common devotion to class goals. Aware of their class position, workers would determine to act together. When transformed into action, this determination would constitute a reflection of the highest form of consciousness, in which *"the mass unites* and forms itself into a class for itself. The interests which it defends become class interests."[32]

Defending class interests would include efforts to redistribute the wealth of society. Here Marx would favor struggles to minimize inequities within the context of industrial capital. Should workmen share Marx's views, they would express a class point of view.[33]

In a study to measure the class consciousness of Detroit workmen, to which we refer below and in successive chapters, we employed several criteria derived from Marx's formulations. *Class verbalization* denotes the tendency of working-class individuals to discuss topics in terms of class. *Skepticism* refers to a belief that wealth is allocated within the community to benefit primarily the middle class. *Militancy* refers to the predisposition to engage in aggressive action to advance the interests of one's class. *Egalitarianism* means favoring a redistribution of wealth so that each individual within the community would have the same amount. These four criteria form the basis of our scale, measuring from low to high degrees of class consciousness.

To measure *class verbalization* we used a battery of eight unstructured questions, each deliberately making no reference to class, so as not to prejudice the answers of the respondent. We asked him for whom he had voted in the most recent election and why, who was his favorite President and why, and so forth. If a worker used class terms in any of these instances, his comments constituted class verbalization.[34]

Skepticism was weighed through the use of the following question: When business booms in Detroit, who gets the profits? If the respondent used categories such as "rich people," "upper class," "big business," or similar references, he was considered class conscious in this regard.

We measured *militancy* by asking the interviewee to project himself into a situation in which workers were about to take action against a landlord, and to indicate whether or not he would join in a series of activities, including picketing. If he answered that he would take part in the demonstration, the study classified him as militant.

Egalitarianism was determined to exist when the worker agreed with the notion that the wealth of our country should be divided up equally.

Linking these various aspects of class consciousness to one another (Table 2-3), we typed workmen according to the degree

Table 2–3.   General Classification of Workmen on Four Aspects of Class Consciousness

WORKERS TYPED ACCORDING TO CLASS PERSPECTIVE	EGALITA- RIANISM	MILITANCY	SKEPTICISM	CLASS VERBALIZATION
Militant Egalitarians	+[1]	+	+	+
Militant Radicals	−[2]	+	+	+
Skeptics	−	−	+	+
Class Verbalizers	−	−	−	+
Class Indifferents	−	−	−	−

[1] Means class conscious.
[2] Means non-class conscious.

to which each had developed a class frame of reference. Seventy-five per cent of the workers then fell into one of the following five categories: militant egalitarians, militant radicals, skeptics, class verbalizers, and class indifferents. Interestingly, one-fourth of those interviewed maintained a point of view inconsistent with this configuration. Although they were clearly "error types," [35] we were able to categorize them on the basis of a point system suggested by Guttman. Accordingly, from a total of 375 workers, 38 qualified as militant egalitarians, 87 as militant radicals, 114 as skeptics, 98 as class verbalizers, and 38 as class indifferents.[36]

Class consciousness, then, can mean a comprehensive class frame of reference. In regard to the most militant workers, consciousness refers to (1) a propensity to use class terms spontaneously, (2) a belief in the direct relationship between heightened pace of economic activity and flow of wealth to the middle class, (3) the commitment to engage in direct action against certain middle-class groups in order to advance working-class interests, and (4) a predisposition to favor economic equality, if only temporarily, as a collective starting point for a group seeking pecuniary gain and occupational improvement. On the other hand, class consciousness for most workmen generally means considerably less.

Conclusions

This chapter has attempted to specify the bases for our holding that economic insecurity and union organization [37] are related to class consciousness, and specifically that the uprooted, the jobless, the less skilled, and working-class racial or ethnic minorities may become highly class conscious, especially when they are members of labor unions. Furthermore, unions help translate consciousness into political action through both class and status-group politics —under certain conditions. How these circumstances were present in Detroit, and how, consequently, they operated to favor the formation of class militancy is the subject we will now consider.

3

Class Consciousness and Politics in Detroit: A Study in Change*

When we observe the sources and consequences of working-class consciousness, we should select a community where conditions favor the formation of class militancy.[1] In this regard, certain cities are better qualified than others. One-industry towns are the most appropriate test sites, especially when these communities concentrate large numbers of workmen in heavy industry and when they become dependent upon a fluctuating demand for their key product. These two considerations are not the only relevant factors to be taken into account, however. When workmen with unpredictable incomes live in various "ghettoes," racial, ethnic, and economic, the community thereby creates a basis for class politics colored by race-ethnic values. We hope to indicate in this chapter how Detroit resembled this model and why it was consequently selected as the place to test our general views of the significance of class politics and its presence as a recurrent phenomenon in certain communities.

Detroit Prior to Automotive Industrialization: c. 1900

About 1900, no key industry dominated the Detroit economy. At that time, commerce and a wide variety of industries supported a

* This chapter is based in part on my "Class Consciousness and Politics in Detroit," *Michigan History*, 48 (December 1964), 289–314.

local population of 285,000,[2] and Detroit was the hub of south-eastern Michigan trade for prosperous farmers who supported tobacco, flour, brewery, shoe, and furniture enterprises. Wage earners worked in the carriage, paint, stove, drug, marine, metal, and other industries.[3] The automotive revolution had already begun, but the industry did not employ a significant proportion of the city's labor force. The middle class, which guided the older industries, consisted largely of independent businessmen, while the working class included many craftsmen, such as carpenters, bricklayers, and metal-workers.

Class position largely determined the distribution of economic rewards, although, as is the case today, the range of rewards within each class was considerable, depending upon occupation. The salaries of clerks, for example, were markedly lower than the profits of most business owners, but somewhat higher than the wages of skilled workers. Within the working class, skilled workers, many of whom were unionized, earned significantly more than the unskilled. At the time, however, a very large proportion of the total blue-collar labor force consisted of non-unionized, unskilled workers.[4] Indeed, Detroit was a non-union town, a place generally safe from "labor interference." [5] This condition was to remain the same until the late 1930's, when the Congress of Industrial Organizations recruited the vast majority of Detroit's industrial workers.

The social composition of the community was essentially Anglo-Saxon, German, Irish, French, and Polish.[6] In one way, this mix of populations was conducive to harmonious class relations. For, while a by no means insignificant proportion of the population was Roman Catholic (especially the Irish, Germans, and Poles), the majority could claim a common cultural and religious background. Predominantly Protestant, most of the ancestors of Detroit's inhabitants had emigrated from Germany * and Britain

---

* However, Detroit's German population has always contained a very large Catholic minority, one almost as large as the German Protestant population.

during the eighteenth and nineteenth centuries. Both employer and employee were presumably influenced by the doctrine of rugged individualism based upon the Protestant ethic [7] and the Horatio Alger myth.[8]

Politically, Detroit, like the rest of Michigan, was predominantly Republican, although the parties of both William Jennings Bryan and Eugene V. Debs could claim minority group support.[9] The Democrats did on occasion win a political campaign,[10] relying upon the Irish and German voters [11] for much of their backing. The Socialist party began at the turn of the century to attract a growing number of voters,[12] a trend which continued to the end of the 1912 presidential campaign, in which Debs polled a record number of Socialist votes, both in Detroit and elsewhere.[13] Even so, compared to the two major political organizations, the popularity and influence of the Socialist party were minimal.[14]

If class consciousness did permeate the minds of a large number of workmen, it failed to find expression in social movements of the sort that occurred during the Great Depression, unless increasing support for the militant Debs be considered an indication of a growing class consciousness. On the whole, the behavior of workers did not suggest any widespread popularity of beliefs inimical to the interests of the business community.

Rapid Industrialization and Prosperity: 1910-29

It is difficult to describe in a few paragraphs the period of Detroit's rapid industrialization and prosperity, since so many changes occurred within such a short span of time. Between 1910 and 1929 vast tracts of farmland on the outskirts of the city were purchased, land was cleared and marshes were filled, factories and tenements were built, laborers were recruited, and fortunes were accumulated by many members of the community. In one decade (1910–20) the population increased from 465,000 to 993,000.[15] By the end of World War I, the technological base of the community had come to rest upon one industry: automobile manufacturing.[16] Henry Ford and other entrepreneurs had established firms and were producing cars that rivaled one another in style and price. Some firms made profits and expanded, but many could not compete and failed.

Despite increased centralization of control within the industry, especially at the end of the 'twenties, oligopolistic conditions did not yet exist. Nor did joint-stock corporations control all of the automobile firms. Many were owned and operated by individual entrepreneurs or by partners.

The economic climate of the community partially accounted for the absence of union or governmental regulation, for the automotive industry produced a prosperity hitherto unknown in Detroit. The *nouveaux riches*, predominantly of Anglo-Saxon and German background, grew in number and moved to the outskirts of the city. The community also contained a working class whose prosperity attracted immigrants from all over the United States, Canada, Europe, and the Middle East. Within a short period of twenty years, from 1910 to 1930, the ethnic composition of the working class changed enormously. Previously Anglo-Saxon, German, and Irish for the most part, it became predominantly Slavic and Southern European, although Northern Europeans continued to fill most of the skilled positions within the working class. The largest of the Eastern and Southern European minority groups were the Poles and Italians, most of whom entered the labor force as unskilled workers. Hamtramck, a Polish-speaking community established on the outskirts of Detroit at the turn of the century, grew rapidly and rivaled "Little Italy," "Little Lithuania," and other ethnic enclaves. These sub-communities, located near the large factories, established their own churches, press, radio programs, and protective and recreational associations, many of which survive today.[17]

Amid these relatively abrupt social and economic changes in the community, labor union organization did not flourish, nor did the Republican party lose its dominant position in Detroit politics.[18] Perhaps militant working-class consciousness could not develop within an economic structure which gave visible support to the Horatio Alger myth. During the late 1920's, the community's class structure appeared to be wide open, as ordinary men on some occasions rose from the ranks of the unskilled to become captains of industry or to fill executive positions within the growing automobile firms. On the other hand, many employers showed little concern for the social welfare of their employees, as has been indicated by Reinhold Niebuhr, a minister in Detroit during this period.[19] To many, poverty and economic insecurity seemed transitory; quite frequently those who were intelligent and worked hard believed they could escape these conditions. Indeed, by the late 1920's, Detroit, with its new skyscrapers and factories, openly displayed the prosperity of America.[20]

Industrial Stagnation: 1930-39

The Great Depression had a tremendous impact on Detroit. Following many business failures, a few automobile firms moved into positions of oligopolistic control over the industry and economic power became more centralized. Day-to-day decisions on style and price were made by fewer businesses, and at the same time, capital within the industry was increasingly concentrated within a smaller number of corporations. During this period of consolidation, many firms either moved toward or declared bankruptcy. Most of these later went out of business, although some were salvaged and absorbed by the larger organizations. In another move, control over the firms' economic activities ceased to belong exclusively to executives, boards of directors, stockholders, and banks. Government agencies and unions demanded and obtained greater power over the industry. With the passage of the Wagner Act (1935), militant labor unions began to share in the control of production.

Economic malaise promoted labor organization within the mass industries during this period. After numerous and unsuccessful efforts to organize these workmen had failed in the early 'thirties, John L. Lewis led the C.I.O. out of the A.F.L. in November 1935. During this period, the C.I.O.'s drive to organize steel, auto, rubber, maritime, packinghouse, and other workers found in the mass industries met with craft union disfavor. Nonetheless, the C.I.O. successfully used militant strategies and tactics to organize these industries. In the automotive industry, the U.A.W. by 1938 had won union contracts from every significant auto producer, with the exception of the Ford Motor Company. And in 1941, the Ford firm gave in and signed a contract with the U.A.W.

This new union concerned itself with a number of considerations besides wages. Unlike craft unions, these new industrial organizations took an active part in setting the pace of work and conditions of the workplace. Management could no longer arbitrarily set the pace of work once unions had won the right to bargain with it on such matters.

Industrial unions came to play an important part not only in the regulation of factory conditions, but in the distribution of wealth within the community. Between 1936 and 1941 unions gained large increases in wages, and subsequently eliminated one of the basic tenets of the automobile industry in an extraordinary break from the past: management was no longer able unilaterally to set wages without union agreement.

We might speculate on why the industrial unions started and how they developed such power. Aside from the Wagner Act, three factors appear to have been of major importance in influencing their growth: widespread material deprivation, vicious job competition, and the all but total elimination of channels of upward mobility within the community. By pre-Depression standards, large sections of the working class suffered considerably during the early 1930's. Part-time employment, unemployment, and poverty were widespread. Beggars were numerous. School teachers were often paid with scrip, while many lawyers went on relief. Soup lines were not sufficient to feed the hungry.

Many workmen who had purchased snappy-looking sport shirts during the "roaring 'twenties" saw themselves and their children dressed in rags. It was not uncommon for workmen to lose their homes or be evicted from rented dwellings.[21]

As the deep poverty experienced by the unemployed became more widespread the work effort of employed workers—including automotive workmen—increased. Knowing that any slackness on their part might well result in their replacement by unemployed workers eager for jobs no matter what the working conditions might be, workers labored at a pace formerly unknown in the automobile industry. Yet, given the paucity of vacancies in the white-collar world, the question of upward mobility became largely academic. For many workmen, the most important consideration was keeping themselves and their families supplied with food and shelter.[22] These conditions paved the way for union organization.

When the Congress of Industrial Organizations made known its goal of recruiting the hitherto unorganized, and began to enlist members in the new industrial unions, workers literally swarmed into the union halls. Employed and unemployed alike supported the new unions, and overnight Detroit became a union town. The programs of these new unions departed considerably from the traditions of the American Federation of Labor, as young militants announced their aims of changing the economic and political structures of not only the shops, but the entire community as well.

While this new leadership rapidly organized the automobile, steel, chemical, and other mass industries,[23] the new militants failed to capture the political allegiance of most workers. Communists and socialists of many varieties streamed into Detroit with two immediate goals: the unionization and political conversion of workers apparently ripe for mass action. They took control of the new labor union structure, but the political loyalty of the rank and file remained behind Franklin D. Roosevelt.[24]

The political structure of the community changed markedly

during this period. Republican control of a large section of the working-class vote disappeared, as the Democratic and, to a lesser extent, left-wing parties grew in importance. In 1932 and 1936 Detroit workers reacted against Hoover and the Great Depression and voted overwhelmingly for Roosevelt. Catholic minority groups fell solidly behind the New Deal. Negroes supported both Roosevelt and other progressives. Negro backing was significant, for by 1930 their voting numbers had begun to influence politicians.[25]

The left-wingers during this period were thus not as effective at the polls as among the working class, where they successfully organized the unemployed, led demonstrations against slum landlords and automobile magnates, directed drives to organize unions, and sponsored giant funerals for workers killed in skirmishes with company police.[26] Speaking out-of-doors, radicals frequently attracted thousands of the unemployed to mass meetings, which sometimes ended in full-scale riots.

Left-wing groups were, on the whole, quite popular in the 'thirties, both with intellectuals [27] and among the masses as well. An incident from 1932 will illustrate this. When members of the security police of the Ford Motor Company killed three workers taking part in a hunger march which attracted four thousand participants and ended at the Ford Rouge plant, the Communist party organized a mass funeral. Horses and carriages were rented, arm bands and flags prepared, and paraders mobilized. The "funeral procession" began on Detroit's main thoroughfare, and an estimated thirty thousand people took part in the cavalcade, which was in fact a Red parade. The Communists had covered the caskets of the deceased with red flags, and many who took part wore red arm bands and carried large placards urging the populace to join the Communist party and support mass organizations.[28] This type of activity was not uncommon in Detroit, especially in the early 1930's.

Many members of the affluent middle class came to fear such workers' demonstrations and other activities sponsored by leftists.

A minority reacted by branding all working-class organizations as Communist or Communist-dominated. To many residents in the chic suburbs of Grosse Pointe and West Dearborn, the C.I.O. and the Communist party were similar if not synonomous.[29] There was some basis for this apprehension, for by any standards the new unions were militant, and their aggressiveness did not go unchallenged. Industrial unions and management used violence and counter-violence before the industrial unions had firmly established themselves. Business groups initiated the use of violence. Shootings, beatings, and the like were repeatedly used by private and public police, hired and dominated by employers, as the Senate investigations of Robert M. LaFollette, Jr., revealed. Legal and corporate authorities frequently blurred the line between private and public use of violence, as various types of police organizations were employed to crush the industrial unions. Police officers and local politicians working with one firm's private police used beating, assaulting, killing, and other violent techniques in order to stop the C.I.O. Naturally, unions on occasion responded in kind.[30]

No doubt much of the upper middle class believed that a coalition of workers and disaffected intellectuals, Communist and non-Communist alike, might develop into a movement capable of challenging capitalism. Although some did broaden their political perspective to the point of accepting New Deal reforms, the possibility of a coalition accentuated the conservative political tendencies of many. Most remained conventional Republicans. A very small minority reacted to the threat from the left by supporting fascist and crypto-fascist movements. Their money and sometimes their membership backed such groups as the Liberty League, America First, the German-American Bund, the Black Legion, and even outright fascist organizations such as the Silver Shirts. Indeed, several of Detroit's outstanding industrial figures subsidized and collaborated with fascist, anti-Semitic organizations and publications.[31]

Brown-shirt organizations also enlisted working-class members, who on occasion armed themselves, engaged in limited military maneuvers (such as drilling and firing light weapons), and awaited the day when they could openly challenge the unions and Communists. Not all of the working-class fascists were anti-union however. Many of them belonged to and supported industrial unions. Father Charles E. Coughlin and his anti-Semitic, anti-capitalistic followers were quite active and numerous during the formative stages of the C.I.O., particularly in the Detroit U.A.W. The fascism of these Detroit workers puzzled Marxists who expected the noble proletariat to be class conscious without being tainted by anti-Semitism. Yet class consciousness and fascist tendencies were obviously not mutually exclusive.[32]

Economic Growth and Prosperity: 1940-55

The period between 1940 and 1955 witnessed economic growth, prosperity, and social change. The technological plant had expanded significantly in the war years, when new and old factories operated at full capacity. Political extremist groups all but disappeared after a brief period of success during and immediately after World War II.

Throughout the period of national emergency, Detroit had been the "arsenal of democracy." Afterward, automotive technology continued to occupy a dominant position within the community. Automobile-makers built plants to meet new market demands. Capital was invested in heavy industry at a rapidly growing rate until the end of the Korean War. During this same period, car production rose to record heights. More cars were being built in more plants by fewer corporations until by 1955, three companies—the General Motors Corporation, the Ford Motor Company, and the Chrysler Corporation—all but monopolized car production.

The social structure altered significantly in these years. A new middle class arose which included a large number of young people of working-class background. All social classes prospered as they never had before, and many moved to the suburbs where they became home owners. Relations between social classes grew increasingly harmonious. The class struggle abated with the end of the post-World War II strikes, although repeated flare-ups between management and workers occurred during and after the Korean War. At the same time, another trend pointed up this harmony. Governmental boards and labor unions often helped minimize class conflict as unions grew more friendly toward companies which were willing to bargain with, and make major concessions to, labor organizations.[33] Prosperity reached almost everyone. Even working-class minority groups improved their standard of living and sent sons and daughters into the middle class.

Prosperity made it possible for members of many of these ethnic groups to break out of the old ghettoes and move to suburbia. This trend was especially noticeable among the Italians and Jews, although a significant proportion of the large and tight-knit Polish community also joined the stream to the edges of the city. The attraction of the suburbs was enhanced by the migration of large numbers of Negroes to the city of Detroit during the period of economic expansion. As the Negroes moved out beyond the central part of the city into districts settled by Catholic and Jewish minorities, many of these moved to the suburbs.[34]

The heavy Negro influx and the white migration to the suburbs sometimes resulted in violent strife between minority groups, especially when racially mixed working-class people were the participants. During World War II, a race riot involving mainly working-class whites and Negroes resulted in the deaths of approximately 30 Negroes,[35] according to official estimates.

On the other hand, all-white groups seldom resorted to violence. They found more subtle ways to express conflicting views on the matter of access to choice residential districts. Residents of Anglo-Saxon and German descent, who dominated the middle-class suburbs, used restrictive covenants and other devices to limit the flow of other ethnic groups into their communities. In Grosse Pointe, a Detroit suburb, real estate interests formally ranked ethnic groups in terms of desirability, and the community acquiesced in their judgment. Members of ethnic groups with low prestige who thought seriously of settling in Grosse Pointe were screened by representatives of the local real estate board. Such criteria as ethnic background and facial complexion were used to ascertain the degree to which applicants conformed to Northwest European standards. Jews, Italians, and Poles were occasionally admitted, but several ethnic groups were entirely beyond the pale, since real estate interests judged them as undesirable.[36] Partly because of this screening process, when minority groups planned to leave the central city, many chose suburbs which accepted them.

Despite the filtered flow to the suburbs—or perhaps partially because of this sorting process—formal political allegiances remained essentially unchanged. The Democrats were still the most popular political party of the working class not only in the central city, but also in many working-class suburbs, such as St. Clair Shores, Roseville, East Detroit, Warren, Livonia, Allen Park, and Melvindale—towns heavily populated by Poles, Italians, and other minority groups who had recently left their ghettoes.[37] These new residents formed a prosperous working class and a new middle class. At the same time, they repeatedly indicated that they had not lost their affiliation with the party of Roosevelt. An exception was their widespread support for Dwight D. Eisenhower during the 1952 and 1956 elections.

Although the Democratic party retained its over-all strength in the metropolitan areas, the extreme left declined rapidly. It was during this period that industrial unions shed their left-wing members and outlook and became powerful respectable forces in local and state politics. Top union leaders severed their left-wing ties or were expelled.[38] Of those who remained in power, most joined the Democratic party, where co-operation with middle-class liberals resulted in the capture of the Wayne County (Detroit) and state Democratic party organizations.[39]

Expressions of working-class consciousness generally declined in this period. Councils of the unemployed, mass rallies, and other forms of militancy disappeared from the political scene. The only political expression of working-class consciousness to remain was a bloc voting pattern discernible in several heavily working-class districts. The once-militant unions functioned increasingly as mediators less influenced by class views on economic problems, except at election time, when they mobilized working-class political loyalties born of the Great Depression in order to win votes for the Democratic party.[40]

Industrial Decline and Uneven Prosperity: 1956–mid-1960's

From 1955 to the early 1960's, Detroit experienced a technological revolution based upon automation. The rapid introduction of new tools and techniques of production eliminated many blue-collar jobs within the automobile industry and other heavy industries such as steel and chemicals. In the case of automobile firms, this process was accompanied by the accelerated centralization of economic control. In addition, the major car firms increased their share of production. The General Motors Corporation and Ford Motor Company, Detroit's two leading automotive firms in the early 1960's, produced 75 per cent of the cars built in the United States.[41] (This was approximately 10 per cent greater than the comparable 1950 figure.) At the same time, the two firms cut the proportion of their capital invested in the city, building many new plants outside Detroit and Michigan at a time when thousands of Detroit auto workers sought employment. During this period of transfer, new factory jobs failed to appear [42] and many unemployed could not find work.

Compounding these problems were periodic economic recessions, increased competition from cars built overseas, and the collapse of several independent automobile firms. Two serious recessions adversely affected Detroit during the late 1950's and early 1960's. At the peak of the 1957–58 recession, 19.5 per cent of the total labor force of metropolitan Detroit was unemployed.[43] In March 1961, at the height of the 1960–61 recession, over 15.2 per cent of the metropolitan Detroit labor force was without work. Moreover, an estimated one-half of this number were believed to be long-term unemployables.[44]

Increased competition from abroad was partially responsible for continued high levels of unemployment even during periods of relative prosperity. From the mid-1950's on, foreign-made cars competed successfully with cars made in the United States. In the decade 1952–62, between 5 and 10 per cent of the cars sold in this country were manufactured abroad. By contrast, foreign manufacturers in 1950 controlled a much smaller fraction of the American market.

Foreign and domestic competition, along with managerial problems, squeezed most of the independent manufacturers out of the automobile business. They left behind a trail of former employees often trained only for jobs demanding minimal skills, paying relatively low wages, and offering little job security.[45] Other firms such as Chrysler, which did not fail, had difficulty competing against foreign manufacturers, General Motors, and Ford. During the late 1950's and early 1960's, Chrysler manufactured between 9 and 15 per cent of the cars built in the United States, while the proportion of the market held by the remaining independents, American Motors Corporation and Studebaker-Packard Corporation, declined markedly from what it had been during the late 1940's. Perhaps Chrysler's problems were most relevant to Detroit's labor force, since a very large proportion of Chrysler employees worked in Detroit and nearby communities.[46]

Economic contraction had an uneven impact upon the class structure. Their savings gone, many members of the working class lost material gains accumulated during the war and postwar years. Among those still employed, many feared temporary lay-offs less than permanent unemployment or future employment in jobs offering significantly less pay and job security. The middle classes were not in this unfortunate position, especially when they were college-trained. For automation had eliminated few of their jobs and had created many new ones designed for the white-collar world. Their formal schooling insured them against extreme deprivation because they could fill a great variety of work roles. Consequently, they were generally successful in finding new employment and comparable rewards if and when a firm no longer needed their services or technological change rendered their occupations obsolete.

Throughout this period, most unions were unable to regulate the pace of automation and factory shutdown. This was perhaps less true of the craft unions at the center of the old A.F.L. than of the industrial unions in the C.I.O. Their diverse positions probably stemmed in part from their differing opinions about the proper activities of a union, opinions which created much difficulty in the negotiations leading to the eventual merger of the two groups in 1955. The A.F.L. traditionally looked upon the union as a business which monopolized prized skills and sold labor at a certain price to an employer. The C.I.O. simply maintained that it organized workers, bargained with management in their behalf, and carried on other activities, but it never considered itself an organization designed to sell labor to management. In fact, industrial unions have generally accepted technological innovation—despite the consequent loss of union membership—as "progress," a stance incomprehensible to a craft union.

The number of industrial union members declined markedly in the decade 1952–62, partially because of the industrial unions' reluctance and inability to challenge the pace of automation and the redeployment of capital to other parts of the country. The decline in the number of workers belonging to unions affiliated with the old C.I.O. in Detroit and elsewhere is illustrated by the following figures.[47] Between 1955 and 1959, the dues-paying membership of the U.A.W. dropped from 1,259,741 to 1,059,639 and loss of membership in other unions in the C.I.O. was also substantial. From the point of view of the U.A.W., the decline in membership must have been appalling, while the future losses loomed as awesome. A Senate report submitted to President John F. Kennedy in February 1961 estimated that 160,000 unemployed automobile workers in Detroit alone would not return to automobile factories.[48] Such was the potential threat of automation to the union.

Many rank and file workers and low-level union leaders responded to loss of jobs and employment security by pressing top-level union leadership to push demands for a shorter work week and an earlier retirement age. In turn, the top leadership has become increasingly aware of the implications that accelerated mechanization and plant relocation had for their jobs, prestige, and power. Since this was the case, many leaders of the industrial unions no doubt ceased to equate accelerated mechanization with progress. Nevertheless, the union elite did not press for a shorter work week, perhaps because the Kennedy administration opposed it.

Throughout this period of economic readjustment, the unions, especially the United Automobile Workers, continued to play an important part in Detroit politics. The unions tended to operate on at least two levels: as a faction inside a formal political organization, and as an independent force with its own political organization. The unions, especially the U.A.W., occupied positions of considerable power within the Detroit, Wayne County, and Michigan Democratic party organization, where they were influential in selecting candidates for public office and in establishing a party program. On the precinct level, the unions worked with the Democratic party and used their own organizations—periodically invigorated before elections—in order to register voters, publicize political issues, and get out the vote. Unfortunately for the unions, the majority of voters did not notice their precinct work, although we cannot say what the Democratic party majority and total vote would have been if the U.A.W. and other unions had not been active in local politics.[49]

Although unions maintained their political influence during this period, their position was potentially precarious. The wealth and power of Ford and General Motors had continued to grow; in addition, management wielded a technological axe: it could eliminate jobs through automation. Firms could abolish many of the jobs of workmen operating within unions which became too demanding. Sidney Lens noted the impact of automation on union bargaining:

> What these technological changes mean for labor's bargaining power must be clear. As the proportion of organized [blue-collar] workers declines in favor of the unorganized technicians and office workers, established unions lose members and finances. In each plant they become weaker relative to the employer with whom they deal; for in case of a strike five hundred men in automated shops can be replaced more easily than five thousand today. Further, the machine tends to become more important to production than the man. If the workers strike in a mechanized plant they can shut the factories down, but in tomorrow's automated shops it may be possible for a skeleton force of nonunion supervisors and office help to run the operation for the period of a strike. That is almost true today in telephone offices; the mere walkout of telephone girls and linemen does not cripple services for a long time. Thus labor's most potent weapon, the strike, is blunted. Finally, automation reduces some of the cohesiveness of the union as workers are separated from each other by relatively large distances within the automated plants.[50]

While unions on the whole were adversely affected, the impact of automation and factory closings hit Negroes especially hard. As is well known, a disproportionately large number of Negroes are unemployed even during periods of community prosperity. Periodic economic recessions exacerbated the problem of Negro unemployment, partly because Negroes were heavily concentrated in semi-skilled occupations in the automobile and steel industries, neither of which offered very steady employment. At the height of the 1960–61 recession, for example, an estimated 39 per cent of Detroit's Negro labor force was unemployed.[51] More importantly, the job market remained small for many of these workers, in part because of their few marketable skills, and also because of employer or craft union discrimination. Consequently, many Negroes were "terminal unemployed," apparently doomed to continuous unemployment for the rest of their lives. Despite this fact, the federal government did not adopt a program to retrain more than a fraction of the workmen displaced by the forces of automation, foreign competition, speed-up, and factory closures.

The Vietnamese war and associated boom have failed to postpone the negative impact of automation on many Negroes and others living in Detroit. Structural unemployment remains a significant problem for hundreds of thousands of Detroiters who have dropped out of (or never entered) the labor force and who consequently have lost (or never gained) Bureau of Labor Statistics status as either employed or unemployed. For these uncounted unfortunates, the increased community prosperity can only heighten their sense of deprivation, as the income gap between the blue-collar employed and unemployed continues to widen. Perhaps the absolute condition of the structurally unemployed does not worsen, but neither does it improve, while the living standards of the employed working class increase. This sense of deprivation would become linked to economic insecurity —specifically occupational insecurity—should the unemployed find themselves in occupations of only momentary demand and hence of short term. "War-on-poverty" occupations and many other service positions are of this order.

Should the occupationally insecure find their way into groups, formal or informal, dedicated to the creation of class-racial struggles and mentalities, the participants might well become predisposed to engage in insurrectionary efforts, especially after they had exhausted the use of other more benign strategies. This explanation of the 1967 Detroit conflagration is admittedly simplistic, but it does touch upon a crucial and necessary source of insurrections, namely, rising but unmet—perhaps unmeetable within present circumstances—expectations.[52]

Conclusions

Detroit has perhaps run the cycle followed by many communities transformed by the industrial revolution. It grew rapidly from a relatively small city with a diversified economy to a large one dependent upon a key industry. The community is now apparently going through a period of technological and political reorganization, the full impact and consequences of which will not be known until the beginning of a peacetime economy in the community and the end of insurrections in the ghettoes (both white and Negro). Unless something is done to eliminate economic patterns of the past, Detroit's future will remain unsettled for some time to come.

4

Uprootedness and Working-Class Consciousness[*]

The Uprooted and the Community

Many of those who seek work in our big cities' industrial plants have emigrated from agrarian regions and therefore fall into the category of uprooted workers.

According to the hypothesis we presented in Chapter 1, uprooted workmen tend to be highly class conscious, especially in the following localities: an *industrializing* community without a tradition of successful working-class movements but with a militant union organization both knowledgeable and powerful, or an *industrialized* community with a history of worker success in labor unions and party organizations.

In either of these cases, the uprooted should be especially militant when they are members of class organizations such as unions. In Detroit, many uprooted workers who are union members are indeed highly militant, as we intend to show in this chapter.

Detroit's Uprooted: Illustrative Categories

Examples of uprooted persons include southern-born Negroes and European-born Poles presently resident in Detroit. With few

[*] Part of the materials in this chapter have appeared in my "Uprootedness and Working-Class Consciousness," *American Journal of Sociology*, 68 (May 1963). This paper was also published in Hiroshi Suzuki's *The Sociology of Urbanization* (Tokyo: Seishimshoto, 1965), pp. 165-79.

exceptions, members of both groups were steeped in *agrarian* cultures before moving to Detroit. Until World War II, the South was essentially a non-industrial area whose culture more nearly approximated an agrarian model. This was also true of Poland, which did not begin to industrialize seriously until after World War II.

Since all our southern-born Negro and European-born Polish respondents were born prior to World War II, they can be considered born in agrarian regions. There are other uprooted as well: Appalachian mountaineers, Sicilian farmers, and Russian laborers who migrated to industrial cities. They often found work in blue-collar occupations and thereby qualify as uprooted.

As you will recall, the prepared share a quite different past from those reared in an agrarian region. Illustrative would be Negro and Polish workers born in Michigan or other sections of the Midwest and East, who either grew up in Detroit or emigrated from regions that have *been industrialized* since at least the 1900's.

The Salience of Uprootedness

The uprooted should express a higher degree of class consciousness than the prepared, and the data presented in Figure 4-1 support this expectation: 52 per cent of the uprooted are either militant radicals or militant egalitarians, while only 22 per cent of the prepared may be classified in this manner.[1] At the other extreme, 13 per cent of the uprooted and 47 per cent of the prepared are non-militants.

When we examine Figure 4-2, the importance of race-ethnicity, the impact of uprootedness remains. First, among Negroes, the southern-born are more class conscious than those born in Michigan and elsewhere in the North. Fifty-eight per cent of these uprooted scored as militants, while 35 per cent of the prepared did so. Among Poles and Ukrainians, those of European background are more likely to express a higher degree of class consciousness than those born in the northern United States.[2]

The percentage differences are somewhat less than the comparable figures for Negroes.[3]

Figure 4–1. Regional Background and Degree of Class Consciousness[*]

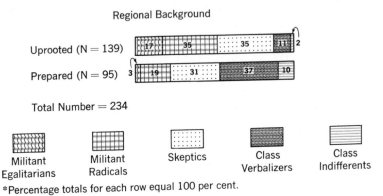

*Percentage totals for each row equal 100 per cent.

Figure 4–2. Ethnicity, Regional Background, and Class Consciousness[*]

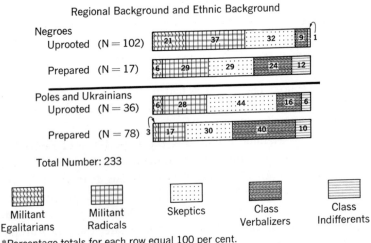

*Percentage totals for each row equal 100 per cent.

The Uprooted as Militant: An Interpretation

The uprooted bring with them few skills and experiences which might help them in their new environment. Consequently, they are readily exploited during part, if not all, of their work lives. This exploitation [4] coupled with insufficient skills effectively limits their chances to obtain secure working-class positions or to move into the middle class. Lack of job security and social mobility creates grievances. At times it engenders collective protests in which the discontented demand an alteration of their condition to more nearly meet their expectations developed prior to movement to the industrial community and to come more in line with the relatively high standard of living maintained by the working class in general.

Many other considerations no doubt contribute to the class consciousness of the uprooted. Of these, one phenomenon deserves particular attention. The uprooted presumably develop an antipathy toward the principal owners of capital goods and land —the dominant classes which have exploited them in both agrarian and industrial regions. In agrarian regions such as much of the southern United States and pre-World War II Poland, personal and family improvement is generally impossible so long as agrarians remain on the farm or the estate. Those with large holdings of land control them through rigid rules and legal structure designed to maintain the unequal distribution of power, wealth, and status. Denied rudimentary rights, subordinate classes find it difficult to express their grievances without being severely repressed by the dominant class or its representatives. For this reason, the agrarians develop a marked dislike for that class.[5] When the dominant class in an industrial community also acts with little regard for their economic and social welfare, these subordinates later broaden this attitude to include all superordinate classes.

Yet we should not overestimate the impact of past membership in a society where there is a high degree of class rigidity. We cannot, for example, say that subordinate-class membership within an agrarian region is the sole source of working-class consciousness for the uprooted. Rather, past residence in an agrarian region contributes to the militancy of uprooted workmen if they are later exploited in an industrial community.

The prepared on the other hand are in a much better position to acquire the occupational skills and urban values of the industrial community. Because of their greater sophistication, they are not subject to the same economic exploitation, blocked social mobility, and job insecurity. In addition, they do not bear a strong dislike for ruling groups found in pre-industrial society, for they never participated in such a form of social organization. The prepared, partly because of these differences in past experiences, fail to develop a general conception of class that might apply to all settings. Hence, far more of them express a low degree of class consciousness.[6]

THE EXTREMELY UPROOTED

The economic problems of former agricultural workers are distressing in the extreme. No other group has faced so many problems on a nearly continuous basis with so little useful experience. If our assumptions are correct, the *extremely uprooted* (those of agricultural, agrarian-region background) should be more class conscious than the *moderately uprooted* (those of non-agricultural, agrarian-region background).

This expectation is supported by Figure 4-3. Southern-born Negroes who have spent some time on a farm prior to moving to Detroit express a higher degree of class consciousness than do Negroes who have never lived on a farm but who come from regions that are predominantly agricultural. Sixty-seven per cent of them are militant, while only 5 per cent score at the other extreme. The same pattern holds for Poles, although the differences are considerably smaller and based upon few cases.[7] Among

Figure 4–3. Past Farming Status, Ethnicity, Regional Background, and Class Consciousness*

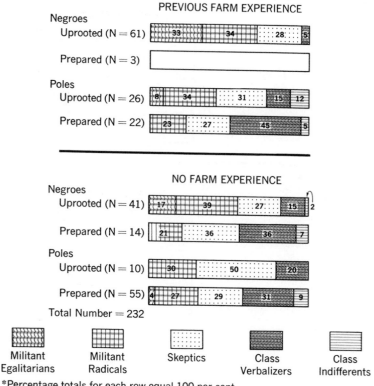

PREVIOUS FARM EXPERIENCE

Negroes
Uprooted (N = 61) 33 | 34 | 28 | 5

Prepared (N = 3)

Poles
Uprooted (N = 26) 8 | 34 | 31 | 15 | 12

Prepared (N = 22) 23 | 27 | 45 | 5

NO FARM EXPERIENCE

Negroes
Uprooted (N = 41) 17 | 39 | 27 | 15 | 2

Prepared (N = 14) 21 | 36 | 36 | 7

Poles
Uprooted (N = 10) 30 | 50 | 20

Prepared (N = 55) 4 | 27 | 29 | 31 | 9

Total Number = 232

Militant Egalitarians | Militant Radicals | Skeptics | Class Verbalizers | Class Indifferents

*Percentage totals for each row equal 100 per cent.

the extremely uprooted Poles, 42 per cent scored as militants.

The extremely uprooted who belong to unions should express an even higher level of class consciousness, since labor groups often use class terms and call for class action to deal with the economic problems common to the working class in general, but accentuated for members formerly from farms in agrarian regions. The information presented in Figure 4-4 supports this expectation. If one examines only union members who have lived

Figure 4–4. Union Membership, Past Farming Status, Regional Background by Ethnic Group, and Class Consciousness (Southern-born Negroes and European-born Poles only) *

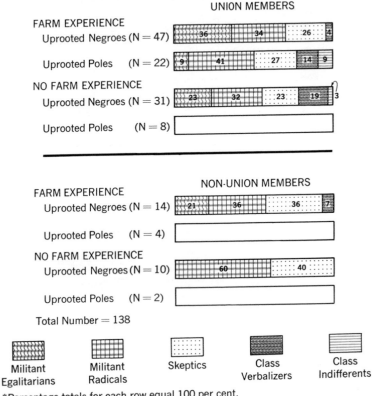

Total Number = 138

*Percentage totals for each row equal 100 per cent.

on farms, 70 per cent of the southern-born Negroes and 50 per cent of the 22 foreign-born Poles are either militant egalitarians or militant radicals. On the other hand, 57 per cent of the southern-born, farm-experienced but non-unionized Negroes fall into the same categories. Unfortunately, lack of a sufficient number of comparable Polish cases does not allow a comparison. The evidence shows, however, that the combination of extreme uprootedness and union membership produces an especially high degree of class consciousness among blue-collar workers of both representative racial and ethnic groups.

The Implications of These Findings

These findings are related to the thoughts of several social scientists on the growth or decline of working-class consciousness in developing and advanced industrial societies, particularly to the question of whether such consciousness takes its most militant form in societies undergoing the transition from an agrarian to an industrial base.

MILITANT WORKING-CLASS VIEWS CONFINED TO
EARLY INDUSTRIAL SOCIETY

Marx had assumed that workers who were accustomed throughout their work lives to the harsh realities of industrial capitalism would have a higher degree of class consciousness than those who had but recently migrated from rural areas. Largely because of this assumption, Marx held that revolutionary enthusiasm would seize the working class of industrialized Germany before a working-class revolution could occur in agrarian-industrial countries such as Russia. Of course, Marx did not say that an embryonic working class would necessarily express a low degree of class *élan,* for he was well aware of the Chartists and other militant British working-class movements. Yet he viewed these early efforts as immature expressions of a working class that was less class conscious than a proletariat steeled by several generations of exposure to industrialization and the agitational activities of labor unions.

By contrast, Engels observed that workers express a high degree of revolutionary consciousness during the early period of industrialization when changes come rapidly and discontinuously to an inexperienced working class. Later generations of workers, Engels theorized, would become less militant, as large-scale industry passed beyond the early period of development and the rate of capital accumulation presumably declined, economic security increased, working conditions improved, and an enlarged industrial base lifted the worker above the bare subsistence level.[8]

Strikingly similar to the views of Engels were those of G.D.H. Cole and Adam Ulam, both of whom investigated British workers during the 1830's and 1840's, when most were of agrarian origin. They contrasted these workers with less rebellious ones of the late nineteenth and early twentieth centuries. Cole traced the revolutionary views of many workmen to the fact that entrepreneurial firms had accumulated capital in a way that severely deprived workmen during England's early industrial development.[9] Ulam's analysis was similar to Cole's. He, too, contrasted stages of industrial development, commented on the marginal quality of the uprooted labor force, and linked both situations to revolutionary politics. He argued that revolutionary thought and action were largely confined to the period of immiserization common to early industrial society, and sharply declined in the succeeding stages. Ulam's argument closely paralleled the one advanced by Cole.[10]

Both Cole's and Ulam's analyses contain many elements of truth; however, they overlook the significance of *economic depressions* in advanced industrial societies. When the business cycle dips sharply, workmen sometimes react in ways which promote class consciousness. New unions are created, older ones become more radical, and workers use direct action to solve their problems.[11] The Great Depression was replete with such instances, and more recent declines (such as the 1957-58 recession) have produced lesser but similar reactions among many workers, especially among the uprooted found in our large cities.

Cole and Ulam also neglected the impact of war or conflicts on class consciousness, especially in societies characterized by the simultaneous presence of backward and advanced forms of technology. War can destroy high standards of living, foster the growth of radical industrial unions, create a sense of deprivation, and in other ways foster revolutionary class politics. This is particularly true in societies where labor unions and labor party leaders have been discredited and where most of the workmen are uprooted, as was the case in Russia between 1917 and 1920.

CLASS CONSCIOUSNESS AND UNEVEN DEVELOPMENT

Leon Trotsky's views on working-class consciousness were considerably different from those expounded by Cole and Ulam, and Marx, Engels, and Lenin as well. During the Russian Revolution, Trotsky observed this important tendency: when peasants entered the industrial working class, they frequently underwent experiences which created militancy. In his *History of the Russian Revolution,* Trotsky stated that working-class radicalism was rooted in discontinuities such as those associated with the leap from backward countryside to advanced factory, from underdevelopment to modernity.

In discussing class consciousness, Trotsky thus related uneven economic development to the growth of revolutionary fervor among the Russian working class during the first two decades of this century. The Russian working class had become militant precisely because it derived directly from the peasantry rather than from experienced artisans, and because consequently it adapted unsuccessfully to rapid economic and technological development and struggled continuously against the political rigidities of tsarism in vain efforts to modify Russian capitalism.[12]

New to an industrial environment, uprooted workers were faced with the problem of adapting to a Russian capitalism committed to the use of modern industrial processes and exploitative techniques introduced by British and French investors. Partly because of foreign control, but also because of the newness of the mammoth enterprises found in large cities such as St. Petersburg and Moscow, workers had no experience with the classical trade unionism replete with local bureaucracy and oligarchy, which tended toward political moderation. Precisely because of the absence of a disciplined and moderate trade union tradition of the sort existing in Germany at this period, the insurgent class potential of the backward Russian workers was transformed by the organizational and ideological preconditions of total cultural revolution into militant action. By October 1917, class consciousness had reached its apogee and found its expression through worker participation in anarcho-syndicalist, social revolutionary, menshevik and bolshevik camps.[13]

Unlike Lenin, who believed that the overwhelming majority of workers would never rise above a bread-and-butter conception of trade unions and politics,[14] Trotsky argued that working-class moderation could not coexist with the abrupt introduction of peasants into an industrial setting. Trotsky's views on the political consequences of telescoped development and what he terms "the privilege of backwardness" should have revolutionized our thinking on class consciousness. Unfortunately, insights such as those expressed in the following quotation have had little influence on social scientists.[15]

> In correspondence with this general course of development of the country, the reservoir from which the Russian working class formed itself was not the craft-guild, but agriculture, not the city, but the country. Moreover, in Russia the proletariat did not arise gradually through the ages, carrying with itself the burden of the past, as in England, but in leaps involving sharp changes of environment, ties, relations, and a sharp break with the past. It is just this fact—combined with the concentrated oppressions of tsarism—that made the Russian workers hospitable to the boldest conclusions of revolutionary thought—just as the backward industries were hospitable to the last word in capitalist organization.
>
> The Russian proletariat was forever repeating the short history of its origin. While in the metal industry, especially in Petrograd, a layer of hereditary proletarians was crystallized out, having made a complete break with the country, in the

Urals the prevailing type was half proletarian, half peasant. A yearly inflow of fresh labor forces from the country in all the industrial districts kept renewing the bonds of the proletariat with its fundamental social reservoir.

. . . Advancing from the sturdy artisans and independent peasants of the army of Cromwell—through the *Sansculottes* of Paris—to the industrial proletarians of St. Petersburg, the revolution had deeply changed its social mechanisms, its methods, and therewith its aims.

As this passage suggests, Trotsky's analysis was an important departure from other socialist views. Trotsky did not assume, with Marx, that a Russian working-class community would become more revolutionary as it matured and emancipated itself from "the idiocies of rural life." [16] On the contrary, he implied that the revolutionary enthusiasm of the Russian proletariat would have deteriorated unless continually renewed and gradually heightened by the influx of peasants ill-adapted to an urban industrial milieu. Trotsky's analysis also differed from the aged Engels's opinions, although the two men did share certain views. Trotsky agreed with Engels that if a young working class were to fail to gain power, and if industrialization were to eliminate agrarian regions, the rejuvenating current of proletarian radicalism might well disappear. Unlike Engels, however, Trotsky did not see an inverse relationship between degree of Russian capitalistic economic development and level of class consciousness; rather, he implied that agrarian regions would continue to be a source of uprooted workers long after the initial period of industrialization. [17]

Trotsky never attempted to apply his interpretation outside Russia. Nevertheless, his analysis helps to explain the distribution of class consciousness not only in early industrial societies, such as early nineteenth-century England, but in advanced ones, such as the United States since World War I. For example, almost all of the workers who took part in the bitter 1929 textile strike in Gastonia, North Carolina, were recent emigrants from agrarian regions. [18] Newcomers from the Piedmont and the Appalachians, these workmen acted with outside Communist organizers to create a union. Much to the surprise of everyone, they helped to establish a labor camp on the perimeter of Gastonia, where they literally waged a prolonged and pitched battle with the local police in order to maintain the camp and to build a union.

Again, an exceedingly large number of workers involved in the 1936 Akron sit-down strikes were from agrarian regions in West Virginia.[19] These workmen plus foreign-born rubber workers—the other major working-class group—worked hard to create a union. If one is correct in assuming that most of the foreign-born rubber workers were also uprooted, the behavior of these workmen is consistent with our expectations.

Similarly, a recent study of the Finnish Communist party by Eric Allardt showed that when rapid economic growth took place in the less developed regions of Finland, left-wing politics became increasingly popular. The Communist party recruited heavily among workmen who had only recently ceased being dependent on farming for their livelihood; and in the one-industry towns located in agrarian regions, the new pockets of Communist agitation assumed a vitality which contrasted vividly with the torpid quality of party life in regions which had been industrialized and politicized for several generations.[20]

Conclusions

Uprootedness, then, would appear to be important in both early and late industrial societies. It is of greatest political significance, perhaps, in early industrializing societies where a disproportionately large number of workmen from technologically backward areas are recruited for industry. Yet the aggressive perspectives of the uprooted wherever located may well stem from material conditions and unmet expectations common to all industrial societies, young or mature. Moreover, whatever the stage of industrialization, great depressions and cataclysmic wars destroy traditions and create vacuums within which uprooted workers can acquire radical perspectives and form revolutionary organizations.

Of those writers who have modified classical formulations to develop analyses appropriate for the twentieth century, Trotsky perhaps has done most to suggest new lines of analysis. His idea of consciousness growing out of uneven development has relevance for today's industrial communities, whose uprooted have leaped from an environment of the mid-nineteenth century to that of the mid-twentieth century, where the landscape is marked by sweeping and unregulated advances in technology.[21]

Yet the uprooted are not the only group to suffer the handicaps associated with labor force marginality. Low marketability, a paucity of esteemed skills, and absence of commitment to established political formulas help create in the unemployed a class perspective on work and wealth. We will now consider how that perspective is reinforced when marginal occupational groups work in plants containing union organizations.

5

The Relevance of Occupational Insecurity*

The term occupational insecurity may be applied to various types of workers—to the blue-collar worker who faces "technological unemployment"; the Negro worker who is a member of a racial group which is predominantly blue-collar in composition and which experiences more than the usual share of job insecurity among the working class; the worker who is downwardly mobile, having moved from a white-collar to a blue-collar occupational position; and finally, a worker who continues to experience or who remains aware of his past economic insecurity as a member of the Depression generation.

These are all relevant aspects of occupational insecurity which we hope to explore in this chapter. Some of the issues which our Detroit study has dealt with are the influence of unemployment on the blue-collar work force as a whole, and on the Negro community in particular; the compound effects of race and union membership on those marginal to the labor force; and the factors that account for militancy among employed and unemployed Negroes. The question of downward mobility has been treated in studies that focus on the political and class views of workers ac-

* This chapter is based, in part, on my "Economic Insecurity and Working-Class Consciousness," *American Sociological Review*, 29 (April 1964), which has also appeared in William Goode's *The Dynamics of Modern Society*.

cording to background, but we will confine our analysis to class consciousness. A related question more distinctly economic in nature is this: Are workers subject to economic insecurity and threats to their jobs in the past (such as those of the Depression generation) more likely to remain class conscious—even in times of prosperity—than those who have experienced less occupational insecurity? The first of these job-related aspects of class consciousness that we will consider is the problem of unemployment.

Trends and Counter-Trends

The early stage of industrial society is characterized by endemic job insecurity among blue-collar workers, considerable struggle among classes, and many indications of working-class consciousness.[1] As industrial society matures, economic crises decline in number and intensity, the class struggle abates,[2] and militancy wanes. Despite these long-term changes, however, extensive occupational insecurity still exists within the advanced industrial community.

Advances in technology and economic organization have helped to establish high standards of living for workers as a whole; these changes have simultaneously created occupational havoc for large sections of the working class. The new prosperity, we have come to know, is accompanied by structural alterations which threaten the livelihood of many who have hitherto benefited from technological progress. In such cases, a combination of automation, plant closures, occupational obsolescence, and cyclical recessions generate short- and long-term unemployment, especially among workmen in primary and secondary industries.

Numerous observers of both early and late industrial societies have commented on the relationship between insecure occupational position and working-class consciousness. Marx argued that successive economic crises would heighten working-class élan.[3] Engels modified this opinion in his later years, stating that a mature industrial capitalistic system would be subject to periodic dips in the economy, but would nevertheless provide an over-all prosperity. This affluence, Engels admitted, would lessen the militancy of workmen.[4] Ironically, Engels was less "orthodox" on this matter than others writing some time after his death. Roberto Michels, for example, argued that life-long membership in the working class constituted one of the greatest sources of anticapitalism in the modern world, precisely because of the precarious nature of capitalistic economy.[5] Many contemporary observers, including Lipset, Lazarsfeld, Barton, and Linz, have shown that in all parts of the world, occupational groups subject to great fluctuations in income have traditionally thrown their support behind leftist parties.[6] Miners, lumbermen, fishermen, and one-crop farmers have time and again backed Socialist and Communist trade unions and social movements.

On the other hand, many social scientists have regarded the structural dislocations of advanced industrial society as minor and without consequence. While noting that "islands" or "pockets" of economic stagnation may exist, these observers argue that relatively few people are involved in what they describe as a "passing phenomenon." Others go so far as to conclude that our affluent society is fast on its way to solving the problems of poverty and economic insecurity. Analysts with this optimistic view frequently refer to the writings of Galbraith in order to buttress their point. Unfortunately, their rosy opinions do not always coincide with his:

> The poverty stricken are further forgotten because it is assumed that with increasing output poverty must disappear. Increased output eliminated the general poverty of all who worked. Accordingly, it must, sooner or later, eliminate the special poverty that still remains. . . .[T]his is not to be expected or, in any case, it will be an infinitely time-consuming and unreliable remedy. Yet just as the arithmetic of modern politics makes it tempting to overlook the very poor, so the supposition that increasing output will remedy their case has made it easy to do so.
>
> To put the matter another way, the concern for inequality

had vitality only so long as the many suffered privation while a few had much. It did not survive as a burning issue in a time when the many had much even though others had much more. *It is our misfortune that when inequality declined as an issue, the slate was not left clean. A residual and in some ways rather more hopeless problem remained.* (Emphasis mine.)[7]

The optimists would have us believe that economic insecurity diminishes in importance with the passage of time. Moreover, they fail to note the present existence of economic forces which promise to eliminate many of the material gains of workers, and which generate discontent and class consciousness, at least within some sections of the labor force.

Interestingly, few economists or sociologists have considered these possibilities, even in periods of recession or depression. However, in spite of the paucity of recent research on these matters, it is clear that the industrial community generates economic insecurity which, in turn, directly affects working-class consciousness. If we assume that unemployed workers will be less secure financially than the employed, then we may hypothesize that the former will be more militant than the latter.

The Relevance of Employment Status

Our study indicates that in most cases the unemployed are more class conscious than the employed. As Figure 5-1 (a) shows, 46 per cent of the unemployed as opposed to 30 per cent of the employed are either militant egalitarians or militant radicals. (The findings in Figure 5-1 are statistically significant at the $<.05$ level.)[8]

Assuming that unstable occupational position engenders class consciousness, we may go on to test whether a racial (or ethnic) group historically subject to tenuous employment expresses a high degree of class consciousness. Negroes in our society are generally in more insecure occupational positions than whites,

Figure 5–1. Employment Status, Race, and Working-Class Consciousness[*]

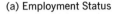

(a) Employment Status

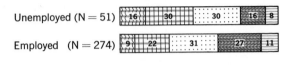

Unemployed (N = 51)   16   30   30   15   8

Employed   (N = 274)   9   22   31   27   11

(b) Race

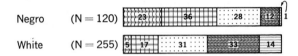

Negro   (N = 120)   23   36   28   12   1

White   (N = 255)   5   17   31   33   14

(c) Employment Status and Race

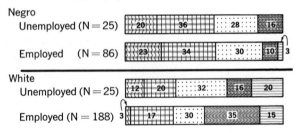

Negro
Unemployed (N = 25)   20   36   28   16

Employed   (N = 86)   23   34   30   10   3

White
Unemployed (N = 25)   12   20   32   16   20

Employed (N = 188)   3   17   30   35   15

Total Number: (a) 325; (b) 375; (c) 324.

Militant Egalitarians   Militant Radicals   Skeptics   Class Verbalizers   Class Indifferents

*Percentage totals for each row equal 100 per cent.

particularly in northern industrial communities, where automation and plant closures have eliminated hundreds of thousands of jobs traditionally held by Negroes in the steel, auto, rubber, meat-packing, and related industries. Given these developments,

Negro workmen in Detroit, for example, should be more class conscious than whites. This study indicates that they are (see (b) of Figure 5-1). Moreover, the differences are considerable: 59 per cent of the Negroes as opposed to 22 per cent of the whites scored as militant, while only 13 per cent of the Negroes compared to 47 per cent of the whites were categorized as either class verbalizers or class indifferents.

Let us further assume that insecure economic status plus economically marginal racial group membership constitute complimentary forces which accentuate the formation of working-class consciousness. If this is correct, then unemployed Negro workers should appear more class conscious than employed Negroes. However, we find that the evidence in (c) of Figure 5-1 fails to support this belief. If anything, the Negro unemployed were slightly *less* class conscious than the employed, while the distribution among whites was as expected. Considered by itself, unemployment does not serve as an important source of class consciousness for Negroes.

In attempting to account for this, we need to consider in addition the impact of union membership. Northern Negroes are heavily concentrated in industrial unions which are a traditional source of class consciousness. If we now consider Negroes exclusively, and simultaneously examine employment status and union membership, it becomes clear that the combination of unemployment and union membership heightens class consciousness. The percentages in Figure 5-2 illustrate the full force of union membership within the Negro community. Eighty per cent of the unionized unemployed as opposed to 27 per cent of the nonunion unemployed were class militants. Admittedly, the number of cases in each category is small; hence, any conclusions based upon such figures are at best tentative. Nevertheless, we cannot overlook the impact of the union.[9] An additional consideration is that working conditions undoubtedly contribute to these differences among Negro workers. Unionized workmen in Detroit have been disproportionately concentrated in large plants, where con-

Figure 5–2. Union Membership, Employment Status, Race, and Class Consciousness (Negroes only) *

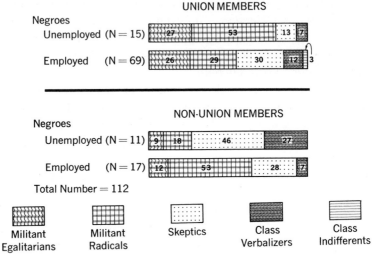

UNION MEMBERS

Negroes
Unemployed (N = 15)   27   53   13   7

Employed   (N = 69)   26   29   30   12   3

NON-UNION MEMBERS

Negroes
Unemployed (N = 11)   9   18   46   27

Employed   (N = 17)   12   53   28   7

Total Number = 112

Militant   Militant   Skeptics   Class   Class
Egalitarians   Radicals   Verbalizers   Indifferents

*Percentage totals for each row equal 100 per cent.

ditions tend to be impersonal and in many ways conducive to the development of class consciousness. Unfortunately, we did not have a sufficient number of cases to weigh simultaneously the significance of union membership, employment status, and plant size.[10]

Unemployment, Race, and Union Membership

At least two important questions emerge from a consideration of these findings: How does occupational insecurity contribute to class consciousness, and how does union membership help to engender militancy among unemployed Negro workers?[11]

Many industrial towns contain conditions which facilitate the formation of working-class consciousness, as when there is widespread unemployment, spatial concentration of large numbers of unemployed workmen, and informal and formal channels of communication between workers. Medium to high levels of working-class unemployment occur when markets contract, plants mechanize, factories relocate, or when businesses fail. At the same time, large numbers of both employed and unemployed workmen are often concentrated in relatively small and culturally homogeneous residential districts. Population density and homogeneity thereby facilitate communication among workers who share common problems, particularly of job opportunity and security. Conversations about such problems are especially prevalent in the Negro ghetto. There, neighborhood organizations often deal with questions such as unemployment, educational facilities, and similar matters.[12] Work groups and unions [13] hold similar discussions. In such groups racial heterogeneity and associated inter-racial hostility probably diminish, but do not eliminate, activities which generate working-class consciousness.

THE UNION AND NEGRO UNEMPLOYMENT

To discuss the importance of labor union membership for unemployed Negroes in industrial towns is to speculate on the impact of industrial unions, since almost all Negro unionists belong to these organizations.[14] In particular, one must focus on the ways in which the rank and file have traditionally viewed class and race issues. They have often defined unemployment as a problem which workmen must continually and collectively face with little or no employer support. Industrial unions have time and again attacked management's opposition to political legislation and union contracts that would increase employment among workers in general and Negro workers in particular. Organizations that have taken this position claim a large audience among working-class Negroes.

Since the early 1940's, the overwhelming majority of Detroit Negro unionists have belonged to industrial unions, where black militants have provided considerable grass-roots leadership.[15] The rank and file and low-level union leaders have been embroiled in numerous struggles with management in a sizable number of large firms. As recently as 1964, union members in Detroit auto plants attacked management on the matter of control of working conditions. It is clear that many Negro and white workers have made demands and become involved in these conflicts. One Detroit worker has discussed the complaints, which led to wild-cat strikes and other forms of protest:

> They dealt with the rate of production as a whole and the amount and type of work each man is supposed to do . . . with health and safety in the plants . . . with the amount of personal time each worker was to have and how it could be used . . . with the hiring, firing, layoff and recall of workers . . . with the building of new plants, the discarding of old plants and the transfer of work and whether and how overtime was to be worked . . . with all aspects of discipline and what authority, if any, management was to have over the worker in the factory. In short, they dealt with every aspect of life in the factory, whether directly in production or not.
>
> If we examine these "local grievances" as a totality, both in the range of subjects with which they are concerned and the consistency with which they are put forward whenever the opportunity presents itself, only one conclusion is possible. The auto workers are striving to substitute their authority and control for the authority and control of management in the process of production.[16]

Participation in this strife engenders militancy. But radical agitation also has helped to shape the views of Negro unionists. During the Great Depression and in the 1940's, Marxist groups concentrated themselves in the largest auto plants and used class politics to influence Negro members of the U.A.W. Consequently, to a far greater degree than some writers would admit,[17] one must take into account the past and, to some extent, the present influence of the Communist party in order to explain the aggressiveness of many Negro unionists. During the formative stages of the C.I.O., Communists were particularly powerful and active in large auto locals with a disproportionately large number of Negroes—for example, U.A.W. Local 600 at the Ford plant in River Rouge, Michigan. In the 1950's, Communist popularity waned considerably, both in the Rouge plant and elsewhere, as the American Communist party's subservience to Soviet policy became publicly evident, as the Reuther machine dismantled the Communist faction within the U.A.W., and as McCarthyites all but eliminated the remnants.

More recently, another organization has come to play an important role in Detroit. This new organization—the all-Negro Trade Union Leadership Council (T.U.L.C.)—had created by 1962 a "black caucus" of approximately 9000 Negroes.[18] It functioned largely within the U.A.W., enjoyed considerable member participation, and undoubtedly contributed to the class and racial consciousness of Negro workmen. The T.U.L.C. has stressed working-class solidarity among Negroes and between races as a partial means of solving problems such as unemployment. Politically, the T.U.L.C. has worked with the Democratic party and other organizations.[19]

Rank and file unionists and Negro voluntary associations clearly have little influence over unemployed and non-unionized Negroes. Consequently, such Negroes are less likely to develop or to use a class-influenced frame of reference. Part of organized labor, at least, has pursued policies which have undoubtedly detracted from its over-all favorable impact on Negro workers. Craft unions, particularly, including those in Detroit, have been biased against Negroes. Because these organizations have visibly practised discrimination, unions in general may become negative reference groups for large numbers of Negroes. Indeed, to the extent that Negro workers mistakenly attribute the policies of craft unions to *all* labor groups, class consciousness may well decrease.

An Additional Consideration

When we first measured class consciousness, we did not refer to class identification.[20] However, when we later substituted this more popular measure of class consciousness,[21] the results, as indicated in Table 5-1, proved to be almost identical with information we obtained earlier. The joint impact of union membership and unemployment also remained the same as in Figure 5-2.

Table 5-1. Degree of Class Consciousness, Employment Status, and Racial Group Membership (in percentages)

VARIABLE CONSIDERED	MILITANT EGALITARIANS	MILITANT RADICALS	SKEPTICS	CLASS IDENTIFIERS	CLASS INDIFFERENTS
(a) EMPLOYMENT STATUS					
Unemployed (N=51)	12	33	29	22	4
Employed (N=274)	8	19	31	31	11
(b) RACIAL GROUP					
Negro (N=120)	18	37	32	10	3
White (N=255)	4	15	32	36	13

An alternate measure of militancy was also devised and based on workers' reactions to the following story: [22]

> Back in 1938 negotiations took place between the Utility Workers' Organizing Committee, and the Consumer's Power Company of Michigan. The union wanted a renewal of its contract with the company, and a year's guarantee against wage cuts. The company refused this and negotiations broke down at the same time as the contract expired. A strike followed, in which the workers took possession of the company's power plants, in the Saginaw Valley area, and expelled the company's superintendents and foremen. During the several days that this stay-in strike lasted, the property of the company

was not damaged in any way. Nor was it a sitdown strike, since the workers continued to operate the power plant, so that interests of the consumers did not suffer. Although the company officials were strongly opposed to this strike action, they settled with the union after a time and it is safe to say that the union won better terms by this action than they would have won in any other way. How do you feel about the actions of workers? I will read you five different choices. You tell me which one of the five is closest to your feeling.

Class-Conscious Responses
1. Approve
2. Approve, but with qualifications

Non-Class-Conscious Responses
3. Cannot decide
4. Disapprove in general, but find points in favor of this action
5. Disapprove

Unfortunately, we were unable to determine whether the favorable responses to the story meant support of the stay-in, plus endorsement of such action today also; approval of this direct action in 1938, but opposition to similar behavior today; or approbation of such action today, but disapproval of this method when used 25 years ago. The third alternative seems improbable, but whether workmen meant the first or second remains unclear. Nevertheless, the results are of interest: the unemployed "approved" the stay-in more than the employed; a disproportionate number of Negroes also endorsed it, unemployed Negro unionists proving particularly militant in this regard. The question thus reinforces our general assessment of unemployed Negro unionists.

The Depression Generation

In examining the interviews of unemployed Negro unionists, we noted not only a general pattern of militancy but also a propensity to use class (and class-racial) terms to describe their attitudes toward a number of matters, including their favorite

President. For example, over 90 per cent preferred Franklin D. Roosevelt, giving the following reasons for their choice:

> I bought a home during the Depression. The moratorium order saved my home. He was the poor man's friend.

> He took the workingmen off their knees and put them in the factory, the W.P.A., C.C.C., and stuff like that.

> I like him best because of his means, ways, and actions. It is the things he did during the Depression. W.P.A., N.R.A. That's right! He made people self-supporting.

> Buddy, let me tell you something. Jobs were hard to find. I've seen hundreds out of work. When Roosevelt got in there, he turned money. Rich people started to spend. F.H.A., W.P.A., and Social Security. I benefited from him. I got jobs.

However, the Negro unemployed were not the only ones to favor Roosevelt. Whites did so as well, and here is what some of them had to say:

> He got rid of the goddamn rackets and bread lines and unemployed.

> He was for the plain, ordinary people. He put the country back on its feet and gave us work.

> He fulfilled all of his promises of the workingman being guaranteed a job. He brought in Social Security and unemployment insurance.

> He did an awful lot for the lower, middle, and upper classes. He got the country back on its feet and everybody earned more money.

> He did more for the workingman than any other President.

> He helped poor people from the Depression. Personally, I lived a good life under him. He did the right thing as President.

> It's simple. He gave the poor man a break.

All these references to Roosevelt suggest that many of the Depression generation are highly class conscious. The significance of generation has been noted by Lipset, Lazarsfeld, Barton, and Linz:

Some American studies illustrate the usefulness of the generation concept. In a study of Negro voting in Harlem in 1944, Morsel (1951) found that 82 per cent of the Negroes under forty-four voted for Roosevelt, as compared with 59 per cent of those over that age. Many of the older Negroes were still responding to an image of the Republican Party as the party of Lincoln. . . .

Studies of the 1948 and 1952 elections indicate that the new political generation, the first voters, are more Republican than those which immediately preceded them. . . .

These results, it is suggested, may be products of a situation in which persons who came of age during the depression or war have developed Democratic ties, whereas those who knew these events only as history and whose first vote was cast in periods of prosperity are turning toward the Republican Party. If, in fact, it is the case that generations tend to vote left or right depending on which group was in the ascendancy during their coming of age, then it may be necessary to reconsider the popularly held idea that conservatism is associated with increasing age. The empirical evidence for this belief was gathered during periods of tremendous social instability, the 1930's and 1940's, when youth turned leftist while their elders tended to retain the more conservative beliefs of their youth. If a society should move from prolonged instability to stability, it may well be that older people would retain the leftist ideas of their youth, while the younger generations would adopt conservative philosophies.[23]

Following the suggestions of these writers and the insights of Mannheim,[24] we can define the *Depression generation* as one whose members experienced the catastrophic consequences of the Great Depression when they were late adolescents or young adults. In this study, we considered all workmen between the ages of 34 and 54 at the time of the interview (1960) members of the Depression generation. On the other hand, we defined the *prosperity generation* as those individuals who reached late adolescence or early adulthood during a period of relative economic prosperity. Thus, workers under 34 years of age were considered members of this generation.

This classification is admittedly imperfect, since a sizable

Figure 5–3.   Generation, Race, and Working-Class Consciousness*

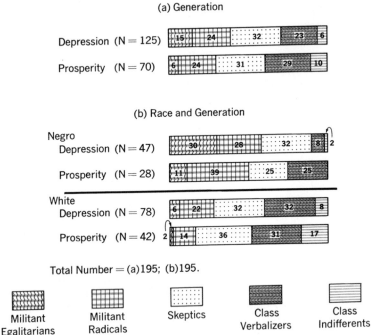

(a) Generation

Depression (N = 125)   15   24   32   23   6

Prosperity (N = 70)   6   24   31   29   10

(b) Race and Generation

Negro
  Depression (N = 47)   30   28   32   3   2

  Prosperity (N = 28)   11   39   25   25

White
  Depression (N = 78)   6   22   32   32   8

  Prosperity (N = 42)   2   14   36   31   17

Total Number = (a)195; (b)195.

Militant   Militant   Skeptics   Class   Class
Egalitarians   Radicals   Verbalizers   Indifferents

*Percentage totals for each row equal 100 per cent.

number of young Detroiters have never prospered.[25] Nevertheless, when we compare these young workers with their Depression counterparts, it would seem that they have experienced
better times.

The information presented in Figure 5-3 confirms that generation may affect attitudes, although considered alone, the percentage differences were not sizable. Thirty-nine per cent of the
Depression generation as opposed to 30 per cent of the prosperity generation scored as militants. (These percentages are
statistically significant at the <.05 level.) This relationship
holds true for both Negroes and whites, as indicated in (b) of
Figure 5-3. Our information indicates, therefore, that economic

insecurity has a lasting effect on many workmen, but that generation membership does not have the same impact on militancy as employment status, race, and union membership.

Downward Mobility

Our investigation raises an additional question regarding the militancy of the declassed and draws upon the experience of class descent. This process involves many dangers. First, a member of the middle class may experience considerable movement from one occupation to another, the totality of which presses him toward the working class. He may try one blue- (or perhaps white-) collar job after another and thereby fail to find a particular niche. Or, as a member of the working class, he may find himself in occupational positions which fail to provide lasting job security. One view holds that downward mobility heightens working-class consciousness, that is, that insecurity experienced as a former member of the middle class makes workers militant. Another view questions whether these workers do, in fact, become strongly class conscious and depart from former standards, including a generally more conservative outlook. It maintains that former members of the middle class seldom accept working-class views, and hope even to regain their past status.

In order to discover which of these views is correct, we should define a key term: downward mobility. For our purposes, it will simply refer to descent from the middle to the working class. Specifically, any worker (1) whose father held a white-collar job when the worker was growing up and/or (2) whose first own full-time job was white-collar will be considered déclassé. The remaining workmen are considered occupationally stable.

The definition proves useful, for we can clearly see (Figure 5-4) that those of middle-class background are markedly less militant than those whose background is working-class. Information gathered by other social scientists substantiates our observations.

Figure 5–4.   Downward Mobility and Working-Class Consciousness°

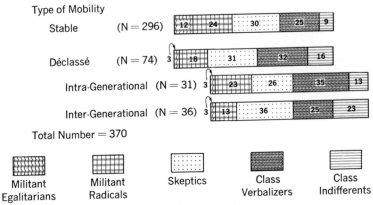

Total Number = 370

Militant   Militant   Skeptics   Class   Class
Egalitarians   Radicals   Verbalizers   Indifferents

*Percentage totals for each row equal 100 per cent.

Lipset and Zetterberg have done an especially good job of piecing together cross-cultural findings on vertical mobility and class perspectives:

> In cases of downward mobility we should not expect, nor do we find, variations among different countries. In all countries, manual workers coming from middle-class backgrounds should be expected to desire to return to the higher class, and hence should be likely to retain middle-class values and patterns of behavior. . . .
>
> The results of voting studies in five countries provide considerable support for the hypothesis that downward mobile persons are less likely to identify with the political and economic organizations of the working class than manual workers who inherit their class status. Thus, the process of social interchange through which some men rise in status and others fall weakens the solidarity and the political and economic strength of the working class. The majority of the men who rise to middle-class status become politically conservative (more in America than in Europe but still a majority on both continents), while a large minority of those who are

reduced to working-class status in the United States, and a majority of men mobile downward in Europe, remain adherents of conservative movements.[26]

The downwardly mobile may be less class conscious for reasons other than the desire to return to their former class position. A high degree of working-class consciousness, for example, frequently involves solidarity *across* racial lines. In the United States this would require a sense of *esprit de corps* embracing both white and Negro workers. Such feelings are uncommon among white déclassés, who are disproportionately prejudiced against Negroes and other minority groups.[27] Among the downwardly mobile who held these views, relatively few were class conscious, although a paucity of cases prevents any useful statistical analysis.

However, our groupings did distinguish among three types of class descent, as indicated in Table 5-2. We may observe in Figure 5-4 that the occupationally stable are more class conscious

Table 5–2. Occupational Background and Mobility Types (Blue-Collar Workers Only)

Occupational Position of Blue-Collar Worker in First Full-Time Job Lasting More Than Three Months	Occupational Position of Blue-Collar Worker's Father When Worker Was Growing Up	
	WHITE-COLLAR	BLUE-COLLAR (OR FARMER)
WHITE-COLLAR	Intra- and Inter-Generational Déclassés	Intra-Generational Déclassés
BLUE-COLLAR (OR FARMER)	Inter-Generational Déclassés	Occupationally Stable

than either type of déclassé. Many of the downwardly mobile are, in fact, non-militant. Forty-eight per cent of the intragenerational déclassé (workers who have shifted from white-collar to blue-collar jobs) fall into this group, and exactly the same percentage of the remaining downwardly mobile are non-militant. By contrast, only 34 per cent of the occupationally stable can be said to be non-militant. The findings are not altogether surprising, for Wilensky and Edwards had approximately the same results in their thorough treatment of the "skidder," or déclassé.[28] Altogether, the evidence strongly suggests that those who experience economic insecurity in moving from the middle to the working class, *fail* to acquire a militant point of view. Previous and extensive exposure to middle-class opinions may perhaps prevent such a change of view.

Conclusions

So far we have demonstrated the relevance of unemployment to the formation of militant class consciousness. Unemployment and union membership contribute strongly toward Negro militancy.

Both whites and Negroes of the Depression generation may hold class opinions in keeping with the economic disorder of their early adulthood. Yet, as we have seen, economic insecurity does not always produce militancy among members of the working class. When workers come from the middle class, their previous experiences seem to dilute their class consciousness.

Occupational insecurity, we may conclude, is not an isolated factor in the formation of class consciousness. With the existence of multiple ethnic and racial communities within the working class, any analysis of class consciousness must take into account the importance of marginal and mainstream working class. In our treatment of the déclassé we have had a glimpse of how ethnocentrism and racism inhibit working-class solidarity. Marx failed to note the full effects of these phenomena, although he observed the conflict:

> Every industrial and commercial center in England now possesses a working class divided into two hostile camps, English proletarians and Irish proletarians. The ordinary English worker hates the Irish worker as a competitor, who lowers his standard of life. In relation to the Irish worker he feels

himself a member of the ruling nation and so turns himself into a tool of the aristocrats and capitalists of his country against Ireland, thus strengthening their domination over himself. He cherishes religious, social, and national prejudices against the Irish worker. His attitude toward him is much the same as that of the "poor whites" to the "niggers" in the former slave states of the U.S.A. The Irishman pays him back with interest in his own money. He sees in the English worker at once the accomplice and stupid tool of the English domination of Ireland.[29]

In the next chapter, we turn our discussion to class-racial (and class-ethnic) communities and problems of class-racial solidarity within the working class.

6

Class Consciousness Among Marginal Minorities*

The Focus

In our large industrial cities, there are many isolated working-class communities subject to racial or ethnic discrimination. Many workmen find that their employers and landlords possess higher prestige, prejudiced opinions, and discriminatory traditions. When class conflict pits one side against the other, the fight may automatically assume a racial or ethnic tone. An example would be conflict between Negro factory workers and white employers over matters of hiring, promotion, and firing, or a fight between black tenants and white landlords over the failure of a landlord to comply with a city ordinance concerning apartment house maintenance. This milieu should help to create class consciousness among blue-collar Negroes in Detroit and other cities where such incidents occur.

Few social scientists have been interested in how class conflict between members of racial groups of different status may be related to degree of working-class consciousness among these minorities. Marx [1] suggested general conditions that fostered

* This chapter is based largely upon a paper entitled "Racial Isolation and Working-Class Consciousness" read before the 1964 meetings of the American Sociological Association.

the development of class consciousness and solidarity—recurrent economic insecurity, relative class isolation, heavy population density, and class homogeneity. After the Second World War, Clark Kerr and Abraham Siegel studied the incidence of strikes in various industries and noted the conditions that related to frequency and intensity of strike action in early industrial societies.[2] They observed that workers in industries that demanded dangerous and dirty labor, offered relatively little job security, and isolated them from middle-class contact tended to become a homogeneous group characterized by intensive interaction. In comparison to other workmen, such workers developed militant unions and utilized the strike more often. Kerr and Siegel found that strikes in the maritime, longshore, mining, and manufacturing industries often assumed the quality of class warfare. The writers implied that these workers shared a high degree of class consciousness, while others in industries which offered better working conditions and job security, more contact with the middle class (and hence less class homogeneity and isolation) developed less militant unions and more moderate bargaining tactics.[3]

During the late 1940's, Theodore Purcell's study of a Chicago packinghouse union repeatedly noted the propensity of working-class Negroes to be more militant than working-class whites.[4] Indeed, the findings of these writers suggest the importance of comparing the class perspectives of Negro and white workmen found in segregated industrial communities.

Marginal and Mainstream Workers: Their Community Counterparts and Views

As we saw in Chapter 1, the marginal working class belongs to a sub-community subject to considerable discrimination and consequent social isolation. Its relations with the middle-class employers and other businessmen are characterized by occupational and housing biases, factors which in turn contribute to their labor force marginality: they are the last hired and first fired.

Mainstream workers differ in that they benefit from discrimination in their favor. At work, home, and play they are relatively well integrated into the labor force and the community. Consequently, we expect mainstream workmen to be less class conscious than marginal workmen, if only because positive discrimination has lessened their labor force marginality.

How well does Detroit's Negro working class approximate our conception of the isolated working-class community? First, the Negro population of Detroit was (and remains) almost entirely working class. In 1957–58, information gathered by the Survey Research Center of the University of Michigan showed that 88 per cent of the one-half million Negroes living in Detroit were blue-collar workers, most of whom were in the auto, steel, and chemical industries. Of these, a disproportionately large number were semi-skilled or unskilled laborers. These workers generally received a poor education, and a sizable number were often unemployed. Unemployment figures for non-whites in Detroit were at least twice as high as for whites, both in periods of prosperity and recession. Whether employed or unemployed, Negro workers had little prestige; in addition, their lack of skills, education, and employment historically left them with little power. Lack of influence plus the presence of racial isolation were partly responsible for their maintaining a sub-culture reminiscent of their southern, agrarian origins.

Thus, a culturally homogeneous population, relatively isolated from contacts with middle-class whites, faced many problems which it subsequently tried to solve by working through religious organizations, block clubs, and Negro labor associations. Of course, the community did not experience total social isolation, for a disproportionately large number of Detroit Negroes belonged to industrial unions. (More than 70 per cent of the Negro unionists sampled in this study were members of industrial unions, mainly the U.A.W.) Largely because a considerable proportion of its population was unionized, many Detroit Negroes earned medium to high incomes, although we could classify a significant minority of the Negro blue-collar population as poverty stricken.[5]

The white Detroit workers corresponded to our definition of mainstream working class. The white working class contained almost every European and Near Eastern nationality and religious group. However, it was predominantly Northwest European* and Slavic.[6] As such, working-class whites constituted approximately 57 per cent of the entire white metropolitan community in 1957–58.[7] Although unemployment had some effect on the mainstream working class, its members were better protected from the vicissitudes of the economy because they were generally better educated, more skilled, and hence more employable. Along with these advantages and mainly because they were white, these workers had better relations with the white middle class. At the same time, racial prejudice and segregated workplaces limited the number and closeness of contacts between white and Negro workers. White workers in auto, steel, and chemical unions [8] did have contact with Negroes on the job, but social relations generally stopped there. Seldom did they extend to neighborhood, school, church, or family.

The Interplay of Race, Earnings, and Union Membership

In the previous chapter, we showed that Negroes were more class conscious than whites.[9] Perhaps of more interest than the percentages involved were the responses of Negro workmen when asked: Who gets the profits when business booms in Detroit?

> You know who gets the profits. The stockholders. The bigwigs get the big fat bonuses the more they produce.

* Northwest European refers to English, Scotch, Welsh, Irish, French, Belgian, Dutch, and German groups.

Figure 6–1.   Earnings, Race, and Working-Class Consciousness*

Low Earners*

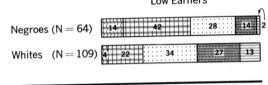

High Earners

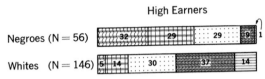

Total Number = 375

* High and low earners are defined as those who in 1959
  made more or less than $5000 respectively.
  (Based upon earnings of head of household.)

| Militant Egalitarians | Militant Radicals | Skeptics | Class Verbalizers | Class Indifferents |

*Percentage totals for each row equal 100 per cent.

The manufacturers. The workers just get a living out of it.
The profits go to the operators.

Let's say the big companies such as consumers' department
stores. The factories of course. They get it because they are
selling cars. In other words, I find out that the big class
has money invested in factories, banks, and loan associations,
and I know they get all the profits.

The owners of big business. (Probe: Would you yourself
benefit?) Yes, when business booms, I do too. It kind of
filters down.

The companies. Cadillac and General Motors.

Everybody gains, but people of wealth gain more. Those
who have, get it.

Stockholders. Everyone benefits when business booms, but
the workingman benefits the least.

The rich man. He's the one that gets the profits.

The upper class. I don't get it. I get the same all the time.

These replies indicate a sensitivity to earning differences and thereby suggest that economic deprivation may be more important than economic insecurity. If deprivation can be measured in terms of low personal income, then its added impact, as indicated in Figure 6-1, does *not* prove to be significant. The combination of race and income does not work out as expected. In fact, Negro workers in the lower income category were on the whole *less* class conscious than those in higher brackets, although the opposite held true for whites. Figure 6-2 indicates, moreover, that while union membership accentuated the militancy of Negro workmen who were high earners, the high-income Negro workmen who were not unionized ($N=10$) were nevertheless quite militant; still, the paucity of these particular workmen in our sample prevents us from drawing definite conclusions. It would appear that the combination of moderately high incomes and union membership accentuates class consciousness among Negro workmen.

Few would doubt that class consciousness among marginal group workmen derives in part from conflict with business. In order to deal with the problems of unemployment and equal opportunity, members of the marginal working class create their own voluntary associations—all of which are culturally homogeneous—to question and, in some cases, to attack the business community. Statements by labor organizations,[10] church groups, and neighborhood associations [11] supplement boycotts, picketing, bloc votes, and other mechanisms of persuasion designed to alter employment policies and sales methods. Marginal workmen who participate either directly or indirectly in these collective practices develop a tendency to see problems in class as well as ethnic or racial terms, to believe that wealth is apportioned in a way that benefits the upper middle classes, to view direct action against business interests as necessary, and to

Figure 6–2.   Union Membership, Earnings, Race, and Class
Consciousness*

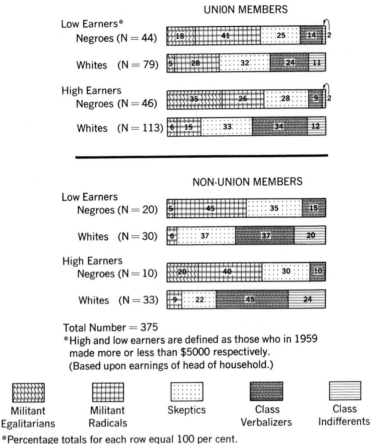

UNION MEMBERS

Low Earners*
  Negroes (N = 44)   18 | 41 | 25 | 14 | 2

  Whites   (N = 79)   5 | 28 | 32 | 24 | 11

High Earners
  Negroes (N = 46)   35 | 26 | 28 | 9 | 2

  Whites   (N = 113)   6 | 15 | 33 | 34 | 12

NON-UNION MEMBERS

Low Earners
  Negroes (N = 20)   5 | 45 | 35 | 15

  Whites   (N = 30)   6 | 37 | 37 | 20

High Earners
  Negroes (N = 10)   20 | 40 | 30 | 10

  Whites   (N = 33)   9 | 22 | 45 | 24

Total Number = 375
*High and low earners are defined as those who in 1959
  made more or less than $5000 respectively.
  (Based upon earnings of head of household.)

Militant   Militant   Skeptics   Class   Class
Egalitarians Radicals   Verbalizers   Indifferents

*Percentage totals for each row equal 100 per cent.

value greater equity in the allocation of wealth. These ideas take
hold among marginal workmen in part because of their separation
from the middle classes and white-collar influence.

Antagonism appears to be strongest among marginal group
workers who have enough money to purchase consumer goods
and services but not sufficient power to eliminate the discrimina-

tory practices of business. Specifically, these particular workers, when compared with their low-income counterparts, clash more frequently with businessmen on such matters as job promotion, fair housing, and educational opportunity. Their moderate incomes help to increase their expectations and move them to make demands upon a business community reluctant to change.

Class-racial conflict between marginal workmen and mainstream businessmen has no doubt influenced the growth of working-class consciousness, but the development of a class perspective also derives from workers' previous participation in industrial unions. As we have already observed in Detroit, these organizations enlisted a very large proportion of Negro workmen during the 1930's and 1940's and stressed the class character of Negroes' problems by focusing on the discriminatory behavior of white employers and the inherent limitations of an industrial system geared more to profits than to employee security. These industrial unions provided an organizational framework for class interpretations of Negro problems.[12]

Labor unions appear to have an impact upon not only marginal but mainstream workmen. However, even unionized mainstream workmen are not very class conscious, and for good reason, since many of their working conditions favor the attenuation of militancy. For example, jobs denied to racial minorities become available to them, and they have better chances of being promoted and retained. Consequently, mainstream workmen have fewer employment problems and when they do, they can frequently count on the aid of helpful friends and employers. Such circumstances hardly promote a militant class perspective, as many writers have noted when they have studied white workers who have benefited from racial discrimination at the workplace.[13]

The Interconnection of Class and Racial Verbalization

Since marginal working-class conflict occurs simultaneously along class and racial lines, certain aspects of *class* consciousness can be correlated with *racial* awareness. Specifically, Negro workmen's differences with white middle-class interests or craft unionists on matters of employment, promotion, and job retention generate both class and racial consciousness. We used a set of eight questions originally to measure class verbalization.[14] We recoded the materials in order to gauge the extent to which workmen used racial terms spontaneously in their replies. Subsequent analysis showed that the answers did demonstrate racial (or class-racial) awareness. One set of Negro answers illustrates the point. We asked the following: Do you think they (city officials) don't pay attention to the needs of some kinds of people? (If Yes) Who is that? Here are some responses:

> Poor people in general, but it's a little harder on Negroes than most. (Probe: How serious is this problem?) Not too serious. Things are getting better, especially housing. I remember the time when you had to live south of Gratiot. (This was an area which contained a majority of Detroit Negroes until World War II.)

> Negroes don't get the break that they deserve.

> Negroes, especially in the city services such as tree clipping, spraying, unpaved alleys, and things like that. (Probe: How serious is this problem?) It's not too serious, but things don't seem to be getting better. They're at a standstill.

> They try to keep us Negroes back far enough so that they will always have us working for them. (Standard probe) Pretty serious problem. Even loan companies and banks take advantage of Negroes to learn their ideas, steal from them, or pass them along to others.

> They spend millions of dollars on rockets, but there are people on welfare who can't put their kids through school— and don't get enough attention. (Standard probe) Pretty serious. A lot of kids who go to schools aren't presentable. You see their clothes, and you guess that maybe they're on the welfare.

> I realize that people have to help themselves, but look at the colored districts. Colored that earn the same as whites

can't get property in nice districts. The line is drawn so you can't get property. They should show some improvement toward the colored race. (Standard probe) Real serious. Future generations are not given much to look forward to. Everybody should have some history and background to them. If you see your fellow man tied down, you lose all desire to better conditions.

The poorer class of people, the working class. (Standard probe) I think it's pretty serious myself.

The working people aren't given an even break. The people, however, don't try to help themselves. They just don't care about helping themselves. (Standard probe) Working conditions are bad, but personally I just can't exactly say why. Personally, I think it is the fault of both the officials and the people.

They don't pay attention to minority groups. They could improve welfare for poor people. (Standard probe) With automation, it's getting really serious. It's driving people away from Detroit.

Although some white workmen expressed themselves in either class or racial terms, others relied upon a class-racial frame of reference.

Lower-class folks, like Italians, Polish, Negroes, and southerners. (Standard probe) It's very serious.

Poor people. (Standard probe) It's very serious. They'll be sorry some day.

In the poorer sections, playgrounds and things like that are run down, but not in the rich sections. (Standard probe) Not too serious.

White working-class people don't get things as would Negroes. For example, the police are tougher on white working people who have dogs in the neighborhood. (Standard probe) We need a new, different mayor in the city. We should have a new head of the transportation department. We need a new government. It's very serious. Corruption must be cleared out.

They don't pay attention to the needs of workingmen. They want to keep him in the lowest place they can. (Standard probe) Pretty serious, and if people don't do anything about it, what good are elections? Right?

Well, the ones with less, the poorer and older neighborhoods. (Standard probe) I really couldn't say what the kind of problems really are, and how bad they are, except from what the newspapers say.

If a workman used one (or more) racial terms when replying to the eight questions, he was coded as engaging in racial verbalization. We then related this to class verbalization. Class and racial consciousness were, in many cases, interrelated; when one occurred, the other did so as well (see Table 6-1). This

Table 6–1.   Race of Worker and Use of Class and Racial Symbols

SYMBOLS	NEGRO (N=120)	WHITE (N=255)
Uses neither racial nor class symbols (N=50)	4%	18%
Uses racial symbols only (N=27)	7%	7%
Uses class symbols only (N=153)	38%	42%
Uses both racial and class symbols (N=145)	51%	33%
TOTAL = 375		

simple correlation does not mean that class consciousness is directly related to race consciousness. This question remains problematic. However, the implication is there.

The Mainstream Working Class: An Amplification

Our treatment of mainstream workmen has so far avoided a number of questions related to the heterogeneity of this category. For example, some ethnic sub-groups comprise what we may call a *semi-marginal working-class* group. Compared to mainstream workmen in general, the semi-marginal ethnic group contains a disproportionately large number of economically insecure workmen, many of whom are unemployed, semi-skilled, or unskilled. Partly because they hold relatively few secure positions, they possess low to medium prestige. In turn, low status helps to isolate them because they have relatively few ties with ethnic groups of appreciably higher or lower prestige, although some ties do extend to other ethnic groups of comparable rank. On the whole, however, affective relations are generally confined to this ethnic community. Friendship and marriage bonds help to cement ties within it, as do voluntary associations and religious organizations.

In contrast are those workmen who belong to an ethnic group whose middle-class members constitute an unusually large percentage of the labor force and whose working-class members are, with relatively few exceptions, steadily employed and highly skilled. The highly middle-class character of the ethnic group and its secure employment position contribute to the relatively high prestige of its working-class members. This promotes easy mingling between these particular workmen and other workers, or with middle-class people of other ethnic groups, particularly those groups similar in prestige. Connections with the middle class are increased as these workmen develop primary ties which cut across ethnic and class lines, producing families and neighborhoods more heterogeneous and middle-class in character. Consequently, when we compare non-marginal group workmen with marginal and semi-marginal workers, the former are less limited by their nationality ties and more ordered by middle-class values.

The Polish (and Ukrainian) workers who lived in Detroit at the time of our study had many of the characteristics of a *semi-marginal* working-class community. As Table 6-2 demonstrates, a disproportionately large number of Polish workers were semi-skilled and unskilled, and our evidence indicated further that a relatively high proportion were unemployed.[15] Generally,

Table 6–2. Occupational Composition of Selected Ethnic Groups, Metropolitan Detroit, 1957–58

OCCUPATION OF HEAD OF FAMILY	NEGROES PER CENT	NUMBER	POLES PER CENT	NUMBER	GERMANS PER CENT	NUMBER	BRITONS PER CENT	NUMBER
WHITE COLLAR								
1) Professionals, Technical, and Kindred Workers	4		9		24		15	
2) Managers, Officials, and Proprietors	3		3		16		20	
3) Clerical, and Kindred Workers	4		13		8		9	
4) Sales Workers	1		6		0		11	
SUB TOTAL	12	(12)	31	(20)	48	(32)	55	(49)
BLUE COLLAR								
5) Craftsmen, Foremen, and Kindred Workers	9		39		27		28	
6) Operatives and Kindred Workers	54		28		15		13	
7) Private Household and Kindred Workers	13		0		8		3	
8) Non-Farm Laborers	12		2		2		1	
SUB TOTAL	88	(80)	69	(44)	52	(34)	45	(39)
9) Not in Labor Force		(7)		(4)		(1)		(7)
TOTALS (Excludes Those Not in Labor Force)	100	(92)	100	(64)	100	(66)	100	(88)

Poles enjoyed considerably less prestige than Germans or Britons. When asked to rank ethnic groups in terms of status, both Polish and non-Polish workers viewed Poles as having low prestige. Table 6-3 shows how different ethnic groups rated their chances to be accepted into a white middle-class country club.

Respondents were asked the following:

> Imagine a situation where a rich country club out in Grosse Pointe is selecting a few new members. It is hard to get into this club because it is exclusive, and there are a lot of people applying to get in. Now, in this one situation it just so happens that every individual who wants to get in the club has almost the same amount of education, income, and occupational skill. These people who want to join up are similar in many other ways as well. However, they do differ in one and only one important way: there are four different nationality groups among the applicants. There are roughly the same number of people of Negro, English, Polish, and German descent. My question is, of these four groups, which nationality group members have:
> (1) the *least* chance of getting into the country club?
> (2) the *best* chance of getting into the country club?
> (3) the *second best* chance of getting into the country club?
> (4) the *third best* chance of getting into the country club?

The percentages (Table 6-3) and the mean rank scores [16] agree on an order of group prestige ranging from highest to lowest in status: the English, Germans, Poles, and Negroes, respectively. Their own group membership notwithstanding, raters agreed on this ethnic hierarchy. For example, the majority of Poles, Negroes, Germans, and English ranked Poles in the third position. It should be noted that other studies have found comparable rankings of ethnic groups.[17] Perhaps more important is the parallel between these ratings and those made by Grosse Pointe real estate interests who, as we have seen, also judged Northwest Europeans the most desirable.

Viewed by those with power as having low status, many of

Table 6-3. Respondents' Judgments on Chances of Ethnic Group Members to Enter Exclusive Club by Percentages*

GROUP SELECTED		NEGROES (N=119)	RATER'S ETHNIC GROUP POLES & UKRAINIANS (N=114)	GERMANS AND BRITONS (N=139)
Best	Negroes	0	1	0
Chance	Poles	8	1	1
	Germans	12	8	12
	English	66	59	55
	Any White Group	7	22	22
	Other	7	9	10
Second	Negroes	0	0	0
Best	Poles	12	7	6
Chance	Germans	53	41	45
	English	11	9	11
	Any White Group	12	27	26
	Other	12	16	12

Third	Negroes	0	1	0
Best	Poles	59	50	60
Chance	Germans	12	7	6
	English	5	2	1
	Any White Group	11	25	22
	Other	13	15	11
Least	Negroes	98	86	96
Chance	Poles	0	1	0
	Germans	0	2	0
	English	0	0	0
	Any White Group	0	0	0
	Other	2	11	4

* Each rating totals 100 per cent.

Detroit's Polish-Americans have come to share this opinion, as indicated by Table 6-3.[18] Undoubtedly this is accompanied by hostility toward members of the middle class who discriminate against them. However, hostility is only one reaction to lower prestige. Another is that Polish-Americans tend to marry within their own ethnic group, or into one of comparable prestige (such as the Ukrainian), or one of slightly higher or lower prestige (see Table 6-4).

The Catholic Church supports this tendency even if only inadvertently, for most of the ethnic groups which comprise the bulk of its membership occupy positions of similar status. By promoting marriage within the Church and maintaining Polish-Catholic associations, the Church has helped to sustain the Polish-American community. In addition, Poles who marry Catholics of non-Polish backgrounds may integrate their spouses into the

Table 6–4. Nationality of Selected Couples and Their Parents, Detroit, 1957–58 (by Percentages)

	Mother								
Ethnic Background of Respondent (from Father)	Negroes	Poles	Germans	Britons and Canadians	Other N. & NW. Eur.	Other E. & S. Eur.	Others	Don't know	Totals
Negroes	100								(99)
Poles		90	3	0	0	6	1	0	(68)
Germans		3	55	22	12	6	2	0	(67)
Britons & Canadians		1	13	56	18	0	9	3	(94)
Totals	(99)	(64)	(51)	(68)	(25)	(8)	(10)	(3)	(328)

Polish-American sub-culture. Numerous Hungarians, Ukrainians, Ruthenians, and Russians have become part of a Detroit sub-community which has (1960) twenty-eight churches where Polish is used exclusively by the priest in at least one of the masses. Although destined to assimilation in the long run, the Polish community quite obviously retains its solidarity. At the time of the study there existed hundreds of Polish-American voluntary associations and two Polish newspapers catering to the metropolitan area's 425,000 Polish-Americans. We should note that these voluntary associations also had ties outside traditionally Polish districts, in such suburbs as Warren and Dearborn.[19] The Polish sub-community thus contained social forces that helped to maintain it; ethnic cohesion also derived from discrimination practised by the Anglo-Saxon community.[20]

British, and to a lesser extent, German ethnic communities made up the mainstream non-marginal working class. In both groups, an unusually large number of workmen were both em-

				Spouse					Ethnic Background of Respondent (from Father)
Negroes	Poles	Germans	Britons and Canadians	Other N. & NW. Eur.	Other E. & S. Eur.	Others	Don't know	Totals	
98					1	1		(88)	Negroes
	60	14	3	16	7	0	0	(58)	Poles
	13	20	27	27	7	1	5	(60)	Germans
	5	14	39	35	7	0	0	(84)	Britons & Canadians
(86)	(47)	(32)	(51)	(54)	(15)	(2)	(3)	(290)*	Totals

* Totals do not include unmarried respondents.

Figure 6-3.   Ethnic Group Membership and Class Consciousness*

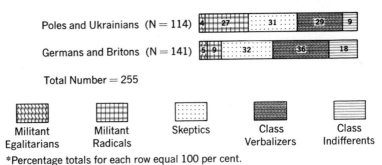

Poles and Ukrainians (N = 114)

Germans and Britons (N = 141)

Total Number = 255

Militant   Militant   Skeptics   Class   Class
Egalitarians   Radicals   Verbalizers   Indifferents

*Percentage totals for each row equal 100 per cent.

ployed and skilled (see Table 6-2, row 5). Furthermore, these
two ethnic sub-communities had relatively large numbers of
white-collar people. Both nationality groups enjoyed more prestige than the Polish community, and their high status is reflected
by their marrying members of ethnic groups with comparable
status. At the same time, we can observe the *absence* of any
religious force to promote the cohesion of these groups and
assimilation of outside members. Those of English, Scotch, Scotch-
Irish, Welsh, and, to a lesser degree, German background have
married outside their own largely Protestant ethnic groups. If
we examine the top prestige groups, we can observe ethnic
disintegration, owing to the absence of homogeneous ethnic
group Catholicism; the shared Protestantism which emphasized
individual rather than group achievement thereby contributed
to a lack of solidarity among those of British and German background.

If, with Kerr and Siegel, we assume that marginality, isolation,
and related considerations produce class consciousness, we should
find that workmen of Polish and Ukrainian background are, on
the whole, more class conscious than German and British workers.
The information in Figure 6-3 substantiates this hypothesis.[21]

Figure 6–4. Union Membership, Ethnic Group, and Class Consciousness*

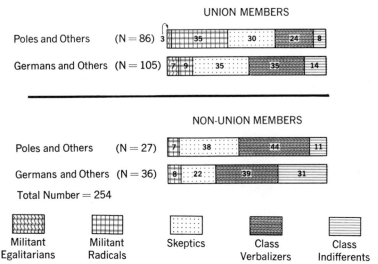

UNION MEMBERS

Poles and Others (N = 86)

Germans and Others (N = 105)

NON-UNION MEMBERS

Poles and Others (N = 27)

Germans and Others (N = 36)

Total Number = 254

Militant Egalitarians

Militant Radicals

Skeptics

Class Verbalizers

Class Indifferents

*Percentage totals for each row equal 100 per cent.

Thirty-one per cent of the Polish-Americans as opposed to 14 per cent of the other ethnic group scored as "militants." Not too surprisingly, class views were most evident among Polish-Americans who belonged to unions (Figure 6-4). A great many of these Polish unionists had weathered the grim period when the U.A.W. organized workers in Detroit auto plants. Their experiences as young workers had created class consciousness, while their sub-community fostered its retention.[22]

Polish membership in the Depression generation has a number of implications, one of which is especially worth our attention. The disproportionately large number of Poles (including Ukrainians) who were members of the Depression generation—the most class-conscious generation—helps to explain why Poles in general were more class conscious than Germans and Britons. However,

Figure 6–5. Generational Membership, Ethnic Group, and Class Consciousness*

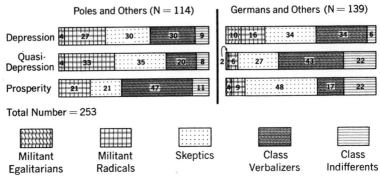

Poles and Others (N = 114)   Germans and Others (N = 139)

Total Number = 253

Militant   Militant   Skeptics   Class   Class
Egalitarians   Radicals   Verbalizers   Indifferents

*Percentage totals for each row equal 100 per cent.

this is not simply a statistical fluke, stemming from the large number of Poles of this generation. Polish workmen were generally more class conscious than Germans (and Britons) at all generational levels.[23]

Among Depression generation workmen (those 34–54 years of age), 31 per cent of Poles scored as militants, whereas for Germans and Britons the comparable figure was 26 per cent (see Figure 6-5). In the older generation (54 years and older in 1960), 37 per cent of the Poles and 8 per cent of the Germans and Britons ranked as either militant egalitarians or militant radicals. Within the younger, prosperity generation (under 34 years of age in 1960), 21 per cent of the Poles and 13 per cent of the Germans and Britons were rated as militant.

Conclusions

Both theory and research indicate that the marginal working class should be more militant than mainstream workmen. This proposition holds true for the industrial community of Detroit, which has a large racial ghetto almost entirely working-class in composition. Specifically, white workers were considerably less militant than Negroes, particularly Negroes who earned moderate incomes and belonged to unions. Perhaps of equal interest is the observation that racial awareness accompanies class consciousness. This finding is not too surprising, since conflict frequently occurs along class and racial lines, as well.

In addition, we discovered that the mainstream working class does not constitute a homogeneous mass of workmen undifferentiated in ethnic background and opinions on class matters. Ethnic sub-cultures exist and in certain ways reflect their class composition. Clearly, the Polish sub-community did contain a relatively large number of highly class-conscious workmen. Of even greater magnitude than the differences in class consciousness between members of this semi-marginal group and the mainstream as a whole, are those differences (measured in percentages) between marginal and semi-marginal, or greater still, between marginal workers and white, mainstream workmen. Thus, the percentage differences separating the German from the Polish workmen were not as great as those which distinguished Poles from Negroes, or whites in general from Negroes. On the whole, race is the most important influence on class consciousness, although nationality differences help to account for variations in attitudes within the mainstream working class.

Class-racial solidarity may be of growing importance in cities such as Detroit, where the Negro working class focuses increasingly on the question of jobs. At the time of the study (1960) the Negro community, especially those members with labor union experience, contained many who were critical of the white business community, discriminatory unions, and to a lesser degree, unions that were unable to arrange greater job security for workers. Negroes may well be turning to racial, working-class organizations for solutions to their problems, and a type of militancy may be emerging based on solidarity among Negro blue-collar workers. This would supplant the view of a working-class *esprit de corps* cutting across racial lines typical of an earlier period of industrial struggle. For the main antagonists of the future may prove to be the white business community and an organized Negro working class.

7

Working-Class Consciousness, Race, and Political Choice*

With the acquisition of high levels of class consciousness, workers often find political channels for the expression of their beliefs. An economic recession or depression—or the aftermath of either one—stimulates worker interest to rally support for a pro-labor candidate.

All of the conditions which we have previously described as tending to create class consciousness existed and promoted class-conscious voting in Detroit in the late 1950's and early 1960's. This includes the 1958 gubernatorial election in Michigan, about which we polled information on workers' voting choices. Widespread unemployment formed the backdrop of the 1958 election; well over 10 per cent of the city's labor force had been unemployed for six months or more prior to November. The problem assumed a class as well as racial character, since it affected most sections of the working class.[1]

A Pro-Labor Politician and Union Push

G. Mennen Williams, the Democratic governor of Michigan between 1948 and 1960, supported such measures as a corporation

* Part of this chapter is based on an article which appeared in the *American Journal of Sociology,* 69 (September, 1963), 171-6.

profits tax and workmen's compensation legislation. He opposed regressive taxation measures and right-to-work proposals, no small task in a state where powerful economic interests have dominated conservative politics. What is more important, he worked vigorously to obtain federal help for the unemployed. His efforts in their behalf were especially evident during the 1958 recession. Williams's views on these matters did not make him a "militant egalitarian," yet we may refer to him as a pro-labor politician in the tradition of Franklin Roosevelt and the progressive Midwestern politicians. Certainly G. Mennen Williams's political views were quite similar to those entertained by dominant groups in the Michigan Democratic party in 1958, when he opposed Paul D. Bagwell, the Republican candidate for governor.

Bagwell supported the interests of the automotive industry's management, a dominant force in the Republican party. In this case, the political ties between the Republican candidate and industry, plus his economic dependence upon these powerful interests, made his moderate stand on unemployment seem unconvincing.

The differences between the two politicians and the importance of the class issue helped the unions and their political organizations (such as the Political Action Committee) to campaign effectively for the pro-labor candidate and mobilize voting support among their own members, especially the more class-conscious ones.[2] On the other hand, lack of contact with most non-union members at their workplace lessened the union's political impact on them, especially on those predisposed to reject appeals that stressed the importance of class interests.

The Pro-Labor Party

The prevailing outlook of the Michigan Democratic party during the years G. Mennen Williams served as governor was quite consistent with Williams's own views—it was (and is) a party clearly progressive and reformist in nature. Pro-labor orientation gained ascendancy about 1948, the time of Williams's first victory. There were a number of reasons for this. First, the labor unions became a powerful influence within the party; in 1948 the state C.I.O. Political Action Committee decided to become actively involved in the Democratic party organization in order to transform it into a political party with progressive policies. The C.I.O. translated this program into action, and subsequently it emerged —particularly, the U.A.W.—as a major power in Democratic party councils.

In 1950 the chairmanship of the state organization went to the highly progressive Neil Staebler. Staebler was an advocate of a citizen-based, "issue-oriented" party, and he instituted various changes in party structure and operation to ensure its commitment to vital issues. In particular, he de-emphasized patronage and favored recruitment and retention on an ideological basis. Governor Williams's active popularization of Staebler's position helped thus to crystallize a reformist and pro-labor point of view within the party.[3]

Both Williams and the Democratic party championed the civil rights of Negroes. In the context of this struggle, status-group politics was at least as significant as (if not more important than) class politics to many Negro workmen. For them, class consciousness was not, then, a major factor (although it proved relevant as a set of attitudes and values), because even the *least* class-conscious Negro workmen supported the pro-labor party and candidate.

Class Consciousness and Class Vote

Despite this racial factor, we may still expect a direct relationship between class consciousness and a vote for the pro-labor politician. Hence, the figures presented in Table 7-1 fail to come as a surprise. (The figures are statistically significant at the $<.05$ level.[4]) In an election in which Detroit workers gave overwhelming support to the reform candidate, 76 per cent of all *militant* workmen interviewed—including non-voters—voiced their support for him (see Table 7-1). At the same time, workers who expressed either a moderate or a low degree of conscious-

Table 7–1. Working-Class Consciousness, Race, Union Membership, and Political Choice

Source of Political Preference	For Williams*	
	PER CENT	NUMBER
WORKING-CLASS CONSCIOUSNESS		
Militant	76	(123)
Moderate	70	(110)
Non-Militant	50	(132)
RACE		
Negro	76	(119)
White	59	(247)
UNION MEMBERSHIP (WHITES ONLY)		
Members	66	(185)
Non-Members	39	(62)

* The percentages are based upon total number of workers who answered the questions, not only on those who voted.

ness gave him somewhat less support. Considering now only those who voted, 95 per cent of the militants, 88 per cent of the moderates, and 69 per cent of the non-militants cast their ballots for Williams.

Apparently, class considerations were of paramount importance in determining most workers' choice of Williams:

> I liked his platform. It was for the workingman.
>
> Because he's more of a man for the poor people. He knows our needs.
>
> I think he's doing a good job for the poor people, I think he's 100 per cent for the workingman.
>
> I thought he was a good governor. He's a staunch supporter for working-class people.
>
> He seemed to do fairly well as far as politics go. He's for the workingman. That's probably keeping him out of the presidential race.

As I told you before, I'm strictly Democratic. Williams is number one. He's for labor. He's for the workingman.

He was giving the workingman a fair shake, where Bagwell wasn't giving us anything.

I didn't vote, but I liked Williams. (Why?) Oh, I don't know.

He seems to be a fair guy. He's honest. If he can do something for the worker, he does it.

Williams is more for the working class.

He's a good man. He always helped the workingman and was the workingman's choice.

The impact of race proved to be especially important in Detroit, where, for several decades, the vast majority of Negroes (irrespective of degree of class consciousness) have voted for politicians committed to strong civil rights programs. Such was also the case in this election in which 75 per cent of all Negroes interviewed supported Williams. Of those Negro workers who voted, almost 100 per cent of the militant were for Williams; what is more interesting is that over 90 per cent of the non-militant did so as well. A low degree of class consciousness thus had little effect on the political choices of Negro voters.

If we examine the impact of class consciousness on white workers only, we find that among voters and non-voters alike, 74 per cent of the militant favored Williams as opposed to 67 per cent of the moderates and 47 per cent of the non-militant.

Of much interest was the *combined* impact of union membership and class consciousness. An analysis of the entire sample of white workers—both voters and non-voters—revealed a predictable pattern of voting support for Williams: militant unionists, 81 per cent; moderate unionists, 72 per cent; non-militant unionists, 52 per cent; militant non-unionists, $N=5$; moderate non-unionists, 50 per cent; non-militant non-unionists, 38 per cent. Militant union members formed the hard core of Williams's support, while non-union members generally voted for Williams or stayed away from the polls (see Table 7-2).

Table 7–2.   Union Membership, Class Consciousness, and
Political Choice

UNION MEMBERSHIP	VOTED FOR WILLIAMS	VOTED FOR BAGWELL	DID NOT VOTE
UNION MEMBER (whites only)	per cent	per cent	per cent
Militant (N=48)	81	2	17
Moderate (N=60)	72	10	18
Non-Militant (N=77)	52	26	22
NON-UNION MEMBER			
Militant (N=5)	—	(2)	(3)
Moderate (N=18)	50	17	33
Non-Militant (N=39)	38	23	39

The Implications of These Findings

Historically, class consciousness has expressed itself politically in
a multiplicity of ways. In the absence of a parliamentary system,
militant workmen have often supported a revolutionary party;
such was the case, for example, in China between 1918 and 1927.
In other situations, a high degree of class consciousness has constituted the partial basis for a labor party founded largely upon
working-class support and dedicated mainly to the pursuit of
ends attainable within a parliamentary framework. This has been
the experience of England, Belgium, and Scandinavia since the
turn of the century. A third alternative is working-class support
of reform politicians not selected by labor but responsive to its demands. This happened in industrial America during the 1930's
when labor supported Franklin Delano Roosevelt, and our results
are completely consistent with this explanation of the political
preferences of class-conscious workmen.

Earlier writers had dealt with some aspects of political behavior,[5] but Goetz Briefs, a Catholic neo-Marxist, clearly de-
lineated these three patterns in the late 1930's.[6] During the
pre- and post-World War II period, Centers,[7] Glantz,[8] Jones,[9]
and Kornhauser [10] studied class consciousness in America and
found that it related to political choice, though not to revolution
or the formation of a labor party. Perhaps the lack of current re-

search stems in part from the assumption that status is a more important influence than class on the behavior of contemporary Americans. Although this assumption may lead to valuable theoretical insights and research findings—as we have already indicated in Chapter 2 [11]—the concern with status does not obviate the importance of class and class consciousness, as we have demonstrated.

Working-Class Consciousness and Solidarity Among Races

Progressive movements in general and industrial unions in particular have always hoped that class consciousness would both affect political choice and improve race relations. Many labor intellectuals cherish the traditional belief that greater class consciousness will be accompanied by a lessening of inter-ethnic and inter-racial animosity. When this happens, they say, then labor organizations and reform movements can forge a permanent alliance on such questions as housing, employment, automation, and schools, as well as on the familiar issue of prejudice and discrimination. Unfortunately, recent conflicts involving labor and minority groups in America indicate that such a *sustained* alliance is not now feasible, although labor and civil rights groups, for example, may periodically join to support politicians or legislation which favor the interests of workers and minorities.

There would appear to be no clear evidence of a relationship between class consciousness and inter-ethnic hostility. In his earlier writings, Marx held that worker participation in a common division of labor over a prolonged period of time would erase this hostility.[12] Later, he revised his opinions, and recognized the black-white division within the American working class, but he failed to comment on its long-term effects. For example, would racial clashes indefinitely postpone the formation of a united labor movement? How might these schisms be overcome? Such questions bothered Marxists even during the nineteenth century. Engels addressed himself to this problem in his later years, revising his opinions as he grappled with its complexity and long-term implications.

Historical evidence shows that Marx's original position was in error. One analyst of the Nazi dictatorship has concluded that many long-term unemployed workers, especially in Berlin, joined Gregor and Otto Strasser's "socialist" faction.[13] The Strasser group was both fervently anti-capitalist and anti-Semitic. Again, Hans Gerth's classic study revealed that approximately one-third of the members of the German Nazi party in 1933 consisted of manual workers.[14] Of these, well over half were members of the industrial working class, the remainder being agricultural workers.[15] Perhaps it is fair to assume that many of the proletarian members of the Nazi party also belonged to the Strasser faction. This was certainly the case in northern Germany—Berlin in particular, as we have said—where the Strassers and their programs were quite popular among certain workmen, especially the long-term unemployed.

Yet we should also remember that during the 1930's many European workers backed political movements opposed to the ethnic hostility characteristic of right-wing political parties. Before the spring of 1933, the vast bulk of German workers supported either the Social Democrats or the Communists, both of which opposed right-wing movements. Roughly the same pattern occurred in Spain, France, Austria, England, Belgium, Holland, and Scandinavia. In all of these countries, working-class parties fought fascism, especially when fascists resorted to violence in order to win political and military victories.

To sum up, historical evidence suggests that while some highly class-conscious workers undoubtedly join organizations with anti-minority group programs, others, equally class-conscious, do not.

CLASS CONSCIOUSNESS AND INTER-ETHNIC HOSTILITY

In Detroit, increases in class consciousness fail to be accompanied by decreases in inter-ethnic hostility.[16] The distribution of re-

sponses, as shown in Table 7-3, does not form any consistent
pattern, unless perhaps a curvilinear one. Yet even this apparent
distribution becomes void when we take into account ethnic
group (Table 7-4) or union membership (Table 7-5).

Table 7–3.   Class Consciousness and Inter-Ethnic Hostility

TYPE OF CLASS CONSCIOUSNESS	DISPLAYS INTER-ETHNIC HOSTILITY per cent	DOES NOT DISPLAY INTER-ETHNIC HOSTILITY per cent	TOTAL NUMBER
MILITANT EGALITARIANS	39	61	(38)
MILITANT RADICALS	32	68	(97)
SKEPTICS	45	55	(114)
CLASS VERBALIZERS	31	69	(98)
CLASS INDIFFERENTS	26	74	(38)

Table 7–5.   Union Membership, Class Consciousness, and
Inter-Ethnic Hostility

TYPE OF CLASS CONSCIOUSNESS	UNION MEMBER Per cent	Number	NON-UNION MEMBER Per cent	Number
MILITANT EGALITARIANS				
Hostile	37	(35)	–	(3)
Not Hostile	63		–	
MILITANT RADICALS				
Hostile	22	(69)	33	(18)
Not Hostile	78		67	
SKEPTICS				
Hostile	47	(86)	39	(28)
Not Hostile	53		61	
CLASS VERBALIZERS				
Hostile	28	(68)	37	(30)
Not Hostile	72		63	
CLASS INDIFFERENTS				
Hostile	29	(24)	21	(14)
Not Hostile	71		79	

Table 7-4. Ethnic Background, Class Consciousness, and Inter-Ethnic Hostility

TYPE OF CLASS CONSCIOUSNESS	NEGRO Per cent	NEGRO Number	POLES & OTHERS Per cent	POLES & OTHERS Number	GERMANS & OTHERS Per cent	GERMANS & OTHERS Number
MILITANT EGALITARIANS						
Hostile	48	(27)	—	(4)	—	(7)
Not Hostile	52		—		—	
MILITANT RADICALS						
Hostile	37	(43)	12	(32)	8	(12)
Not Hostile	63		88		92	
SKEPTICS						
Hostile	47	(34)	40	(35)	47	(51)
Not Hostile	53		60		53	
CLASS VERBALIZERS						
Hostile	50	(14)	27	(33)	27	(51)
Not Hostile	50		73		73	
CLASS INDIFFERENTS						
Hostile	—	(2)	0	(10)	38	(26)
Not Hostile	—		100		62	

Conclusions

In considering the impact of class consciousness on political choice in a modern industrial town, we have seen how class-conscious workers support a pro-labor candidate when the times, the candidate, the unions, and the party demand their vote.

However, because of inter-ethnic hostility, class consciousness has presently a limited range of political consequences. The absence of bonds of solidarity among workmen of different racial and nationality groups prevents workmen, labor organizations, and reform groups from collaborating on a sustained basis, even when faced with common problems.

Nevertheless, when white workers are highly militant they often support the rights of minorities, despite their prejudices. This was shown in the 1958 Michigan gubernatorial election. Significantly, racial prejudice did not prevent white workmen from helping to elect a politician dedicated to advancing the cause of civil rights as well as of labor. In such instances class consciousness proves more important than inter-ethnic hostility, and temporary coalitions between representatives of labor and of reform movements become feasible.

8

From the Bottom Up

We have already demonstrated that within the Negro community, many workmen express extremely high degrees of consciousness, which they translate into political choice. We have attempted to account for Negro class consciousness by emphasizing the impact of job discrimination, uprootedness, and union membership on workers who are able to discuss their common problems at the workplace and in their neighborhoods. But how does grass-roots leadership organize workers into a politically active community? To answer this question, the author became a participant observer in the Detroit block-club movement.[1]

Contrary to the opinion that the city, especially the working-class section, is marked by "the relative absence of intimate personal acquaintanceship, the segmentalization of human relations which are largely anonymous, superficial and transitory . . .,"[2] we believe that collective problem-solving on the neighborhood level is not impossible. Moreover, many Negro working-class districts have the potential for creating enough solidarity to foster political militancy. This is particularly true of neighborhoods that support neighborhood organizations, contain many union members, consist largely of uprooted workmen, and face an economic crisis.

130

For our model of neighborhood organizations we will use the Detroit block-club movement. This movement originated in the mid-1950's and concerned itself with problems widespread within the Negro ghetto: rats, urban renewal, unemployment, bank foreclosures on home mortgages, negligent landlords, inadequate recreational facilities, segregated schools, poor police protection, and the like.[3] Detroit block clubs [4] began as an answer to the problem of how to prevent central city neighborhoods from becoming slums.

As is well known, urban blight has been a problem in large American cities since World War II. In part, it spreads when many families who live in near-slum areas do not know how to maintain and upgrade their own blocks and neighborhoods. The problem of developing and upholding standards of house maintenance was difficult when city officials and working-class families could not communicate with each other. Prior to the mid-1950's, most large cities had few ties between city officials, administrators, and planners on the one hand, and citizens in slum neighborhoods on the other. Thus, planners could not co-ordinate their actions with those who sought help or with those who would be receptive to suggestions on neighborhood upkeep.

In response to this lack of communication, a section of Detroit's city planning commission revised its traditional policy on neighborhood preservation and, in the mid-1950's, established local organizations built around the block and neighborhood. Twelve members of the commission set up a special sub-unit to organize the grass-roots block clubs. They contacted neighborhood leaders who had some interest in social problems and who were active in church groups, P.T.A.'s, labor unions, and settlement houses. In many cases, individuals approached the team of city planners first, in the hope that the latter would help organize their block. Once the initial contacts were made, the city planning commission staff and organizers attempted to establish homogeneous groups on the block level by recruiting home buyers and home owners. Most of the home owners had moved to run-down neighborhoods after World War II and had invested their wartime savings in a down payment on older, single family houses. The block-club organizers assumed that these potential home owners would be more motivated to upgrade and preserve the character of the neighborhood than those who rented. In addition, the home owners' common backgrounds allowed them to communicate readily with one another. (Generally southern-born Negroes, they were almost all factory workers and union members, with the overwhelming majority belonging to the C.I.O.) The social scientists and social workers who initiated the block-club movement encouraged housing maintenance and worked to promote close friendships within the community.

Upgrading, Recreation, and Protection

Although block clubs dealt with social problems in general, they emphasized neighborhood conservation and home improvement. Anyone living on a block where a club existed could join it, providing he paid his dues. Meetings attracted from 5 to 90 per cent of the inhabitants of the block, with the clubs generally enjoying their largest turnout during their early period of organization. Attendance later tapered off until the active membership included not more than 10 to 20 per cent of those living on the block.

The block clubs' conservation activities were extended to the schools to involve parents in efforts designed to promote the interests of their children. Block clubs and elementary schools sometimes jointly sponsored a "clean-up day," on which the entire neighborhood turned out to clean up alleys, streets, and lawns. On one occasion, the local elementary school, including the principal, assistant principal, and band, co-operated with parents in nearby block clubs to clean alleys inside the school district. School representatives took pictures of the alleys before, during, and after the collective assault on garbage cans, old debris, and the like, and the activity was symbolized by the theme of a "war on rats," a graphic way of attacking the removal of alley litter. On D-Day in this gray neighborhood, the school band led a "company" of children armed with swords made of painted cardboard.

The local school had helped to arouse the youngsters' interest in the campaign. In art and English classes, teachers encouraged pupils to express their concern through drawings and poetry. The children responded by portraying a variety of scenes, most of which contained pictures of rats. The "rat theme" made students, parents, schools, and block clubs participants in community reform.

Block clubs did other things to promote intimacy among families living in the same area. They often sponsored parties, which were informal gatherings. Friends met to play cards, dance, or engage in similar types of recreation with the proceeds going to the block club or perhaps to a member with a medical bill. There were also outdoor parties, generally held within the confines of a blocked-off street. These all-day affairs were almost wholly child-centered: there were picnics on the pavement, and youngsters competed in bag races, fifty-yard dashes, and other events organized by their parents. Free soda pop, popcorn, and ice cream purchased by the block club contributed to the carnival mood. Such entertainments attracted as many as fifty to one hundred children and their parents, thereby giving block-club organizers the opportunity to get acquainted with parents reluctant to attend block-club meetings. Children thus became the basis for the extension of club membership.

Once organized and solidified by recreation activities, block clubs expanded their services and enhanced local prestige by sponsoring paint-up, fix-up, and weed-up campaigns. A person with skill in carpentry might contribute his services to help other families in his block club. Those families reciprocated by performing such tasks as house-painting, seed-planting, and the like. Sometimes the specific form of this reciprocity would be discussed and stipulated at meetings of the block club. Tactics were also reviewed: which houses were in need of repair, the choice of paints, and the division of labor for projects. The results were visible improvements in the neighborhood and greater cohesion among families, who could take pride in their collective achievements.

Block clubs learned to deal successfully with legal authorities and city departments, and in this way obtained many benefits to the community. For example, some block clubs sponsored baseball teams which they financed through parties. Block-club officers persuaded recreation and other city officials to allow the block club to convert vacant lots into baseball diamonds. The police and city officials found that a policy of co-operation was rewarding, and block clubs often worked with precinct police officers to protect neighborhoods from local and outside criminals.

In some cases, the clubs supplemented the efforts of protective authority; during a crime wave, for example, one club provided a protection service for those who had to walk in the neighborhood at night. The club provided escorts and asked families to leave their porch lights on. Seventy-five per cent of the households co-operated even though only one-fifth of the adults in the area were active in the block club.

Prevention of crime occasioned yet other types of collective action, such as the neighborhood meetings with police officials co-sponsored by block clubs. Unfortunately, these gatherings did not attract those whose behavior block-club members found most reprehensible, namely, criminals and delinquents. Nonetheless, the meetings did help to strengthen ties within the clubs and between clubs and the police, especially those in charge of the precinct.

Although these efforts were successful in integrating a sizable number of families into block clubs, too frequently the meetings by-passed an important category: older white people, who were reluctant to take an active part, often because of poor health or racial attitudes. In order to obtain their verbal support, if not their participation, block-club members sometimes offered to shovel snow from their sidewalks or helped older persons with minor repair work around the house. These efforts had some effect, at least from the point of view of the block club, for these outsiders did subsequently participate in some campaigns. Still, it was difficult to obtain the continued involvement of older people.

Young couples also tended to remain inactive, but even here block clubs on occasion evolved techniques for integration, such as offering baby-sitting services. Of course, block clubs did not deliberately set out to manipulate people through any of these devices. Rather, they experimented with different solutions and when one worked, the clubs accepted it. The block clubs depended upon the process of collective problem-solving.

Upgrading and Politics

The movement was eventually forced to become political in order to protect and extend its interest in neighborhood welfare. Questions of zoning, urban renewal, police protection, school boundary gerrymandering, and the like were of vital interest to the block-club families, and over half the clubs became politically involved in at least one of these issues. Certain clubs, particularly on Detroit's west side, became very active politically. When municipal organizations erected barriers to the achievement of their goals of neighborhood conservation, the block clubs sought to change these policies. Representatives were sent to speak before local groups to put pressure on the municipal government. At election time, almost all the clubs became active—some sponsored meetings for candidates; often the clubs arrived at an informal or explicit decision to support a particular candidate.

Many city politicians reacted negatively to what they considered annoying block-club demands. These politicians finally abolished that section of the planning commission that had organized and maintained the clubs. The city had created a problem-solving agent which it could not control. In fact, the block clubs sometimes opposed the proposals of the city planning commission. Moreover, because they fought pressure groups such as organized real estate interests, which traditionally worked closely with the planning commission, the city council, and powerful economic interests, the clubs invited opposition. Yet, to the amazement of many, hundreds of block clubs continued to flourish without the support of the city planning commission.

DEPENDENCE OF CLUBS ON THE NEIGHBORHOOD COUNCIL

Aid from neighborhood councils helped the clubs survive. The neighborhood council generally consisted of (1) elected delegates representing between 25 and 40 block clubs in the neighborhood and (2) a number of others acting on behalf of prominent voluntary associations in the area. Like block clubs, each council met monthly to discuss its problems and those of the particular clubs.

The neighborhood councils duplicated many service functions of the block clubs: they sponsored parties, dances, and the like. In addition, they gave advice to block clubs on a variety of topics: how to obtain a stop sign for a street intersection; how to complain about poor garbage collection; how to obtain surplus government paint; how to plant grass seed; how best to uproot weeds. To instruct block-club delegates on some of these matters, some neighborhood councils called upon leaders of home-improvement groups in the upper middle-class white suburbs.

Ties with the middle class assumed other forms as well. Neighborhood councils co-operated with police precincts, church groups, political organizations, and leaders of labor unions. Yet they were not always asking for advice; sometimes they made political demands on these groups. The councils sent delegates to meetings of the Detroit Common Council, where they confronted and debated with representatives of city agencies, real estate interests, and other groups. The councils became involved in local elections, and supported candidates for mayor, city council, governor, and Congress, although their endorsement was more often covert rather than explicit. Although they expressed a wide range of political interests, councils were most effective in swinging political support to candidates for municipal office. During the 1961 campaign, the councils, along with other Negro groups (including the Trade Union Leadership Council, church organizations, the NAACP, the Cotillion Club, and the Negro press), worked successfully to unseat a mayor and a police commissioner opposed by Negroes because of alleged toleration of police brutality. In this mayoralty race, neighborhood councils helped a young reform candidate by marshaling the support of Negroes, who constituted 30 per cent of Detroit's electorate. In the election of the Common Council, also conducted on the basis of a city-wide vote, a former member of the city planning commission and the original organizer of the block clubs had the least number of votes among the nine elected. However, he was among the top three in precincts well organized by block clubs.

Neighborhood councils became politically involved in still other ways. For example, some west side neighborhood councils donated time and funds to carry on legal suits against a Detroit school board, which, they claimed, gerrymandered school districts along racial lines. The councils also instigated and supported boycotts against firms that discriminated against Negroes.

NEIGHBORHOOD AND DISTRICT COUNCILS

Neighborhood councils sometimes elected delegates to a residential district council, whose membership consisted also of representatives of social agencies and settlement houses, school teachers, and police officers. These non-delegates on the whole steered the group in a way that promoted better relations with schools, social agencies, unions, and churches. They acted as a moderating influence on what otherwise might have been an organizational center and central clearing house for militant groups.

At one meeting of the district council, for example, rank and file delegates passed a resolution condemning Chrysler Corporation for working men overtime while many former auto workers who had been laid off remained unemployed. Several of the non-delegate officers were given the responsibility of forwarding this complaint to the Chrysler Corporation and the U.A.W. The officers maintained, however, that such a resolution was improper, and that it would upset relations with industry. Unknown to the delegates, they chose not to forward the complaint. Again, more moderate non-delegates held meetings and workshops on matters such as automation and unemployment, but they generally restricted the range of key participants to exclude militants such as the Reverend Albert Cleague,[5] a black nationalist and a leading member of the Detroit executive board of the NAACP.

District council leaders could not punish neighborhood councils and block clubs through such measures as personal explusion or charter suspension. Because district councils could not levy serious sanctions, individual block clubs and neighborhood councils enjoyed considerable autonomy, which allowed them to be as radical or militant as they wished. In this respect, the structure of the block-club movement was far different from labor unions, which have concentrated and centralized power at the top of their organization.

Block Clubs and the Creation of Radical Views

The views of Negro block-club members on collective action can be understood more clearly when they are related to the industrial and agricultural changes that have been taking place in America since the end of the Second World War. Rapid mechanization of agriculture in the South displaced large numbers of rural workers. Industrial positions in the North provided many with a standard of living markedly superior to their former one. However, the 1958 recession threatened this new-found prosperity. Widespread unemployment and economic insecurity made many of Detroit's Negro unemployed consider the probable consequences of economic depression. As we have showed earlier, in many instances, these conditions engendered the creation of political militancy.

What may occur is a spontaneous endorsement of grass-roots action—even when it leads to class or class-racial warfare. We have already noted that under certain conditions economic insecurity breeds hostility toward the economic order, and leads to antagonism among political groups and commitment to political radicalism.[6] All these attitudes appeared in a study we conducted in two predominantly Negro neighborhoods in Detroit during the summer of 1958.

While economic insecurity cannot, of course, be equated with a readiness to engage in violent behavior, an important precondition for the initiation of violence may well be the development, within a group, of a definition of the conditions under which violence becomes a probable or expected outcome of economic crisis.

BLOCK CLUB, ECONOMIC INSECURITY, AND RADICALISM

Our study, conducted in May and July of 1958, was based upon interviews of heads of households. The initial aim was to explore the problem by covering a single neighborhood in which there was considerable indigenous political activity and militant leadership within the block club. Soon after, we decided to repeat the study in a neighborhood matched, as far as possible, on all variables except block-club organization and political activity. Although this research site was not wholly free of political organization, it did provide a contrast to the political activity of the first neighborhood.

The west side area we chose coincided with the boundaries

of a block club which had recently added the functions of a political pressure group to its principal concerns of cleaning up the area and sponsoring recreational and other social activities. This club had joined with others in Detroit in an attempt to persuade the governor to declare a moratorium on home mortgage payments for the unemployed. Three militant leftists residing in the neighborhood were active in the block-club movement, both in the local and city-wide groups.

The east side neighborhood had no such club. Although its meetings were decidedly political, they were poorly attended, having, at the most, twenty-five people. The west side group, on the other hand, organized one political action meeting which attracted an audience of three to four hundred.

In many ways, however, the two neighborhoods were similar. Almost all residents were home owners or home buyers. In addition, between 75 and 85 per cent of the respondents in both areas were Negroes. The vast majority of these were born in the South and worked in blue-collar, unionized occupations, mainly in the automobile industry. From 50 to 60 per cent of the Negroes interviewed in both settings were unemployed or working part-time; and many of the remainder feared unemployment. In all, we interviewed 92 from both neighborhoods.

In our 1960 study, 120 of the sample were Negroes residing in neighborhoods very similar to those studied in 1958.[7] We used comparative information from the more recent study conducted during a period of heightened economic activity to contrast workers' views on the economic order under different economic conditions.

We asked all workers the following question: If a bad depression were to happen, what do you think would happen in this country? When workers anticipated violence, their replies were classified according to the form the violence was expected to take—either collective (revolution, rioting, civil war, and so on), or individual (killing, robbing, stealing, crime waves, etc.).[8] Previous research suggested that predictions of violence would be frequent in both neighborhoods, since the two areas (1958 studies) had suffered extensive unemployment.[9] It also seemed probable that expectations of *collective* violence would be more prevalent in the neighborhood that was highly organized and largely guided by militants. In addition, we assumed that unemployed Negroes would take more extreme views than comparable whites, since the frequency and consequences of unemployment were more striking among the former than the latter. In the 1960 study, it was hypothesized that these radical views would be more widely shared among Negroes interviewed in 1958 than in 1960, when unemployment had declined.

THE INCIDENCE OF POLITICAL MILITANCY

In general, the information gathered supported these predictions. A large percentage of those interviewed in both neighborhoods in 1958 felt that some form of violence would take place if and when a serious depression occurred. Sixty-three per cent of the Negroes in the west side neighborhood and 58 per cent on the east side expected violence. Even more significant, perhaps, is the breakdown. On the west side, 35 per cent predicted collective violence and 28 per cent mentioned individual forms. A not unexpected reversal of attitudes was found among east side respondents: only 22 per cent foresaw collective violence, while 36 per cent expected individual action. In the 1958 sample, the Negro unemployed (almost all of whom were unionized) proved to be singularly concerned with violence. On the west side, 71 per cent of the unemployed as opposed to 53 per cent of the employed expected violence to occur. The east side Negroes concurred in this opinion, although the percentage differences were not as great.[10]

In general, Negroes tended to expect violence more than did whites, although a comparison of the 1958 and 1960 samples showed that for the 1960 recovery period, both Negro and white workmen were less inclined to expect unrest.

Many of the replies to our question were remarkably strident. More importantly, when workmen expected collective and violent action, they showed a tendency to overlook—but not to dismiss—the relevance of the central government during such crises. Perhaps some assumed that a serious economic depression could not occur if the government were careful, but that in the event this did happen, the people should attempt to settle their problems through collective action. Such action might precipitate federal help designed to relieve the lower classes of their economic problems. Whatever their assumptions, the replies often remained inchoate and the radical ideas uncrystalized. Nonetheless, we found that of those who foresaw the possibility of collective violence, a disproportionately large number also favored government ownership of all industries.[11] In all, their replies blend militancy with doubt about government ability. Why such views should develop is a complex question not easily answered. Yet we have tried to give a partial explanation.

In a city where the lives of many working-class people, particularly Negroes, are seriously affected by industrial unions, the successful creation of block clubs may derive largely from organizational experiences and successes with unions. In this chapter we have shown that when Negro workers join block-club organizations to solve neighborhood problems, many develop a collective and radical outlook. In thus far demonstrating the connection between block clubs and political militancy, and the positive effects of the clubs in solving some of the working-man's problems, we have said little about the negative aspects of block clubs, particularly as they relate to a multi-racial working class.

Perhaps the most important weakness of the block clubs is their one-sidedness.[12] Since Negroes are ghettoized within certain residential districts, and since neighborhood councils and block clubs are organized on a spatial basis, the clubs may promote class-racial consciousness among Negroes, but they cannot produce a similar frame of reference within white working-class groups beyond the ghetto and the block clubs. The block clubs thus contribute to the furtherance of consciousness in only one sector of the working class.

"Property protection associations" organized on a neighborhood basis may appear in white neighborhoods, but they bring about racial strife among blue-collar workmen found in the community. These racial antagonisms inside the blue-collar world make difficult but do not prevent the formation of organizations that bring black and white workmen together to focus on their common difficulties.

Epilogue

The two considerations that scored highest on our table of zero order correlations were uprootedness and ethnic background.* Those who witnessed the insurrections in Watts in 1965 or in Detroit and other cities in 1967 do not need to refer to tables in order to view present militant class consciousness as an outgrowth of minority group–employment issues. The young, structurally unemployed participated in the demonstrations. But the arrest records of Negro demonstrators in those cities show that many were *fully employed;* this raises new questions for those who speculate on the direction of working-class consciousness in the late 1960's. What, for example, are the limits of union influence on class consciousness? Are unions failing to resolve hard issues of economic insecurity, one cause of militancy? Has coalition politics failed, and will workers turn to insurrectionary methods?

This book was written on the assumption that working-class people in Detroit could work within the existing political structure in a non-violent way to free themselves from economic exploitation and racial discrimination. New militant politics, continuing labor problems, and disillusionment with traditional democratic methods—the facts of 1968—challenge this assumption. Any discussion of consciousness today must comment on the potentiality of revolutionary political effort. In this section, therefore, I would like to re-examine some of the sources of class consciousness.

* See Appendix C.

144

I.

When, where, and how are militant forms of class consciousness likely to occur in the near future? Our findings suggest that class attitudes will be strongest where marginal members of the labor force have forged plant and/or neighborhood organizations within communities where there is a history of class and class-racial struggle. For some, the location of the struggle will be in the fields and ranches of states such as Texas and California where farm workers once again attempt to build a union. For many others, the arena will be the sub-section of the plant, where workmen use the work-group union organization as a means of obtaining greater control over working conditions and pace of work. For large numbers of manual workers, the contest will be fought in the big-city neighborhoods where Negroes and other minorities try to gain more control over businesses, housing, and jobs.

THE CALIFORNIA FARM WORKERS

Working-class consciousness derives in part from union organization, particularly when the union is new, the strikes aggressive, and the unionists uprooted. Specifically, groups such as the California farm workers found in the lower San Joaquin Valley would appear to be on their way to solving their problems through labor union organization, non-violent picketing, collective bargaining, and party politics. These Mexican-Americans are presently putting on the most successful drive among farm workers since the massive, but broken efforts of the 1930's. (In New York, Puerto Ricans appear to be following a similar path, although they are less class conscious and organized than either the San Joaquin Valley Mexicans or the big-city Negroes.)

Today, AFWOC (the Agricultural Farm Workers Organizing Committee) led by Cesar Chavez and Larry Itliong is carrying on a strike to organize Mexicans, Filipinos, and other minorities laboring in the sun-baked fields of California's Central Valley. Supported by Walter Reuther, the California AFL-CIO, the

U.A.W. (United Auto Workers), the I.U.D. (Industrial Union Department of the AFL-CIO, itself led by Reuther), and the I.L.W.U. (International Longshoremen and Warehousemen's Union), the strike may build a union among minority farm workers. In the process, the strike and the union, if this book's assumptions are correct, should also foster class consciousness, class politics, and status-group political action.

The Delano strike and others of its kind in California have concentrated on the organization of workmen who have been uprooted from agrarian regions—northern Mexico, the rural Philippines, west Texas, rural Louisiana, and so on—relocated on California's large mechanized farms, subjected to recurrent layoffs and agricultural automation, and rankled by racial discrimination in regard to work and housing. Hence, these men are ready for a union. If this attempt at unionization succeeds, it will undoubtedly mark the beginning of a serious and non-violent effort to bring millions of minority group Americans into labor unions and into class-conscious thinking in general.

But should the class-conscious frame of reference become significant for these farm workers, would it not be a very temporary thing? The success of the farm workers would presumably so seriously diminish economic marginality that in the long run they would cease to be militant and perhaps accept a moderate level of consciousness, one that would go no further than a mild form of class verbalization or class identification. In effect, their level of consciousness would decline and become approximately the same as that of most white workers.

Perhaps union success would have this impact. We suspect that it would, although long-term differences with management might arise out of a new area of dispute once bread-and-butter issues have been settled. Perhaps conflict between the growers and farm workers over pace and conditions of work would become paramount and help to maintain a militant frame of reference.

But why should we expect widespread and prolonged union successes among farm workers, either in their efforts to diminish job insecurity or to increase control over working conditions? The farm workers of California have spent over seventy years trying to organize a lasting union, and they have failed in every instance, largely because of the power of the growers. Given this past, farm workers' unions might once again fail, and hence be unable to create solutions to problems faced by farm workers.

Still, there are other possibilities, or so it would seem. Federal legislation and programs may impart valuable occupational skills to farm workers, elevate most of them out of the rural proletariat and into the upper working and middle classes, where marketability of scarce skills rather than union protection would give them job security with high remuneration. Perhaps the celebrated war on poverty is the answer for rural workers and growing numbers of young structurally unemployed.

Given the magnitude of potential federal economic resources, plus the sincerity of commitments made by leaders on the matter of retraining, one might argue that the government will soon translate economic potential into reality. Even if labor's drives to organize rural (and urban) workers should fail, the war on poverty would eliminate widespread insecurity by providing skill training programs and lucrative jobs, thereby giving minorities the pecuniary means necessary for breaking out of their ghettoes. In so doing, the government would pre-empt the creation of community divisions and get militants off the aggressive path to economic and social justice.

This is one alternative to direct unionization or militant action. It is even possible for proponents to foresee programs to ameliorate the effects of automation—by building up skills to counter the long-term effects of thinning the work force among rural manual workers.

Unfortunately, there is not likely to be enough government money and technical personnel available for this. To succeed, tens of billions of dollars would have to be spent annually and carefully for proletarianized minorities to achieve the kinds of scarce skills necessary to elevate them without union support into the skilled blue- and white-collar worlds. Further, can we believe that U.S. taxpayers would be willing to undergo such prolonged economic austerity in order to carry on an upgrading effort for people with whom they do not want to live and about whom they know little more than their stereotypes suggest? Clearly, the unorganized farm workers cannot depend upon the government. They must build and use their unions, much as Detroit workers did thirty-five years ago.

II. Is Labor Failing the Worker?

For the unionized, class consciousness derives fundamentally from workers' economic problems. Had Detroit's labor unions been completely successful in eliminating job insecurity, neighborhood grievances, and structural unemployment, militant consciousness would have become part of the community's history. But unions have not done so. Hence consciousness remains.

In this regard, a major consideration is the contradiction between heightened pay scale and continuing occupational as well as job insecurity. The U.A.W. in Detroit has been successful in increasing wages and benefits such as pensions. Over the last decade, the real wages of auto workers have risen not only on an hourly but also on a yearly basis. As a result, many U.A.W. and other industrial as well as craft unionists enjoy a life style similar to that of the lower middle class.

But these improvements have not eliminated structural insecurities for employed workers. Automation still threatens many who believe that its full effects will not be felt until after the completion of the Vietnam war. They anticipate massive layoffs and express concern over potential loss of daily and weekly wages should unemployment become long-term—as was the case in Detroit after both World War I and II, and following the Korean War.

Job insecurity is experienced also in terms of lack of control over pace and kind of work. Many feel that increases in pay should be accompanied by greater power to specify work norms, to determine the speed of production, and to improve factory conditions. Efforts to resolve this pay-work contradiction have recently been undertaken in the teaching profession, where union leaders have pressed for greater teacher control over policies of schools. Auto union leaders do not, however, share this frame of reference on control of workplace. A major limitation of trade unionism is its inability to resolve this aspect of job control.

Detroit's top labor leaders avoid fights over factory conditions. Walter Reuther and other leaders such as Emil Mazey have discouraged tough bargaining on matters of dignity at work, although U.A.W. negotiators have pressed and found the Big 3 auto companies willing to make major concessions on wages and fringe benefits. Perhaps because of managerial flexibility on these matters, leaders in the auto unions have made their most aggressive demands in areas such as a "guaranteed annual wage." During major negotiations over contracts, while leaders fight and win on bread-and-butter issues, union locals are forced to settle factory disputes after "the broad lines of settlement" are reached, thereby publicly placing local union militants in the position of appearing as recalcitrant and unreasonable.

Workers often try to settle job grievances through the use of traditional tactics—periodic work stoppages, wild-cat strikes, production slow-downs, and refusals to recognize contract agreements arrived at by top union officials who have ignored plant conflicts. In turn, management has often punished those it deemed to be undisciplined union workers, usually those who attempt to determine pace and conditions of work. Punishment, both real and threatened, constitutes a form of economic insecurity, since it can lead to firings. This has happened to a considerable number of Detroit chief stewards and thousands of rank and file members over the decades, so there is an objective basis for working-class apprehension and bitterness.

Even when labor unions are relatively effective in dealing with problems of factory conditions, they nonetheless fail to resolve many problems facing working-class people at the neighborhood level. (The frame of reference of working-class consciousness includes more than the workplace.) Labor organizations usually do not deal directly with the problems created by landlords, merchants, finance companies, and the like. The unions may pay lip service to efforts taken by neighborhood people to solve these problems, or they may try to use their political power to pass legislation to help, but they are not working on a day-to-day basis to get rid of rats, prevent rent increases, stop loan sharks, fight for home payment moratoriums during recessions, eliminate rezoning efforts sponsored in part by profit-oriented merchants, work with police captains, or aid in other local concerns.

These tasks are left to the neighborhood organizations. They often use conflict mechanisms to deal with neighborhood irritations—demonstrations, boycotts, and other forms of direct action that become a further source of class consciousness not only among many working-class Negroes but whites as well, especially when they are in or near the bottom of the class-racial heap.

Of course, one might argue that private business firms will settle these grievances by creating semi-public development corporations to be subsidized in part by the government; these firms will create jobs and thereby eliminate neighborhood actions judged as disturbances by those in positions of authority. This argument is questionable, since the job problem is but one source of ill feeling. Neighborhood problems exist quite apart from whether its residents are employed at gainful occupations.

Detroit industrial unions, especially the U.A.W., have elevated and will continue to elevate a majority of Detroit's blue-collar unionized Negroes. More precisely, militant Negroes have participated in building unions that in turn have paid off in terms of benefits for unionized Negroes. Among Negroes (as well as among whites) there has been a particularly close relationship between working-class consciousness and bloc voting for political candidates supporting programs favored by workers. We noted that at certain times class-conscious labor helped to put into office candidates who supported programs favored by labor and minorities, two categories by no means mutually exclusive.

In Michigan, ex-Governor G. Mennen Williams helped these groups in many ways. Anti-labor laws were constantly defeated, despite the anti-union mood in the country during the late 1940's and early 1950's. Organized workers, both white and black, benefited from legislation pushed through under his leadership. Bills on improved workmen's compensation and industrial accident insurance were passed because of Williams's efforts. No doubt large sections of the community's unionized Negro population have associated bloc voting along class and racial lines with material improvements. Consequently most of them will undoubtedly continue to vote Democratic, especially when a pro-labor candidate runs for office during an economic recession.

But what about the non-unionized others, the young people both black and white, especially the tens of thousands of young Detroit Negroes who have failed to benefit from union activities either during the Williams administration (1948-60) or the subsequent period? They were and are beyond the pale of organized labor and hence not covered by U.A.W. contracts (that specify average incomes well over four dollars per hour, including fringe benefits) and state labor legislation aimed at improving the economic security of *unionized* workmen. Detroit contains numerous young blacks who have never belonged to an industrial union, worked in plants covered by them, marched in integrated union picket lines, voted for pro-labor candidates, and/or acquired a militant-unionist perspective.

Since the industrial unions do not organize either the young unemployed or service employed, the labor unions have been generally unable to help them. Neither have the block clubs done much, nor has the Michigan Democratic party, despite its good intentions. The regular political processes mean little to these young people. As a result, such youths were in the vanguard of the looting and violence in the Detroit ghetto last summer. It is evident that they are ready to try insurrectionary activity.

Union influence on voting behavior can be seriously undermined by increasing numbers of *un*unionized and militant youth, since the views and actions of the aggressive young are often, if only partially, accepted by the unionized middle- and older-generation Negroes. It should not be forgotten that young unemployed Negroes often have friends and relatives who work at Ford, General Motors, Chrysler, and the feeder plants, and that these workers are taking advantage of the war prosperity by buying homes, new cars, appliances, and the like. The employed blue-collar workers are capable of empathizing and sympathizing with their relatives, friends, and acquaintances. They can, for they have lived inside a black community where the employed and the unemployed are often neighbors linked in more ways than most white persons can imagine. These ties, their confinement within the black community, their common feelings, likes, and dislikes, their shared awareness of how blacks get kicked around *even when employed* prepare the sympathetic job holders to side with the long-term unemployed against small business, the police, the National Guard, and even the U.S. Army. Were large numbers of employed, unionized Negroes to prefer *insurrection* to voting, they would act counter to union recommendation; they might very well become alienated from their unions. The reproaches of the aggressive and angry young might thereby be able to do to the U.A.W. Negroes what management has never been able to do, namely, to erode their sense of loyalty to their union. Should these ties weaken, so might their traditional class frame of reference, for a severe decline in union loyalty would lead to a questioning of these class values.

Should a substantial number of Detroit's unionized Negroes lose their class-union militancy and embrace a markedly class-racial variety, with the grievances of the black underdog, the whole union structure in Detroit would be shaken, for union leaders need such militant unionists to win major and prolonged strikes, particularly in the automobile industry. Detroit workers and their unions are thus deeply caught up in the conditions that are producing such upheavals in the Negro communities today. Progressive labor must deal directly with the problems facing the black minority in America.

When underdogs are convinced that the C.I.O., the Trade Union Leadership Council, the NAACP, the Democratic party, and like established organizations cannot find them jobs other than demeaning tasks without union job protection, pay, and prestige, the peaceful politics of coalition is in serious trouble. During the Detroit insurrection last summer one complaint kept recurring: young Detroit Negroes don't want just any job; they want jobs with dignity, in part because the town is filled with lucrative jobs. To get employment like this, they are willing to work through government aid programs. But if that does not work, many will lose what little respect they still have toward government, its problem-solving ability, and its rules—especially the ones on the sacredness of preserving a law and order judged by young Negroes as most lopsided in its partiality.

Ironically, by channeling scarce tax dollars away from domestic labor struggles, the federal government has spurred class consciousness. By raising false hopes and then committing itself to spending large sums abroad and cutting back on poverty programs at home, the federal government has inadvertently fostered militant forms of working-class consciousness in our larger cities. The government promised minorities more occupations and jobs than it could deliver. In so doing, it helped to change what working-class groups expected, what they were minimally willing to accept. Consequently, many have been disappointed. When these people are organized and led by militants already present in a ghetto, they can and will raise hell.

Should guerilla action find recurrent expression and widespread support in future episodes inside the Motor City, such action would diminish non-violent forms of class consciousness discussed at length in this book, for this kind of consciousness would no longer be able to find successful voting expression. Hence, this class perspective would decline from disuse. Also, if insurrections continue, a significant minority of *white* supporters of progressive legislation may move permanently over to support conservative, if not reactionary, political candidates. This shift in votes would be sufficient to guarantee repeated labor setbacks *at the polls and at the workplace,* thereby producing a double source of demoralization.

The conclusion is clear: the fortunes of the U.A.W. may well rest upon the elimination of black unemployment.

Appendix A: Questions Used to Measure Working-Class Consciousness

Questions on Working-Class Consciousness and Illustrative Replies

The following list of questions was used to measure the various aspects of class consciousness. Questions are considered in the following order: class verbalization, skepticism, militancy, and egalitarianism.

CLASS VERBALIZATION

Class conscious, N=298. References made to class categories, including economic groups, on one or more questions. Not class conscious, N=77. No reference to class categories.

1. All things considered, what do you think of Detroit as a place to live?

> O.K. It's got some good things and some bad things.

> Right now, pretty bad. I think we're catching it worse than any other city as a whole. For people with property, however, it's good.

> All right, but mostly for niggers who will take over everything soon.

> It's the best city to live in for a certain kind of work. It's good if you want to work on automobiles.

I think it's a pretty nice place. The living is good, I guess.

Well, I've been here all my life. Detroit is a fairly nice place. Work is not as good as it used to be. Industry has moved out and what not.

It's a pretty nice place. I'm living here and doing all right.

It's a good place for work, but not so hot if you don't want to work.

If there was more work, it would be a great place.

I think it's strictly a working man's town. If you have any ambition at all, it's a good working man's town.

Outside of high taxes, it's not so bad.

I think it's a fairly good city. It's convenient and there's a lot of activities. There's equal opportunity for everyone.

I think it's a good place to live.

2. What do you think of city government?
   2a. First of all, what are its good features?

It does things if the club gets behind them. (What do you mean by club?) The neighborhood improvement club.

The police department is very good. Recreation for the kids is good. The city keeps it clean for people with property. Detroit is cleaner than Chicago.

It's all right.

I like the police department and the highways. The garbage collection is tops.

I've never given it much thought.

It's got fairly good government. Of course, I have my own disagreements with the police department. Other than that, I think it's a fairly good government.

It's a working town and it's getting better for Negroes on working conditions as it progresses.

There are no good parts.

I can't answer.

It's democratic. We are all allowed to take part in it. All the citizens can.

They've done an excellent job in promoting business and trade. They've been very fair in their decisions.

I think they're trying to modernize.

It's a democratic type of government.

We have a lot to be dissatisfied with, but the government still makes an effort. The upkeep of streets and other services aren't bad.

Wages. It's been generally fairly good.

It's been good for me, but then, I'm not particular.

Non-partisan government is good.

There is good recreation and police and fire department. The government is honest. Also, the water department is good.

I'm satisfied. I don't have any complaints.

I like the way of refinancing and keeping taxes as low as possible.

The mayor and councilmen are standard, and I see nothing wrong with them. I might dislike some individuals, though.

I like the non-partisan city council. Also, there is no race problem to speak of here. I have no complaints.

They don't do anything. There's nothing good about it.

The government of Detroit is about as good as it will ever get.

2b. What are its bad features?

There's too much graft. (Like what?) The government steals people blind. We're taxed on everything. Government is a lot of hooey!

I don't like the new proposed income tax.

When you get two sides, each knocking each other around, there is no co-operation.

There aren't enough medical services, such as clinics and hospitals.

In general, I think the police is the worst part of city government.

There are lots of them. The city shouldn't let all those plants move out without reconciling with them on cutting taxes. They let employment get away from here, and it sets the city back.

I can't think of any bad things.

There's nothing bad about it. I think it is a good place to live.

I don't think too much of the police department. That's not the opinion I have of all policemen, though.

I once thought it was a very prejudiced place. Some of the city services such as paving alleys and side streets are poor.

It tries to keep the little man from getting anything. It taxes the little man too much.

The high cost of living that the city allows to the utility operations and also to the department on home ownerships. The city's requirements are too rigid.

The common council doesn't get around to the out-of-the-way areas to check up unless there's a complaint. The better areas get better service.

In a city of this size, the government tends to lose touch with the people at large. An individual's grievances can't be heard easily.

Public transportation ain't so hot. You have to wait for a long time when you want to catch a bus.

Our councilmen are elected by the entire city. The councilmen should be elected by district. It would be a better representation of the people.

When aldermen were from each area, it was better. I don't like Miriani (the mayor). If he would have his picture taken a few less times, I'd like it.

There aren't enough council members from the east side.

There's a bad transit system. There isn't enough bus service.

I don't approve of slum clearance. It's chasing Negroes into all areas. The city should first build places for Negroes to live in. Right now, Negroes are moving in near here.

I can't think of any.

Sometimes the police get involved in scandals. The slum situation is bad, but they're doing as much as they can with the finances available.

3. Do you think city officials show favoritism to any groups of the population?

IF YES

3a. What is that?

They're all out for themselves. They don't give a God-damn about anyone else!

If you're a relative to them, you get a good break.

White people.

Up in the northwest section, they show lots of favoritism. They let merchants down here and in the slum area do without services. In the northwest section, the streets are kept up better, and so are the alleys.

I don't study those sorts of things.

Some people in the police department are not fair. They don't give mixed couples an even break.

The white people. This is especially noticeable in their residential neighborhoods, say above Seven Mile Rd., for example.

They show favoritism to immoral women and children.

The moneyed people. The big interests.

They favor the west side more than the east.

They favor the colored on such things as jobs. Also, colored get off easier when they are arrested.

They tend to favor the colored, but then, any government would have to.

The colored. When colored complain, people jump because of the NAACP. It's an easier time getting welfare for Negroes.

Colored people. It's a joke, the preferential treatment they get.

4. Do you think they (city officials) don't pay attention to the needs of some kinds of people?

IF YES

4a. Who is that?

The working man. They want to keep him in the lowest income bracket they can.

The colored. Some of the conditions are awful. (Like what?) Oh, housing and slums. They're not as anxious to help the colored man as they are the white man.

When it's close to elections, they are OK to everybody. (How about when it's not close to elections?) I don't know. I guess they pay attention.

Older people like myself.

They don't pay attention to the needs of unemployed people.

The group that are past forty-five and fifty years of age.

The white people. The colored people get more welfare, but don't have any proof.

My age group, between forty and sixty-five. People that are unemployed and can't get jobs.

In taxation. Personal property tax is not profitable. A person's property is his own business. A guy who owns his own business has to pay tax on property and equipment. (Respondent used to own his own business.)

Poor people with large families. Instead of helping them, they take money from them.

Colored people.

The people, those at the bottom.

Alcoholics, dope addicts. That takes in Skid Row. The officials could show a little more consideration rather than just jail them. From my experience, this is the case. I've worked in a mental hospital as an attendant. They jail them and push them around until they almost crack. They then put them in a hospital to patch them up. It's very serious, especially after the Korean conflict. So many young veterans are using dope. There are a lot more than you heard about in World War II. A lot of dope-taking is going on in high schools, too.

5. Do you think any persons or groups of people enjoy special powers or privileges in Detroit, more than the average person?

The people that have the money. If you don't have money, you don't get much privileges.

The American white man. But Jews and Italians and Syrians have difficulties like we do, but we are at the lowest point.

Rich people.

Real estate people.

Officials of the city.

The people in the higher economic bracket, the wealthy people.

Negro people don't get an even break.

Wealthy groups, especially whites. You can see them in the Seven Mile areas, Sherwood Forest.

Labor groups have more than average power. There are some abuses by big unions. Politicians help these labor groups, but not as a whole.

Colored. They can do almost anything, murder, robbery, and get probation—which is a joke.

Political club members get all kinds of favors. One time when I lost a job during the Depression, I knew somebody and three days later I got a job on the WPA as a supervisor.

I hear that the Catholics do, but I don't know. There's no proof.

Detroit Edison, J. L. Hudson, the large automobile manufacturers, and the utilities.

The organized groups. The higher classes of people.

The politicians. The taxpayers have to pay for their privileges.

Businessmen. (Anybody else?) I couldn't name anyone else.

The "hundreds crowd." I don't want to name them. From traffic ticket favors all the way up.

The wealthy.

Well, I think the businessmen have more power than the working man. (Anybody else?) I can't think of anybody else.

People who have more money could enjoy more power.

The colored have a lot more power in Detroit than the white.

The Italians, but it's also the voters' fault. The mayor is Italian. Union officials are mostly Italian. The ones that were caught stealing were Italian.

6. With elections coming up this fall, people are getting more interested in politics. What is your party preference? Are you a Republican or a Democrat?

IF REPUBLICAN OR DEMOCRAT

    6a. Why is that?

IF NOT REPUBLICAN OR DEMOCRAT

    6b. In general, do you consider yourself closer to the Republicans or Democrats?

    6c. Why is that?

       (Responses for Democrats and Democratic-independents only)

The Republicans are good for rich people but not for average people.

Because the Democrats are the party of the common people. They do more for common people.

I feel that the Democratic candidate is more for the little fella, and I am a little fella.

The Democratic party lets the little guy get some of it instead of letting it trickle down from the top.

It's the lesser of two evils. There isn't really much difference. They're both dominated by the same people.

It's more for working people. The Republicans are for business people and corporations.

Because, generally men who represent the Democratic party are more aware and in a position to do something about needs of common men, working men like myself.

Since I am a laboring man I think they are closer to the laboring man.

The Democratic party is more for the working man. It's not like the Republicans, who favor the rich.

All my friends are Democrats. I always think of F.D.R., and he was a Democrat.

The Democrats are more for the people.

I've been that way all my life. My parents were Democrats.

The Republican party was founded by big business. Democrats are more for working people.

I changed in 1934. The Democrats did more for the people. They gave us work. They gave us WPA and the CCC camps.

I was raised a Democrat and always believed in the Democratic way. I've always voted Democratic.

They favor labor more in my opinion.

My dad voted Democratic. Also, I like Democratic ways.

I think that the Democrats are a good party. My father was Democratic. That's probably the main reason.

I don't know. I don't like the Republicans.

Because I'm a Catholic and most Catholics are Democrats.

They do more for the laborer and the small man.

Because my father was a Democrat.

Well, I don't know. I'm a Democrat because they have more consideration for the working man.

The Democrats are more for the working man.

It takes in middle-class people. They get more benefits.

I'm labor.

We've had eight years of Republicanism, and we need a change. I believe in the Democrats. They do more for the working man.

I'm a working man. All of them are Democrats.

Not much reason. Things are the same with either party. I'm just a Democrat.

I associate with others who are Democrats, and besides, I think the Democrats are a working man's party.

Being a working man, I'm a Democrat.

I gotta vote for one or the other. They're both bad. There were once some real good Republican politicians, but they all died.

7. A lot of people did not vote in the governor's race two years ago when Williams and Bagwell ran against each other. Did you vote?

IF VOTED

    7a. Who did you vote for?

    7b. Why did you vote for him?

IF DID NOT VOTE

    7c. Which one of the two did you prefer, Williams or Bagwell?

7d. Why did you feel this way?
(Answers for support of Williams only)

Because he's a Democrat.

Williams is all right. He's a Democrat.

I'm a Democrat and I've liked his past performances as far as labor and whatnot are concerned. Williams seems to be fair as far as race relations are concerned.

He's always done a good job. I think he holds his job up good. He does a good job for Michigan.

He would make speeches that all the people could understand, and he came to my neighborhood.

I'm a Democrat, that's all.

He's the best governor we've had since I've been here. Williams, you can talk with him or call him. He'll come down to the church to talk, too.

Because he was a Democrat. He has been doing a good job against a handicap of a Republican legislature.

I didn't think Bagwell was the man.

I think he's done a great job while he was in office. They condemn him for a lot of things that weren't his fault.

Because I've liked his program and his administration.

He's been in for so long. Actually, I don't know why.

He's the best governor in every way.

Because he's more of a man for the poor people. He knows our needs.

Because I thought he conducted a good administration. He was good and helpful to labor, and labor needs all the help they can get.

Because he's a Democrat, and I think he's a good man, too.

Williams had experience. He had a better background than Bagwell.

Williams has been doing a good job. He tried to do everything for us. The income tax, for example, is good for poor people.

Same reasons that I like the Democratic party. Coming from his background, he took the common man's viewpoint.

I figured he represented the working man and not the wealth.

He has good principles. He is a man in no class. He is just a good man. He's an exception. He associates with all classes and deals with their problems.

Well as far as I'm concerned, he's for the working man.

I thought he was a good man. Everybody I talked to thought he was good. He can fight for Michigan. (Anything else?) He can get factories to stop moving out.

I like him, and he's a good man, favorable to everybody. I've talked to him, and he's fair-minded.

Because he was a good administrator. But he didn't have any backing. I wanted to make a majority so that the legislature could operate.

Because I thought he was honest and would make a good governor.

We were in a mess at the time, and I believed that if we went with him for another term he would straighten us out. Much to my regret, he hasn't.

Williams has done much for the state as a whole. He's been good.

He's always been a mixer. He mixes with the common people. He's a down-to-earth man.

He's a good Democrat. He gets around. You can have a party in your basement, and he'll come down and say "hello" to you. That's more than the rest of them will do.

He's a good guy. That's all. If he runs again, I'll vote for him.

He does a good job. He made a lot of things possible for the poor working class. The unions are with Williams.

I liked Governor Williams's platform. It was for the working man. He worked hand in hand with labor. He has money and is dedicated to work. He certainly doesn't need money.

He's done a lot for the state. He's been blamed for a lot but one man doesn't dictate laws. Poor representation in the state doesn't allow for decent representation of voters.

His record was good. He has done a lot for the colored people. He's taken a lot of good stands.

I think he's a good governor. I couldn't find anything wrong with him. I didn't know anything about Bagwell.

I thought he was a man that could take care of the job. He did a good job before.

I thought he was the best man. He always had an efficient government and always stood up for the working man.

8. Who was the best President we ever had? (90 per cent chose F.D.R.)

    8a. Why do you say that?

    (Answers for Roosevelt supporters only)

Because of what he did during the Depression. When he was in office he did a lot for the country.

Because he put us right back on our feet. I lost my home and every dime I had, and I regained it because of him. He put people back to work.

He did a lot. He brought the nation out of the big slump, but probably any other person in there would have done the same thing.

He was a good guy. He did lots for poor people.

Except for Abraham Lincoln, he was the greatest. Roosevelt did a lot of things for the people during the Depression— when I only had a nickel in my pocket.

He did a good job for the times.

He did more for the working man than any other President of the United States.

I remember the CCC camps and NRA programs that he set up to get us out of the Depression.

He took us through those war years and gave us our eight-hour day and NRA.

During the Depression, he helped people get jobs and make a better living.

He was the best for the working man. He brought in social security, ended Prohibition, and brought in FHA.

It was good when he was President. He got the country on its feet.

He brought us out of the Depression and into a level of economy we had never known before.

He gave every working man more than any other President has.

He did more for the poor people. He was for them.

Because he did more for the common people than anyone. He was not for the big guy.

He built up social security and old-age pensions and things like that.

The main reason: When he got in, I got a job.

He was a man who considered all people and did something about it. He was a man of action.

He could carry the public. He put programs on to help the country get on its feet.

He was with the poor people. He brought us up to where we are. Truman was O.K. too.

He did the most for the people. He distributed wealth, got everybody back on their feet. Color, creed, nationality, profession didn't mean a thing to him.

He was a great war leader. He had more social reforms than any other President. These are the things that we live under today.

He understood people. He did many things. He helped the country out of the Depression, but most important, through his understanding he helped world peace.

He was the poor man's friend.

The majority liked him. He stayed in a long time, and he did a lot for the poor people.

He got me jobs, work.

He did more for the people.

Well, because at the time he became President the whole world was in a bad way economically, and his first concern was for the whole people.

He stepped in when things were in a bad way and did a lot to straighten things out. He recognized that the little men were the backbone of the country. The projects set up by him were to help the little man.

He put everything up. He put people up. In my neighborhood, a $15,000 house can be bought for $800 down because of Roosevelt. Nobody else like him, nor will there ever be.

He brought the country back so that the poor people could get work and something to eat.

During the war he ran the government quite well. He was a good war-time and peace-time President.

He really brought the country out of a slump. He started a lot of good things for the country. He was a fair-minded President, as far as different people were concerned.

He did a lot of good for this country. He certainly did a lot more than the rest.

The way he opened up a lot of jobs and got everything going.

SKEPTICISM

1. When business booms in Detroit, who gets the profits?
   Class conscious, N=203. Big business, upper class, rich people, and similar class categories.

Not class conscious, N=143. Everybody, everyone, or all the people.

Everybody gets a little bit. I do, too.

The people get the profits. There's a lot of overtime. There's no recession.

The companies.

The stockholders. (Anybody else?) Well, the working man lives pretty good then.

The stores, grocery stores. (Anybody else?) Anyone who's selling like that. For example, car manufacturers.

The companies. Cadillac and General Motors.

The businessman. Because he sells the goods, he profits. He pays fifty cents and charges one dollar.

Upper-class people, because they have something to offer, like real estate, warehouses.

The businessmen, both little and big business.

The middle man.

Everyone profits by it.

The owner.

The owners of companies.

The rich man.

Manufacturers get most, but everyone benefits.

Everybody gains, but people of wealth gain more. Those who have, get it.

It's spread around quite well. Business profits, but workers only get wages which don't change.

The manufacturers, whoever is selling. Labor also benefits through more work.

The business people. Manufacturers, storekeepers, small businessmen.

The profits are shared. Workers get their share.

Everybody.

Everybody. It's pretty even.

Businessmen get the money.

Stockholders. Everyone benefits when business booms, but the working man benefits the least.

Everybody benefits.

The business owners.

I don't know. I really don't.

The rich man. He's the one that gets the profits.

Everybody in business.

That I couldn't tell you. As long as I get my wages, I don't worry.

The rich get the profits, but everybody gains somewhat.

I think we all share in the profits. In good times everybody gains.

Everybody—businessmen, workers, and so on.

It's 50-50 for the manufacturers and the laborers.

Companies and businesses, but it seeps down to workers and equals out.

Everybody in general—businessmen, owners and what not.

General Motors and Ford.

They all get it. Most of the chain stores do well. The government gets some in income tax.

Businessmen, not me.

The industrialists.

Stockholders. (What do you mean?) People who own various companies in town.

Everybody.

The working class. It has more money to spend.

Businessmen and government.

All these factories. Big factories make the profits. The businessman.

The rich man.

Everybody gets some, but businessmen get more.

The upper classes. I don't get it. I get the same all the time.

Everybody does when business booms.

All of us.

The guys that own the stores.

The businessman, the companies.

Everyone—small business, big business, and working-class people.

MILITANCY

This aspect of consciousness was operationally defined by asking all respondents to project themselves into the following situation and then asking them how they would react:

Question:
Public opinion people like myself often ask the people we talk with to use their imagination in answering a question. Now imagine the following situation. Almost all of the people in your neighborhood are factory workers and rent their homes or apartments. People in your neighborhood have been complaining about high rents and poor housing in your neighborhood and the landlords refuse to do anything about it. If these working-class people in your neighborhood were to get together and form an organization to try and do something about these problems, that is, try to force the landlords to change things for the better,

would you support this group or figure it was none of your business?

If the respondent said he would support this group, or if he was unsure, he was asked a series of questions, the last one of which was: Would you take part in a neighborhood demonstration such as picketing the landlord to do something about it?

Class conscious, N=133. Yes, would picket.

Not class conscious, N=208. No.

Other, N=34. Unsure and other responses.

EGALITARIANISM

The following question was used to weigh egalitarianism. Only the most positive response was classified as constituting class consciousness.

Question:

Do you agree or disagree with the following statement: The wealth of our country should be divided up equally so that people will have an equal chance to get ahead.

Class conscious, N=96. Agree.

Not class conscious, N=248. Disagree.

Other, N=31. Unsure and other responses.

Appendix B: The Survey Sample

The Sample

In the spring and early summer of 1960, we interviewed blue-collar residents in Detroit. We selected these workmen from seven ethnic neighborhoods and used a list random sample procedure to select workers from within these districts. Three of the areas were predominantly Negro, three Polish, and one Northwestern European. Although we took random samples within each one of the seven districts, what we found cannot be considered as distinctly "representative" of the entire Detroit community. On the contrary, our information only suggests the views of people studied within each of the ethnic groups.

The sample design can best be summarized in the following order: (1) the reason for developing a stratified sample, (2) the time of research, (3) drawing the sample, and (4) the quality of the interviewing.

Why Stratify?

Statistical pragmatism is the main reason for using stratified sampling. This form of statistical realism has marked our approach to research on class consciousness. We have assumed that workers from racial and nationality groups that are disproportionately working-class should be more militant than workers found in ethnic groups characterized by disproportionate concentrations of white-collar workers. As we have already mentioned, we take for granted that the Negro working class is part of a proletarianized group, while workmen of Northwest European background are found in nationality groups more middle-class in character. Consequently, we have hypothesized that the Negro and white minorities should differ markedly in their class-influenced attitudes. In order to test this notion, we stratified the sample so as to include Negro and German-British districts, thereby ensuring an adequate numerical representation from both groups. Obviously, we had prediction tables in mind when we took over two-thirds of the total sample from these two groups.

Sample Districts

We constructed the sample so as to maximize comparability between districts: we did not include suburban or working-class slum districts (see map). All the interviews were conducted within the city of Detroit, but beyond the central core of the city (one of the most dreadful slums in North America), bounded by East and West Grand Boulevard.

We should note that the sample choice resulted in the selection of a large number of older workers. As is well known, residential districts in the central city frequently contain a large number of older people, whereas the young and middle-aged are generally concentrated in the suburbs. Of course, there were exceptions; for example, the study sample contained a relatively large number of young Negroes.

Time of the Study

We selected our sample and did most of the interviewing during the late spring and early summer of 1960. Although the inter-

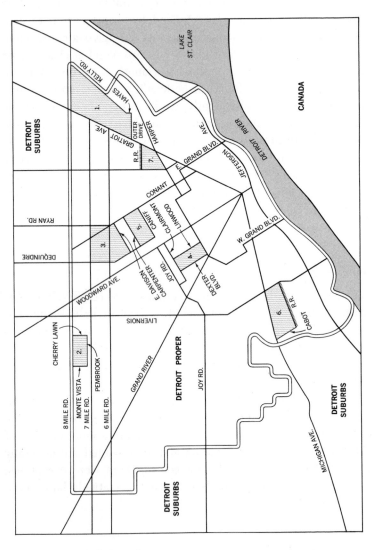

Sub-Sample Districts, Detroit, 1960

viewing took place during a period of relative economic prosperity, the community's economy was not up to par. Following the 1957-58 recession, the percentage of unemployed had dropped from an August 1958 peak of 20 per cent for the total labor force, to 6 per cent in April and May of 1960. Many workmen, nevertheless, failed to find work when the automobile industry recovered. At the time of the study, Negro and Slavic workmen were a disproportionately high percentage of the unemployed.

How Was the Sample Drawn?

SELECTION OF ETHNIC CORE AREAS

We emphasized ethnic concentration and deprivation in selecting groups for the study. Also, the ethnic groups had to represent a broad range in income.

Three sources of information guided our selection: the personal observation of non-experts, the advice of ethnic specialists, and published materials on the distribution of ethnic groups in the city of Detroit. By pooling our information, we decided to concentrate on two proletarian groups, Negroes and Poles. Both groups satisfied the two selection criteria, for they were residentially nucleated and socially low in status.

In order to balance our sampling, we also interviewed Anglo-Saxons and Germans, both prosperous ethnic groups. Locating them precisely was something of a problem, although we found from experts and census data that these working-class groups were heavily concentrated on Detroit's upper east side, an area more heterogeneous than the Polish and Negro districts. Yet because this neighborhood was the only one of its kind in Detroit, we decided to proceed and to draw a sample from this district.

ELIGIBLE RESPONDENTS

We interviewed only blue-collar workers with particular ethnic and regional backgrounds: those of German, British, Canadian,

Polish, Ukrainian, and Negro descent were eligible for the interview. We excluded southern-born whites, since their ethnic background was different from that of other Anglo-Saxons and Germans.

In order to choose the eligible, we traced the descent line through the respondent's father. Where this line was mixed, we selected the nationality group with the higher prestige; thus, if a respondent's father was German-Polish, we classified the respondent as German. Fortunately, only a small number of respondents claimed mixed nationality on their father's side.

We included Canadians in the sample because of the extreme difficulty of separating them from those of British descent. We included other Canadians as well—those of French or Scandinavian descent—but they were few in number.

We also brought Ukrainians into the sample, and for the purposes of analysis, we treated them in the same category as Poles. A pragmatic consideration dictated this decision. Many Poles claim ancestors born in the Ukraine, while some Ukrainians maintain that their forefathers came from Poland. Added to this is the fact that the border separating the Ukraine and Poland shifted back and forth several times during the first half of the twentieth century. One can imagine the chaos that might have resulted had there been an attempt by the interviewer to separate Poles from Ukrainians. Another side to this problem is the fact that Detroit Ukrainians tend to live adjacent to and often within Polish districts.

From each of the seven districts we drew separate samples. Unfortunately, the number of potential respondents chosen from each district depended in part upon the reception given the interviewers. We had to curtail interviewing in one ghetto area (District 2) after a gang chased one of the interviewers away. District 2 was not unique; in District 7 many respondents were exceedingly unco-operative. In spite of the general hostility of the respondents in this district, the interviewers attempted to complete the schedules.

In another district (District 1), a very large proportion of potential respondents turned out to be members of white-collar occupations or ineligible ethnic groups. We therefore had to select a disproportionately large number of respondents from the district.

The selection of the sample proved to be an on-going process. Our staff had originally planned to interview 100 respondents from each of the following clusters: (1) Negroes, (2) Poles and Ukrainians, and (3) Germans, Britons, and Canadians. At the same time, anticipating our statistical analysis, we had planned to include in each of the three clusters 50 respondents whose total personal income was less than $5000 in 1959. In the case of Negroes and Poles, this task did not prove to be a problem, since they were often in low-income brackets. Unfortunately, but expectedly, proportionately fewer Germans, Britons, or Canadians earned less than $5000. It was therefore necessary to over-sample the district where they were heavily concentrated until we had interviewed 50 respondents who made less than this sum.

Another problem—this one on data validity—was the possibility of bias arising out of an interview in which the participants belonged to diverse and sometimes antagonistic ethnic groups. However, we avoided this whenever possible by having Negro staff members interview Negro respondents, and vice versa. We did this in order to minimize racial barriers to communication within this racially conscious community. Still, in many cases, we found it necessary to use white interviewers among Negro workmen. Interestingly, when we compared the Negro interviews obtained by both whites and Negroes, there seemed to be few, if any, differences in results.

In an interview involving both middle- and working-class participation, it is likely that not a few manual workers would be reluctant to express trenchant comments unless a deep sense of concern moved them to do so. Should class bias occur, it would work against worker expression of militant views. Presumably this curtailment of free expression could have occurred quite frequently, especially with Negro workmen and white interviewers.

To compensate for the small sampling, we focused on particular segments of the working class—only male, manual workers found in certain ethnic groups, located beyond the core of the central city but within its outer boundary.

The following table presents the ethnic background of interviewed workers. One hundred nineteen claimed to be Negroes, while one informant insisted he was Irish-Negro. For the purposes of analysis there were 120 Negroes. All but ten of the 114 Slavs were of Polish extraction. One hundred forty-one of those interviewed were of Northwest European origin, with the majority claiming German ancestry. Two respondents insisted on referring to themselves as "Americans," though information obtained from neighbors indicated that their background was English.

Table 1. Interviews Completed, by Sub-Sample District and Ethnic Group

ETHNIC GROUP	SUB-SAMPLE DISTRICT							TOTAL NUMBER
	1	2	3	4	5	6	7	
NEGROES	0	12	51	52	4	0	1	120
SLAVS								
Poles	33	0	5	0	35	22	8	103
Ukrainians	0	0	3	0	3	3	1	10
Combination of Pole and Ukrainian, or Either with Some Other Group	1	0	0	0	0	0	0	1
NORTHWEST EUROPEANS								
Germans	71	0	1	0	3	2	0	77
German and other	3	0	4	0	1	0	0	8
English	16	0	1	0	0	1	1	19
Scotch	6	0	0	0	0	0	0	6
Ulster Irish	2	0	0	0	0	0	0	2
Welsh or Combination of British, or British and Some Other Ethnic Group	15	0	1	1	1	0	0	18
CANADIANS								
British	6	0	0	0	0	0	1	7
French	3	0	0	0	0	0	0	3
Other Canadian	1	0	0	0	0	0	0	1
TOTALS	157	12	66	53	47	28	12	375

Appendix C: Statistical Methods

Zero-Order and Partial Correlations as They Relate to the Sources of Consciousness

In the following two tables we present information that supports key hypotheses advanced in this study. Both the significance levels and the zero-order correlations confirm the study's expectations in every instance. As Chapters 4 through 8 have already indicated, the significance levels for the first eight hypotheses are less than .05. The zero-order correlations go as high as .41. In computing these measures of correlation and levels of significance, we have used Kendall's Tau [1] as a measure of correlation and a test of significance based upon Tau.[2] Parenthetically, this significance test is more powerful than X^2.

We should comment on the statistical procedure used to calculate these zero-order correlations. We have collapsed the five categories in the dependent variable to three: (1) militant egalitarians and militant radicals, (2) skeptics, and (3) class verbalizers and class indifferents. We followed this procedure in order to balance the number of rows and columns in the distribution table. The upper limit of Kendall's Tau reaches unity only when these numbers are equal. If most of my independent variables

1. Hubert M. Blalock, *Social Statistics* (New York: McGraw-Hill Book Co., 1960), pp. 321–4.
2. Sidney Siegel, *Nonparametric Statistics for the Behavioral Sciences* (New York: McGraw-Hill Book Co., Inc., 1956), pp. 220–22.

Table 1. Relationship Between Class Consciousness and Selected Independent Variables

SELECTED INDEPENDENT VARIABLE	KENDALL'S TAU MEASURE OF CORRELATION	SIGNIFICANCE LEVEL BASED ON KENDALL'S TAU
Ethnicity	.39	.001
Union Membership	.14	.001
Uprootedness	.41	.001
Downward Mobility	.12	.001
Generation	.10	.01
Skill Level	.19	.001
Employment Status	.09	.01
Personal Income	.09	.01

Table 2. Relationship Between Class Consciousness and Selected Dependent Variables

SELECTED DEPENDENT VARIABLE	KENDALL'S TAU MEASURE OF CORRELATION	SIGNIFICANCE LEVEL BASED ON KENDALL'S TAU
Voting Preference	.17	.001
Inter-Ethnic Hostility	.04	.05

had five categories, the collapsing would not have been necessary, since they would match perfectly the five gradations of class consciousness. Unfortunately, our independent variables contained either two or three categories. We should mention that this collapsing does not consistently increase or decrease the zero-order correlations. For example, in the case of ethnicity, Kendall's Tau drops from .39 to .32 when the full five categories of consciousness are used, but in the case of union membership, the correlation coefficient increases from .14 to .16 when we follow the same procedure.

As expected, the use of partial correlation analysis reduces the impact of all the independent variables considered. We have used a measure of partial correlation presented by Blalock (p. 336) in order to gauge the extent to which critical social forces reduce the impact of the major variables (Table 3). When we relate ethnicity to class consciousness, for example, while con-

Table 3. Partial Relationships and Class Consciousness

Selected Variable and Variable Which Most Reduces its Impact on Class Consciousness		KENDALL'S TAU MEASURE OF CORRELATION	KENDALL'S MEASURE OF PARTIAL CORRELATION
INDEPENDENT VARIABLE	CONTROL VARIABLE		
Ethnicity	**Uprootedness**	.39	.23
Union	Plant Size	.14	.13
Uprootedness	**Ethnicity**	.41	.26
Downward Mobility	Ethnicity	.12	.08
Generation	Ethnicity	.10	**.05**
Skill Level	Ethnicity	.19	.10
Employment Status	Ethnicity	.09	.06
Personal Income	Ethnicity	.09	.04

trolling for uprootedness, we reduce the correlation coefficient from .39 to .23 (Table 3). We selected uprootedness for this analysis because it had the best over-all impact of reducing the correlation coefficient of the ethnicity–class consciousness relationship. We show other controls in Table 3 that reduced the influence of the other independent variables considered. Size of plant diminished the importance of union membership, while other variables had less of an impact when we used them as controls. To cite another example, the relationship between uprootedness and class consciousness decreased considerably when the ethnic partial control was applied. Both uprootedness and ethnicity survived the influence of one upon the other. Thus, they operate as independent variables with considerable weight. The results therefore support our assumption of multiple causation.

The Combined Impact of the Sources of Consciousness

By approaching working-class consciousness through the use of multi-variable analysis, we can examine the statistical impact of a plurality of factors, all considered at the same point in time. In this way it becomes possible to think in terms of the amount of variance explained simultaneously by a host of independent variables. The multiple correlations in Table 4 indicate the combined impact of eight key variables considered in this study. For example, the combination of race-ethnicity, union membership, and uprootedness explains one-third of the total variance of class consciousness. Our analysis has already indicated their relative importance. The remaining five variables explain the additional amount of class consciousness accounted for in the study. On the whole, our analysis of these considerations has revealed their lesser importance. It should be remembered, however, that these five variables have this impact only after we have taken into account (1) ethnicity, (2) union membership, and (3) uprootedness. (In other words, the remaining five variables only account for the difference between .33 and .41.) Had we presented the

Table 4. Multiple Relationships and Class Consciousness

	INDEPENDENT VARIABLES RELATED TO CLASS CONSCIOUSNESS							
RACE/ETHNICITY	UNION MEMBERSHIP	UPROOTEDNESS	DOWNWARD MOBILITY	GENERATION	SKILL LEVEL	EMPLOYMENT STATUS	PERSONAL INCOME	MULTIPLE CORRELATION, OR R^2
X	X							.168
X	X	X						.332
X	X	X	X					.346
X	X	X	X	X				.356
X	X	X	X	X	X			.391
X	X	X	X	X	X	X		.400
X	X	X	X	X	X	X	X	.407

cluster of five variables prior to our taking into account the importance of ethnicity, union membership, and uprootedness, those five would have explained a greater part of the variance than they do in their present order. However, no other combination of considerations explained anything approaching .33 of the variance.

A problem facing any social scientist using multiple correlation technique is the statistical utility of his arithmetical gymnastics. This study has used the multiple correlation technique as a heuristic device. We obtained measures of multiple correlation discussed in Table 4 through the use of The Dwyer Square Root Method. (See "The Square Root Method and Its Use in Correlation and Regression," *Journal of the Americal Statistical Association,* 40 [1945], p. 502.) This measure of association assumes an interval scale. However, we used information that is at best ordinal. To our knowledge, there is no multiple correlation measure which can both treat data on an ordinal level and relate eight variables serially to a dependent variable. Consequently, we have used a measurement that assumes an interval scale. When we violate the rules of measurement in this way, we obtain correlation coefficients that are suspect. That is, they are no longer precise measures of relationships. However, we may think of these correlation coefficients as essentially descriptive in the sense that they give some indication of the relative importance of each variable as well as the joint impact of all eight factors. And, we repeat, we have presented the multiple correlation coefficients only for heuristic purposes.

Multi-variable analysis of this kind has further weaknesses. However useful, statistical measures can do little more than indicate *what* is relevant in determining attitudes. The statistics tell us little about *how* groups acquire their views. They also fail to indicate why such perspectives should be shared, or why certain relationships occur in one community and not in another. Nor do they suggest *when* a key relationship will take place within a community. Obviously, then, we must not depend exclusively upon statistical results for explanation.

Appendix D: A New Way of Viewing Consciousness Inside the Working Class

Our treatment of working-class views does contain certain weaknesses, and perhaps when we again study working-class consciousness, we might profit by making a distinction among type, level, dimension, degree, and cumulation of consciousness, as indicated in the diagram. As for *type,* consciousness might be viewed in class, racial, or class-racial terms, depending upon the analytic interests of the observer, although the investigator can observe all three phenomena simultaneously. We should also examine the incidence of low, medium, and high *levels* of consciousness. For example, in this study, class verbalization constituted a dimension found at a low level of consciousness, skepticism fell in the middle range and militancy as well as egalitarianism, respectively, ranked in the higher positions. (Class verbalization constituted a low level because it would appear to be easily acquired, at least more so than skepticism, militancy, and egalitarianism, in that order.) These four dimensions of consciousness, however, do not exhaust the logical possibilities. For example, we were able to substitute the *dimension* of class identification for class verbalization at a low level of consciousness within our larger measure, thereby indicating the flexibility of both concept and measure of working-class consciousness.

Type, level, and dimension constitute three approaches to the subject. In addition, there is the summarizing notion of *degree.*

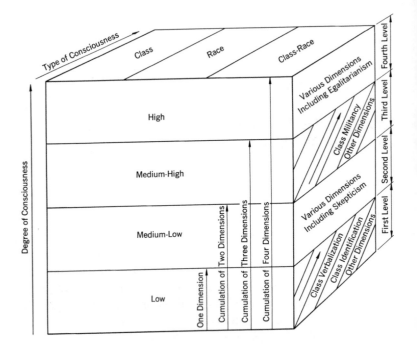

Degrees and Dimensions of Working-Class Consciousness:
a Schematic Presentation

In order to discuss degree of working-class consciousness, we
might conceptualize consciousness in terms of its cumulation of
one, two, three, or four (or more) dimensions. For example, we
have classified the militant egalitarian as one who has scored
positively on class verbalization, skepticism, militancy and egalitarianism, and hence expressed a high degree of class consciousness. Each dimension of consciousness, such as class militancy,
could also be treated in terms of level, dimension, degree, and
cumulation of consciousness, perhaps in a way not too different
from the manner in which we have charted the larger measure.

Notes

INTRODUCTION

1. Writers have made distinctions between different types of workmen and generalized accordingly. Many generalize with such abandon, however, that one wonders where analysis ends and stereotype begins. For an example of this kind of confusion, see Seymour Lipset's analysis in *Political Man* (Garden City: Doubleday & Company, Inc., 1960), pp. 45–76, 97–130, 131–78, 220–84.
2. Perhaps the best analysis of bureaucratic paternalism can be found in Charles H. Silberman's *Crisis in Black and White* (New York: Random House, 1964), pp. 308–55.
3. See John C. Leggett and David S. Street, "Economic Crisis and Expectations of Violence" in William Gomberg and Arthur Shostak, *Blue Collar World* (Englewood Cliffs, N.J.: Prentice Hall, 1964), pp. 498–504.
4. The lack of a sense of guilt, indeed, the tendency to celebrate the insurrection and struggle, has been aptly analyzed by Michael Parker in his "Watts: The Liberal Response" in *New Politics*, 4 (Summer, 1965), 41–9.

CHAPTER 1

1. A number of writers have discussed the place of the union, and we will have occasion to observe their views. The writer who first impressed me on the significance of trade unions and other working-class organizations was C. Wright Mills, the young Mills that I associate with the essays in *Power, Politics and People, New Men of Power,* and *Anvil and Student Partisan.*

    In an essay called "A Marx for the Managers" Mills deals with the revolutionary lower classes and how they elevate their leaders into power. He implied that they do so through struggle organizations like labor unions and soviets. See "A Marx for the Managers" in *Power, Politics and People*, edited by Irving Louis Horowitz (New York: Oxford University Press, 1963), p. 71. Also in the same volume see "The Trade Union Leader: A Collective Portrait," pp. 77–96; "The Labor Leaders and the Power Elite," pp. 97–109.

2. See Adolf Sturmthal's discussion of Yugoslavia in *Workers Councils* (Cambridge, Mass.: Harvard University Press, 1964), pp. 86–8.

3. Oscar Handlin was the first to popularize this rubric in *The Uprooted* (Boston: Little, Brown and Co., 1952).

4. See Karl Marx, "The Eighteenth Brumaire of Louis Bonaparte," reproduced in part in Lewis Coser and Bernard Rosenberg, eds., *Sociological Theory: A Book of Readings* (New York: Macmillan Co., 1957), p. 374 in particular. Relevant would be Clark Kerr and Abraham Siegel's "The Inter-industry Propensity to Strike— An International Comparison," found in *Industrial Conflict*, Arthur Kornhauser, Robert Dubin, and Arthur M. Ross, eds. (New York: McGraw-Hill Book Co., 1954), pp. 189–212. Seymour Lipset has presented considerable information which supports Kerr and Siegel's observations on conditions conducive to consciousness. See his *Political Man*, pp. 175–6, 205–7, and particularly 87–8.

5. Given my definition, the category mainstream working class does not include workers located outside the advanced urban-industrial community. Consequently, miners, lumbermen, and other rural workers fail to qualify for either of the two categories devised for the urban-industrial setting. The study of class consciousness and political radicalism among manual workers in rural regions demands a thoroughgoing analysis. For an excellent pathfinding work, see Eric Allardt's treatment of left-wing militancy among manual workers in northern and eastern Finland, "Regional Imbalance and Working-Class Consciousness: An Ecological Study," a paper presented at the International Congress of Political Science in Paris, September 1961.

6. We use nominal scales in an attempt to sort elements on the basis of a certain characteristic. As we do, we make decisions about which elements are most similar and which most different. In this regard Hubert Blalock has pointed out:

Our aim is to sort them into categories which are as homogeneous as possible as compared with differences between categories. If the classification is a useful one, then the categories will also be found to be homogeneous with respect to *other* variables. For example, we sort persons according to religion (Methodists, Presbyterians, Catholics, etc.) and then we see if religion is related to prejudice or political conservatism.

Social Statistics (New York: McGraw-Hill Book Company, Inc., 1960), p. 12.

7. On the matter of ordinal scale of measurement, Blalock has observed:

It is frequently possible to order categories with respect to the degree to which they possess a certain characteristic, and yet we may not be able to say exactly how much they possess. We thus imagine a single continuum along which individuals may be ordered. Perhaps we can rank individuals so precisely that no two are located at the same point on the continuum. Usually, however, there will be a number of ties. In such instances, we are unable to distinguish between certain of the individuals that we have lumped together to a single category. We are able to say, however, that these individuals all have higher scores than certain other individuals. Thus we may classify families according to socioeconomic status: "upper," "upper-middle," "lower-middle," and "lower." We might even have only two categories, "upper" and "lower."

Social Statistics, p. 13.

CHAPTER 2

1. See Selig Perlman, *A History of Trade Unionism in the United States* (New York: The Macmillan Co., 1923).
2. Alfred G. Meyer used a related distinction in his treatment of Marx's works. He analyzed their theoretical framework in terms of two approaches, one concerned with causal relationships and historical sequence, the other focused primarily upon structural relationships and functional ties. See his *Marxism* (Cambridge, Mass.: Harvard University Press, 1954).
3. Marx has treated the relation of change to consciousness in a variety of contexts; see "The Communist Manifesto," in *Capital,*

The Communist Manifesto and Other Writings, Max Eastman, ed. (New York: The Modern Library, 1932), pp. 315–55, and Karl Marx, "Wage, Labor, and Capital," *Selected Works*, Vol. 1 (New York: International Publishers, 1933), pp. 268–9.

4. See Perlman, pp. 265–95.
5. Perlman, pp. 3–129.
6. See Robert F. Brooks, *When Labor Organizes* (New Haven: Yale University Press, 1942); Carroll R. Daugherty, *Labor Problems in American Industry* (Boston: Houghton Mifflin Co., 1936); Alfred W. Jones, *Life, Liberty and Property* (Philadelphia: J. B. Lippincott Co., 1941), pp. 24–53; Art Preis, *Labor's Giant Step* (New York: Pioneer Publishers, 1964), pp. 3–81.
7. After presenting Perlman's position on this matter, Sidney Peck noted a surprising similarity between the views of Perlman and Lenin:

> A somewhat similar perspective is expressed by the advocates of "scientific socialism." In the work of V. I. Lenin, one of the more orthodox exponents of Marxism, a view emerges of working-class ideology which in many respects is akin to the thesis of the Wisconsin School. Lenin distinguishes between two types of working-class mentality, i.e., trade union consciousness and social democratic consciousness. In *What Is To Be Done*, he sees trade union consciousness developing as a reaction to the conditions of exploitation inherent in capitalism. The trade union emerges as an organizational instrument which the working class utilizes in bargaining with the bourgeoisie over the sale of labor-power. Thus, trade union consciousness is a spontaneous response to the oppressive conditions which force the worker to exchange his labor-power for subsistence commodities.

> From this spontaneous concern to improve their bargaining power and conditions of work comes unanticipated consequences: trade unionism serves to organize and discipline the masses and trains them to work together. In this respect, trade union organizations emerge as the citadels from which the working class can move to attack the arsenals of capitalism.

> But the ideological motivation to attack the system as a whole does not arise as a spontaneous outgrowth of working-class mentality. Rather, Lenin suggests, it arises outside of the

working class as a natural and inevitable outcome of the development of ideas among the revolutionary socialist intelligentsia.

Sidney Peck, *The Rank and File Leader* (New Haven: College and University Press, 1963), pp. 36–7.

8. "The Eighteenth Brumaire of Louis Bonaparte," in Karl Marx, *Selected Writings in Sociology and Social Philosophy*, T. B. Bottomore and M. Rubel, eds. (London: Watts and Co., 1956), pp. 188–9.

9. Perlman, pp. 265–95.

10. Alfred W. Jones, pp. 250–80.

11. Brooks, pp. 99–201; Daugherty, pp. 354–452; Jones, pp. 54–139.

12. Jones, pp. 315–17.

13. Pope observed that workers had developed "class consciousness in a social sense, due chiefly to the isolation of mill villages." Liston Pope, *Millhands and Preachers* (New Haven: Yale University Press, 1941), pp. 216–61.

14. Marx's comments on the Indian peasantry are perhaps less well known than those on the French agrarians. Wittfogel has paraphrased Marx on this matter:

> In two articles published in the *New York Daily Tribune* in 1853 Marx discussed the character of Asiatic society and the possibilities of its progressive dissolution. In these articles he cited India as representative of "Asiatic society" and the Hindus as having certain crucial institutions in common with "all Oriental people." He argued "climate and territorial conditions" made "artificial irrigation by canals and waterworks the basis of Oriental agriculture." And he observed that water control "necessitated in the Orient, where civilization was too low and the territorial extent too vast to call into life voluntary association, the interference of the centralizing power of the government."
>
> Thus it was the need for government-directed water works that according to Marx gave birth to the Asiatic state. *And it was the "dispersed" condition of the "Oriental people" and their agglomeration in "self supporting" villages (combining small agriculture and domestic handicraft) that permitted its age-long perpetuation.* (Emphasis my own.)

See Karl Wittfogel, *Oriental Despotism* (New Haven: Yale University Press, 1957), p. 374. For Marx's classical statement on the European peasantry, see his "The Eighteenth Brumaire of Louis Bonaparte," taken from Lewis Coser and Bernard Rosenberg, pp. 374–6.

15. Richard Centers, "The American Class Structure, A Psychological Analysis," found in Guy E. Swanson, Theodore M. Newcomb, and Eugene L. Hartley, eds., *Readings in Social Psychology* (New York: Henry Holt and Co., 1952), p. 304.

16. See Mark Abrams, "Press, Polls and Votes in Britain since the 1955 General Elections," *Public Opinion Quarterly*, 21 (1957–58), 543–7. Lipset discusses the general characteristics of the "deference voter." He tends to be old, to have little education, to live in relatively small communities, to be employed in small companies, farm or personal service, and to be a non-conformist. See Seymour M. Lipset, "Must Tories Always Triumph?" *Socialist Commentary* (November 1960), p. 11.

17. Neal Gross studied a cross-section of the Minneapolis population in 1950 and addressed himself to the following problem: How do people identify themselves in terms of social class when subjected to both open- and closed-ended questions? When the open-ended question on class identification was used in the early part of the interview, only 11 per cent of the total population maintained that they were working class; one-third claimed middle-class membership; one-fifth held that they did not know to which social class they belonged; one-seventh claimed that there were no social classes in America; another one-seventh identified themselves within a wide range of classes, from the "employer class" to the "common" or "poor" class. Later in the interview, however, Gross found that when the respondents were asked to identify their class position from among four closed-ended alternatives (upper, middle, working, and lower class) the proportion who identified themselves as "working" increased considerably. Also, a small number of those who had initially considered themselves working class in the open-ended question later chose middle class from the closed-ended list of alternatives. See Neal Gross, "Social Class Identification in the Urban Community," *American Sociological Review*, 18 (1951), 398–404.

18. In a post-World War II study of Danielson, Connecticut, Lenski found that prominent citizens did not agree on the number and composition of social classes in this small semi-industrial community. Gerhard E. Lenski, "American Social Classes, Statistical Strata or Social Groups," *American Journal of Sociology*, 58

(1952), 139–49. Looking at "Citrus City," California, in the early 1950's, Thomas Lasswell drew the following conclusions: (1) no uniform set of clearly defined criteria exists by means of which the respondents judge class composition; (2) a generally recognized number of social classes does not exist; (3) there is no community consensus on the social strata found within it. Thomas E. Lasswell, "A Study of Social Stratification Using an Area Sample of Raters," *American Sociological Review,* 19 (1954), 310–13.

During the mid-'fifties, J. Haer dealt with the problem of delineating social-class awareness of respondents in Tallahassee, Florida, a political, administrative, and university center in the Deep South. The study found that (1) only four-fifths of the population believed in the existence of social classes; (2) a wide variety of criteria were used to identify social classes, although the main criteria—used in less than a majority of instances—were economic; (3) an extremely large proportion of the respondents either could not place themselves within a particular class or thought of themselves as middle class; (4) the respondents frequently could not consistently identify themselves as belonging to one class or another; (5) only slightly more than half of the respondents could successively name social classes, suggest the distinguishing features of these classes, and place themselves consistently within the class order they described. John L. Haer, "An Empirical Study of Social Class Awareness," *Social Forces,* 36 (1957), 117–21.

19. Manis and Meltzer, observing trade union members in Paterson, New Jersey, in 1950, concluded that class images there were not salient, and that many respondents could not state or agree among themselves on the number of social classes in this industrial town. However, unlike that of Citrus City, this study showed that workmen used economic criteria in a majority of instances to define the composition of social classes. Manis and Meltzer also found that many respondents had rather deferential attitudes toward the middle class, while at the same time most of them maintained a belief in the cohesion of the labor union. On the whole, then, most workmen expressed *a low level* of class consciousness. Jerome G. Manis and Bernard N. Meltzer, "Attitudes of Textile Workers to Class Structure," *American Journal of Sociology,* 60 (July 1954), 30–54.

20. The fact that most workmen did not develop or maintain a clearly consistent frame of reference in times of prosperity does

not eliminate the political impact of the few militant workmen, as a study by Manis and Meltzer in the late 1940's shows. Their survey of textile workers indicated that militant workmen generally favored labor legislation and voted in a way that was consistent with their personal and class interests. Specifically, Manis and Meltzer determined the percentage of workers who favored government ownership of the textile industry. Of those who were highly class conscious, 43 per cent were in favor, while the corresponding figure for those not very class conscious was found to be 20 per cent. Also, 76 per cent of those who scored high in consciousness preferred the Democratic party, while slightly less than half of those who scored low in consciousness expressed this preference. Jerome G. Manis and Bernard N. Meltzer, "Some Correlates of Class Consciousness Among Textile Workers," *American Journal of Sociology*, 59 (September 1963), 182.

Oscar Glantz's 1952 study of Philadelphia provided further information on the salience of consciousness. It should be noted that he defined class consciousness not in terms of social-class identity but by (1) allegiance to either business or labor and (2) orientation toward either the N.A.M. or C.I.O. positions on controversial issues. He concluded that class-conscious workers were more likely to vote Democratic than those without a class perspective. See Oscar Glantz, "Class Consciousness and Political Solidarity," *American Sociological Review*, 23 (August 1958), 375–83.

21. Morris Rosenberg, "Perceptual Obstacles to Class Consciousness," *Social Forces*, 32 (October 1953), 22–7.

22. See Friedrich Engels, "Why There Is No Socialist Party in America," in Karl Marx and Friedrich Engels, *Basic Writings on Politics and Philosophy*, Lewis S. Feuer, ed. (Garden City: Doubleday and Co., Inc., 1959), pp. 457–9.

23. Marx referred to the context of class consciousness in a number of places. See Karl Marx, *The German Ideology*, Parts I and III (New York: International Publishers, 1947); "Preface to a Contribution to the Critique of Political Economy," in Karl Marx, *Selected Writings in Sociology and Social Philosophy*, p. 52; and "Poverty of Philosophy," in the same volume, pp. 186–8.

24. See Harry Elmer Barnes, *An Introduction to the History of Sociology* (Chicago: University of Chicago Press, 1958), pp. 192–7. Relevant also is an essay by Irving Louis Horowitz, "Introduction: The Sociology of Ludwig Gumplowicz," in Ludwig Gumplowicz,

Outlines in Sociology (New York: Paine Whitman Publishers, 1963), pp. 40–44.

25. Joseph A. Schumpeter, *Social Class and Imperialism, Two Essays* (New York: Meridian Books, 1955), pp. 134–5.
26. Otto Bauer, *Die Nationalitätenfrage und die Sozialdemokratie* (Wien, I: Brand, 1907), pp. 187–234.
27. Marx used hard (objective) criteria to define class in the Communist Manifesto. See "The Communist Manifesto," in *Capital, The Communist Manifesto and Other Writings*, pp. 324, 329, 345–6. Also Karl Marx, *The Eighteenth Brumaire of Louis Bonaparte* (New York: International Publishers, 1926), pp. 50–67, especially p. 62. However, in the same analysis he used class identity—not objective criteria—as the basis for defining class:

> In so far as millions of families live under economic conditions of existence that divide their mode of life, their interests and their culture from those of the other classes and put them in hostile contrast to the latter, they form a class. In so far as there is merely a local interconnection among these small peasants, and identity of their interests begets no unity, no national union and no political organization, they do not form a class. They are consequently incapable of enforcing their interest in their own name, whether through a parliament or through a convention.

Karl Marx, "The Eighteenth Brumaire of Louis Bonaparte," taken from Lewis Coser and Bernard Rosenberg, pp. 374–6.

Later, shortly before his death, Marx suggested his dissatisfaction with this matter. See *Selected Writings in Sociology and Social Philosophy*, pp. 178–9.
28. See Lewis Corey, "The Middle Class," in Reinhard Bendix and Seymour M. Lipset, *Class, Status and Power* (Glencoe: The Free Press, 1957), pp. 371–81; C. Wright Mills, *White Collar* (New York: Oxford University Press, 1951), pp. 63–76.
29. Both Marx and Engels emphasized the importance of workers' struggles to achieve better living conditions. For illustrative material see Frederick Engels, "Introduction to the German Edition of Karl Marx's *The Civil War in France*," found in *Capital, The Communist Manifesto and Other Writings*, pp. 373–4.
30. See his "The Chartists," in *Selected Writings in Sociology and Social Philosophy*, p. 200.

31. See excerpts from *The German Ideology,* pp. 74–5.

32. Emphasis my own. See excerpts from "The Poverty of Philosophy," in *Selected Writings in Sociology and Social Philosophy,* pp. 186–7.

33. See Karl Marx, *Capital, The Communist Manifesto and Other Writings,* pp. 342–3.

34. See Appendix A for questions and replies used in measuring working-class consciousness.

35. "Error types" refer to patterns of response inconsistent with those presented in Table 2-3. For example, workers who scored "plus" on class verbalization, "minus" on skepticism, and "plus" on both militancy and egalitarianism would constitute error types. Again, workmen who answered positively on verbalization and skepticism, negatively on militancy, but affirmatively on egalitarianism would also be counted as error types.

    These and other unusual patterns of response may, in some cases, have occurred because the workmen did not understand the questions posed by the interviewer. However, this was not always the case, for some inconsistent answers represent a lack of consensus among workmen on what constitutes a high degree of militancy. Some considered picketing more extreme than favoring equality. These workers might value the latter but eschew personal participation in picketing demonstrations. On the other hand, our evidence indicates that most workmen viewed picketing landlords as less extreme than favoring the equal distribution of wealth.

36. For further information on the construction of these categories, see John C. Leggett, "Working-Class Consciousness in an Industrial Community" (Unpublished Ph.D. Dissertation, University of Michigan, 1962), pp. 73–135.

37. Admittedly, our treatment of unions is limited by the absence of theoretical and empirical materials on various *types* of unions, e.g., "syndicate" as well as "trade union"; *forms* of strikes, e.g., "economic" or "political"; and *nature* of workers, "isolated" or "integrated." However, in Detroit, where workmen belonged to various forms of *labor unions* and where they almost invariably conducted *economic strikes* within industries whose labor force was generally *highly isolated* in Kerr and Siegel's terms (auto, chemical, steel, and related workers made up over three-quarters of the blue-collar labor force) unions generated relatively high levels of working-class consciousness.

CHAPTER 3

1. With very few exceptions, most studies of class consciousness have taken place in small and medium-sized towns with a diversified economic base. To our knowledge, social scientists have never used survey techniques to study class consciousness in large cities that qualify as dependent upon a key industry. However, we should not overlook an excellent analysis that dealt with class consciousness in Buffalo, New York, and focused on the World War I period—Elwin H. Powell's "Reform, Revolution, and Re-action: A Case of Organized Conflict," in Irving Louis Horowitz's *The New Sociology* (New York: Oxford University Press, 1964), pp. 331–56. Also relevant and informative is Sidney Peck's study of the relative militancy of Milwaukee union stewards, in *The Rank-and-File Leader*. However, neither Buffalo nor Milwaukee has been a one-industry city.

2. *Thirteenth Census of the United States: 1910. Abstract of the Census with Supplement for Michigan, 1912* (Washington, D.C., 1912), p. 64.

3. See George B. Catlin, *The Story of Detroit* (Detroit: The Detroit News, 1923), pp. 650–58, 705, 721; Allen Nevins, *Ford: The Times, The Man, The Company* (New York: Charles Scribner's Sons, 1954), pp. 74–5. Sidney Glazer has noted the quickened pace of industrial development and population growth in Detroit between 1865 and 1900, when the city grew not only as a maritime distribution and commercial center, but also as a manufacturing one with markets located primarily in Michigan. See his "The Beginnings of the Economic Revolution in Michigan," in *Michigan History*, 34 (September 1950), 193–202. For an analysis of Detroit as a trade center during this period, see John A. Russell, "Study of Michigan's Marketing," in *Michigan History*, 13 (Winter, 1929), 32; William Stockton, "Fifty Years of Industrial Progress in Detroit," in *Michigan History*, 10 (October 1926), 609–10.

4. Sidney Glazer has analyzed the less than successful efforts of the Knights of Labor to organize skilled labor during the 1870's and 1880's and the more rewarding exertions, especially among craft workers, of the American Federation of Labor. See his "The Michigan Labor Movement," in *Michigan History*, 29 (Spring, 1945), 73–8.

5. Nevins, pp. 380–84.
6. Floyd Streeter, *Political Parties in Michigan* (Lansing: Michigan Historical Commission, 1918), pp. 161–77; Peter Ostafin, "The Polish Peasant in Transition: A Study of Group Integration as a Function of Symbiosis and Common Definitions" (Unpublished Doctoral Dissertation, University of Michigan, 1948). Streeter has observed that the greater portion of early settlers of Michigan were of "American nationality," emigrants from New England and New York. See his "The Factional Character of Early Michigan Politics," in *Michigan History*, 2 (January 1918), 165. Hugo Erichsen wrote: "From 1860 to 1880 the Germans in the city numbered nearly one-third of the population and were quite prominent in the social and political life of the town." See "My Memories of Old Detroit," in *Michigan History*, 17 (Spring, 1933), 208–10. The French originally constituted a majority of Detroit's population. As late as 1830, the French still numbered one-half. See Leigh G. Cooper, "Influence of the French Inhabitants of Detroit Upon Its Early Political Life," in *Michigan History*, 4 (January 1920), 303.
7. See Gerhard Lenski, *The Religious Factor* (New York: Doubleday and Company, 1961), pp. 6–8, 26–8, 311–23.
8. An interesting discussion of Detroit's elite between 1870 and 1900 that refers to dozens of leading figures whose names strongly suggest that a disproportionately large number were of English, Scotch, and German background is James F. Dickie, "Reminiscences of Detroit," in *Michigan History*, 14 (Autumn, 1930), 579–650.
9. Edgar E. Robinson, *The Presidential Vote, 1896–1932* (Stanford: Stanford University Press, 1947), p. 234.
10. Hazen S. Pingree, a "progressive Republican" before Theodore Roosevelt, was mayor of Detroit from 1889 to 1897. From 1897 to 1905, Democrats controlled this position; however, Democratic success constituted "a brief resurgence," one not again experienced until the 1930's. See Stephan B. and Vera H. Sarasohn, *Political Party Patterns in Michigan* (Detroit: Wayne State University Press, 1957), pp. 3–23. Also see Charles R. Starring, "Hazen S. Pingree: Another Forgotten Eagle," in *Michigan History*, 32 (June 1948), 129–50.
11. For a discussion of the Irish and German vote during this period, see Streeter, pp. 161–77.
12. However, German-American social democrats were organized in

Detroit as early as 1877, if not before. See Sidney Fine, "The Ely-Labadie Letters," in *Michigan History*, 36 (March 1952), 2.

13. *World Almanac and Book of Facts*, 1913 (New York: Press Publishing Company, 1912), pp. 739–40.

14. The Progressive party received substantial voting support in Detroit and elsewhere in Michigan during the 1912 presidential election, as indicated by the following figures on the total Michigan vote: Theodore Roosevelt, 39 per cent; William Howard Taft, 28 per cent; Woodrow Wilson, 27 per cent; others (including Socialists), 6 per cent. Parenthetically, it should be noted that the party of Roosevelt could not elect candidates to state offices in this rock-ribbed Republican state. See Alice Porter Campbell, "Bull Moose Movement in Michigan," in *Michigan History*, 25 (Winter, 1941), 34–47.

15. *Thirteenth Census of the United States: 1910. Abstract with Supplement for Michigan*, 1912, p. 64; *Fourteenth Census of the United States: 1920. Composition and Characteristics of the Population by States*, Volume 3 (Washington, D.C., 1922), p. 488.

16. William W. Potter, "Fifty Years of Michigan Progress," in *Michigan History*, 8 (October 1924), 431–41; Earl B. Fuller, "The Automobile Industry in Michigan," in *Michigan History*, 12 (April 1928), 280–96; "The Automobile Industry in Michigan," in *Michigan History*, 8 (July 1924), 219–65.

William Stockton has supplied us with a useful measure of the impact of the automotive revolution on the growth of industry in Detroit. Whereas in 1890 the United States Census ranked Detroit seventeenth in value of products produced in industrial centers of the country, nine years later the city stood sixteenth; in 1904 it was twelfth; in 1909, ninth; in 1914, sixth; and in 1924, third. See his "Fifty Years of Industrial Progress in Detroit," in *Michigan History*, 10 (October 1926), 607–9.

17. Lois Rankin wrote a most useful article on ethnic minorities and their socio-economic positions during the first three decades of this century. She included the following nationality groups in Detroit: Bulgarians and Macedonians, Finns, Greeks, Hungarians, Italians, Yugoslavs, Lithuanians, Poles, Roumanians, Russians, Syrians, and Ukrainians; but she did not deal with the French-Canadians, other Canadians, Cornish, Dutch, English, German, Irish, Jews, or Scandinavians. Miss Rankin noted that Detroit's foreign-born in 1930 constituted slightly more than 25 per cent of the city's population, and that only New York with

33 per cent and Chicago with 26 per cent ranked higher. Her article treats each group in terms of its location, occupation, religion, voluntary organizations, family life, relations with other minorities, and ties with the larger community; see "Detroit Nationality Groups," in *Michigan History*, 23 (Spring, 1939), 129–84. Also see R. Clyde Ford, "The French Canadians of Michigan," in *Michigan History*, 27 (Spring, 1943), 243–57; John C. Vismara, "Coming of the Italians to Detroit," in *Michigan History*, 2 (January 1918), 123; Leo M. Franklin, "Jews in Michigan," in *Michigan History*, 23 (Winter, 1939), pp. 77–92; Erdmann D. Beynon, "The Hungarian Population of Detroit," in *Michigan History*, 21 (Winter, 1937), 89–103; June N. Miljeric, "The Yugoslav People," in *Michigan History*, 25 (Autumn, 1941), 358–64.

18. The Democratic and Socialist parties declined in influence soon after the end of World War I and did not become important again until the 1930's, although Robert M. LaFollette received a large vote in 1924. Sarasohn, p. 24.

19. Reinhold Niebuhr, *Leaves from the Notebook of a Tamed Cynic* (Hamden, Connecticut: The Shoe String Press, 1956), pp. 78–89, 94, 111–13, 128–9, 143, 149–50; June Bingham, "Reinhold Niebuhr in Detroit," in *Christian Century*, 78 (March 8, 1961), 279–98.

20. Many writers extolled the new technology and prosperity. See, for example, William W. Potter, "Fifty Years of Michigan Progress," in *Michigan History*, 8 (October 1924), 441. For many Detroit workers, the "roaring 'twenties" proved to be a period of considerable optimism and recurrent "hangovers"; Clayton W. Fountain, *Union Guy* (New York: The Viking Press, 1949), pp. 25–34.

21. A sense of relative deprivation has been aptly described by Sidney Glazer:

> The panic [the Great Depression] affected the automobile industry in an unusual manner, since the total annual hours of workers had to be reduced drastically. It was possible for most of the other industries to give at least partial employment, but a large number of automotive workers were entirely without employment. Many had purchased homes and had made other investments during the boom twenties. Thus, the average worker not only found himself unemployed, but

feared that his accumulated savings would be lost. Likewise, the loss of a standard of living, previously taken for granted, caused considerable uneasiness and a general feeling of insecurity.

See Glazer, "The Michigan Labor Movement," in *Michigan History*, 29 (Spring, 1945), 81.

22. Relevant here is an autobiographical account of how one Detroit worker experienced the 1930's, in Fountain, pp. 34–130.

23. Especially useful is Sidney Lens's analysis in *The Crisis of American Labor* (New York: The Sagamore Press, 1959), pp. 172–95.

24. Irving Howe and Lewis Coser, *The American Communist Party* (Boston: Boston Press, 1957), pp. 368-82.

25. John C. Dancy, "The Negro People in Michigan," in *Michigan History*, 24 (Spring, 1940), 221. For material on the past, present, and projected growth of the Negro population of Detroit, see Thomas F. Hoult and Albert J. Mayer, *The Population Revolution in Detroit* (Detroit: Institute for Regional and Urban Studies, 1963), p. 10.

26. Communists even made some headway within a respectable tool- and die-makers' union, the Mechanics Educational Society of America, at the height of the Great Depression. See Sidney Fine, "The Tool and Die Makers Strike of 1933," in *Michigan History*, 42 (September 1958), 310–11, 318–19.

27. For a discussion of American intellectuals and their attraction to the left, see Seymour M. Lipset, *Political Man*, pp. 310–44.

28. Keith T. Sward, *The Legend of Henry Ford* (New York: Rinehart, 1948), pp. 231–42.

29. *Labor Policies of Employers' Associations in Violation of Free Speech and Rights of Labor*, Parts 4–8, in *Report of the Committee on Education and Labor*, No. 6, 76th Congress, 1st Session (Washington, D.C., 1939).

30. Sward, pp. 372, 385–400.

31. Sward, pp. 146, 160, 450–63.

32. Morris Janowitz has discussed the mass support of the Black Legion and similar organizations found in Michigan in "Black Legions on the March," in *America in Crisis*, Daniel Aaron, ed. (New York: Alfred A. Knopf, 1952), pp. 305–25. See also Lipset, *Political Man*, pp. 131–79.

33. See Arthur Kornhauser, Albert J. Mayer, and Harold L. Sheppard,

When Labor Votes (New York: University Books, 1956), pp. 11–20.

34. Hoult and Mayer, pp. 11–12.

35. Alfred McClung Lee and Norman D. Humphrey, *Race Riot* (New York: The Dryden Press, 1943), p. 84.

36. See "Pointe Realty Plot Charged by Bufalino," Detroit *News,* February 6, 1961; "Adams Rips Quizzing of G. P. Home Buyers," Detroit *News,* April 19, 1961. (Paul Adams was the state attorney general.)

Ethnic discrimination has continued but in a more subtle form. A recent issue of the *New York Times* (March 12, 1967) commented on the slow pace of change. Only two Negro families (beside Negro servants) are known to live among the 55,000 Grosse Pointe residents. The article goes on to point out:

Ingrained restrictive methods came into the open in 1960 when an official of the Grosse Pointe Property Owners Association, testifying at a hearing, said that prospective home buyers were routinely rated according to a point system with a radical [*sic*] pattern.

Private investigators hired by the Association awarded or withheld points according to a would-be resident's action, dress, education, job and "swarthiness," it was disclosed.

To get into Grosse Pointe, a prospective home buyer needed 50 points if he was of Polish extract, 65 points if his background was Italian or Greek, and 85 points if he was Jewish, it was learned. There were no gradings for Negroes.

Exposure of the point system meant its end. It was abandoned on orders from the Michigan Corporation and Securities Commission. But more subtle—and no less effective—restrictive attitudes and practices have remained. One consequence is, as a Grosse Pointe hostess here remarked the other night, "Everyone looks alike—watch the people at this party, they might all be cousins, and they're all WASPS."

Grosse Pointe is still predominantly white Anglo-Saxon Protestant . . .

37. This continued political loyalty is consistent with the findings of
    Bennett Berger, *Working-Class Suburb* (Berkeley and Los An-
    geles: University of California Press, 1960), pp. 80–90, 110.
38. Irving Howe and B. J. Widick, *The U.A.W. and Walter Reuther*
    (New York: Random House, 1949), pp. 149–72.
39. Especially relevant is Stephan B. and Vera H. Sarasohn's analysis
    of how the automotive interests increased their influence within
    the Republican party of Michigan during the 1940's and early
    1950's, and how the industrial unions, particularly the U.A.W.,
    joined the liberals during the same period in a powerful coalition
    made up of the Wayne County and Michigan Democratic party
    organizations. See their excellent study, *Political Party Patterns
    in Michigan*, pp. 26–68.
40. One should not overlook Sidney Lens's discussion of the decline
    of militancy within industrial unions during the 1940's and
    1950's, pp. 70–172, 195–252.
41. "Auto Dealer Stocks Continued to Drop in May," *Wall Street
    Journal*, June 7, 1961. During the first six months of 1963, the
    General Motors Corporation and the Ford Motor Company
    captured 79 per cent of the car market, while the Chrysler Cor-
    poration held 13 per cent according to "Auto Sales Pace in June
    Rose 8% from the 1962 Month," *Wall Street Journal*, July 5,
    1963.
42. William Haber, Eugene C. McKean, and Harold C. Taylor, *The
    Michigan Economy, Its Potential and Its Problems* (Kalamazoo:
    The W. E. Upjohn Institute for Employment Research, 1959),
    pp. 3–58, 61–140, 233–49.
43. *Michigan Labor Market*, 13 (September 1958), 5.
44. *Michigan Labor Market*, 16 (April 1961), 4. See also "160,000
    Won't Regain Auto Jobs," *Detroit News*, February 2, 1961.
45. Relevant here is a study conducted by Wayne State University
    sociologists, who focused on what happened to Packard Motor
    Company workers after the Detroit plant closed. See Harold L.
    Sheppard, Louis A. Ferman, and Seymour Faber, *Too Old to
    Work—Too Young to Retire: A Case Study of a Permanent Plant
    Shutdown*, Senate Special Committee on Unemployment Prob-
    lems, 86th Congress, 1st Session (Washington, D.C., 1960),
    pp. 13–39.
46. Of those laid off by Chrysler, many joined the long-term unem-
    ployed. Of these, the majority were undoubtedly Negro, some

of whom we quoted on pp. 4–5. Of those quoted, some may have taken part in various forms of collective behavior associated with the recent Detroit insurrection. For a pathfinding discussion of various forms of crowds, movements, and other forms of collective behavior, see Herbert Blumer's "Collective Behavior," in *Principles of Sociology*, Alfred M. Lee, ed. (New York: Barnes and Noble, Inc., 1951).

47. "Restless Reuther: He May Try to Replace Meany as AFL-CIO Chief," *Wall Street Journal*, June 21, 1961.

48. "160,000 Won't Regain Auto Jobs," Detroit *News*, February 2, 1961.

49. Kornhauser, Mayer, Sheppard, pp. 17–20. For statistical material on Detroit voter indifference to the grass-roots political activities of both Republican and Democratic precinct organizations, as well as independent political activities of the unions, see Daniel Katz and Samuel Eldersveld, "The Impact of Local Party Activity Upon the Electorate," *Public Opinion Quarterly*, 25 (Spring, 1961), 16–20.

50. Lens, p. 283.

51. "Joblessness High for Negro in U.S.," *New York Times*, March 5, 1961.

52. For a preliminary discussion of recent U.S. insurrections, see John C. Leggett, Richard Apostle, Albert Baronas, and David Driscoll, "Total Cultural Revolution, Class-Racial Consciousness and Current U.S. Insurrections" (a paper read before the 1967 meetings of the American Sociological Association).

CHAPTER 4

1. Admittedly, today's prepared are often tomorrow's unprepared (while the contemporary unprepared may be yesterday's prepared)—and hence often without the skills associated with participation in a secure occupational position. Under conditions of rapid technological change and occupational obsolescence, unless the prepared workers acquire high and general levels of knowledge, their head start as big-city urbanites may prove to be of very short-term significance in acquiring occupational positions offering stable employment opportunity. Today we have reason to believe that many of Detroit's insurrectionary youth are "un-

prepared" even though they were objectively "prepared" eight years ago.

2. In addition, we should note that a series of statistical controls failed to upset the relationship between uprootedness and class consciousness. Length of residence, union membership, generation, and several measures of economic position did not erase the importance of uprootedness.

3. An examination of Figure 4-2 indicates that *ethnicity* is of importance even when one takes into account the impact of uprootedness. Uprooted Negroes were more militant than their Polish counterparts, while Negro prepared stood in the same relation to Poles born in the northern part of the United States.

4. Exploitation here refers to poor pay, abysmal working conditions, long work days, little job security, repressive managerial practices, and the like. Our definition is not based on the Marxian theory of surplus value. For a lucid and negative appraisal of the Marxian concept of exploitation, see Eduard Heinmann, *History of Economic Doctrines* (New York: Oxford University Press, 1964), pp. 144–52.

5. A number of writers have analyzed the political and economic unrest of European peasant populations undergoing industrialization. Unfortunately, left-wing analysts have not often linked peasant dissatisfaction with the landed aristocracy to peasant efforts at political and economic organization. For a critical analysis of the "green" (peasant) revolutionary movements which swept Eastern, Southern, and Central Europe during the late nineteenth and early twentieth centuries, see David Mitrany, *Marx Against the Peasant* (Chapel Hill: University of North Carolina Press, 1951).

   It is true, of course, that peasant groups are content with their circumstances under certain conditions; however, this is seldom the case when industrialization rationalizes agricultural production, concentrates land ownership, and links both production and ownership to world market conditions controlled by imperialist power. See Irving L. Horowitz, *Three Worlds of Development* (New York: Oxford University Press, 1966), especially pp. 164–92.

6. Werner Landecker has developed a quite similar interpretation of the sources of class consciousness. Although his explanation is more general than the one advanced in this study, it presents a point of view consistent with my own:

It seems then that in one form or another a large proportion of the population perceive their present social positions as stepping stones to higher levels. Under such conditions, one will tend to view oneself or one's family as being potentially above the transitional level occupied at the present time. Only if prospects for up-mobility seem to be dim do people come to think of themselves as being in the same boat with others of similar status and as being part of a distinct class. It seems then that the frequency of up-mobility which is assumed to occur stands in an inverse relation to the prevalent degree of class consciousness. *The higher the apparent frequency of up-mobility is, the lower the degree of class consciousness will tend to be.* (Emphasis mine.)

Ronald Freedman *et al., Principles of Sociology* (New York: Henry Holt and Co., 1952), p. 462. See Landecker's Introduction to Chapter 12.

7. Again, extreme uprootedness has an impact even when one takes into account previous agrarian conditions such as land ownership, occupational position, and farm size.

8. See Karl Marx and Friedrich Engels, "Letter to Karl Kautsky, November 8, 1884," in *Correspondence 1846–1895* (New York: International Publishers, 1946), p. 422.

9. Cole contrasts this situation with the easing of pressures on workmen at mid-century, when the emergence of corporate capitalism led to the joint-stock corporation. The joint-stock corporation could obtain capital from wealthy individuals and large banks more readily than the individually owned firm. After this change, workers were less likely to undergo rank exploitation arising from the need by employers to accumulate capital from funds that might otherwise have been used for wages. Cole's analysis of the embryonic and mature British working class is contained in his *A Short History of the British Working Class* (London: George Allen and Unwin, Ltd., 1952), especially pp. 121–39.

10. Adam Ulam presents a poignant analysis of conditions in England that prompted uprooted workmen to take leftist positions on the question of industrialization and power; see *The Unfinished Revolution* (Cambridge, Mass.: Harvard University Press, 1960), pp. 58–90. J. L. and Barbara Hammond have also analyzed the conditions and spirit of revolt common to uprooted workmen of early nineteenth-century England in *The Town*

Labourer, 1760–1832 (London: B. Longmans, Green and Co., 1949), Vols. 1 and 2. E. P. Thompson dealt with the class conciousness of skilled artisans in the early part of the nineteenth century. In his analysis he points to their concern with the question of political freedom; *The Making of the English Working Class* (New York: Pantheon Books, 1963), pp. 711–832.

11. See Harold Wilensky and Charles N. Lebeaux's *Industrial Society and Social Welfare* (New York: Russell Sage Foundation, 1958), pp. 27–132, for a discussion of the conditions uprooted workmen faced during the early period of industrialization in the United States.

12. Trotsky makes two important points about the character of stage skipping; first, he indicates its self-contradictory character, and second, he points to *state* barriers faced by the subordinate class:

> The possibility of skipping over intermediate steps is of course by no means absolute. Its degree is determined in the long run by the economic and cultural capacities of the country. The backward nation, moreover, not infrequently debases the achievements borrowed from outside in the process of adapting them to its own more primitive culture. In this the very process of assimilation acquires a self-contradictory character. Thus the introduction of certain elements of Western technique and training, above all military and industrial, under Peter I, led to a strengthening of serfdom as the fundamental form of labor organization. European armament and European loans—both indubitable products of a higher culture—led to a strengthening of tzarism, which delayed in its turn the development of the country.

Leon Trotsky, *History of the Russian Revolution* (New York: Doubleday and Company, Inc., 1959), pp. 3–4.

13. Ruth Fischer has written one of the best analyses of the variegated political character of the Russian working class during this period in *Stalin and German Communism* (Cambridge, Mass.: Harvard University Press, 1948), pp. 25–51, 148–70.

14. Vladimir I. Lenin, "What Is To Be Done," from his *Selected Works*, Vol. 2 (New York: International Publishers, 1943), especially pp. 51–115.

15. Leon Trotsky, pp. 9–10. Nonetheless, Trotsky's notion of discontinuities has had an impact in a number of other academic fields, including general evolution. Elman Service, in an essay on "The

Law of Evolutionary Potential," drew heavily upon Trotsky's
ideas concerning "the privilege of backwardness," in Marshall D.
Sahlins and Elman R. Service, *Evolution and Culture* (Ann
Arbor: University of Michigan Press, 1960), pp. 99–100.

16. See Karl Marx, "Communist Manifesto," in *Selected Writings in
Sociology and Social Philosophy*, pp. 184–5.

17. Harold Isaacs shared many of Trotsky's views on and interest in
the revolutionary politics of laborers. In his classical analysis of
China's early industrialization and complex politics, Isaacs stressed
the importance of combining stages of industrial development
in accounting for the revolutionary behavior of hundreds of
thousands of workers in Shanghai, Wuhan, and Hong Kong during the 1920's. In essence, Isaacs applied Trotsky's analytic
framework to China, tracing its uneven progress from the early
part of the nineteenth century through the 1930's.
        William Ayers gathered considerable material in support of
Isaacs's views, noting how the bulk of Chinese workmen had
only recently entered the industrial labor force—itself largely
a twentieth-century phenomenon. Ayers dealt at length with the
ways in which Chinese workmen clashed with the British, especially in industries that aided the promotion of militant class
consciousness. Harold Isaacs, *The Tragedy of the Chinese Revolution* (Stanford, Calif.: Stanford University Press, 1951), especially
pp. 1–74. William Ayers, *The Hong Kong Strikes, 1920-26*
("Papers on China, Regional Studies Seminars," Vol. 4 [Cam-
bridge, Mass.: Harvard University Press, 1950]). Also see his
Shanghai Labor and the May 30th Movement, Vol. 5 in the
same series (1950).

18. Liston Pope, pp. 213–306.

19. Alfred W. Jones, pp. 61–6.

20. Erik Allardt, "Traditional and Emerging Radicalism" (mimeographed paper), p. 21; *Social Struktur och Politisk Aktivitet*
(Helsingfors: Soderstrom and Co., 1956), p. 84; and *Patterns
of Class Conflict and Working Class Consciousness in Finnish
Politics* (Helsinki: Institute of Sociology, 1964), especially pp.
112–30.

21. Of course, one might argue that today's uprooted will give birth
to tomorrow's prepared, and hence, the problem of uprootedness
may well be transitional. However, as we have suggested (foot-
note 1), tomorrow's prepared may become the following day's

unprepared, a category of workmen located in a position in many ways similar to the generation of uprooted.

CHAPTER 5

1. See Chapter 1, pp. 9–13, for a discussion of different stages of industrial society.
2. Many analysts have commented on the demise of the class struggle. In particular, Eduard Bernstein has questioned the "crisis theory" of capitalism, noting that the general trend of both productivity and the standard of living under capitalism is upward, and that economic disturbances seldom interfere with these developments. More specifically, he described the transformation of the German socialist movement from a revolutionary organization to a bureaucratic mass party and related this structural change to economic improvements. See Peter Gay's excellent treatment of his analysis, *The Dilemma of Democratic Socialism, Eduard Bernstein's Challenge to Marx* (New York: Collier Books, 1962), pp. 121–51, 184–98.
3. Karl Marx, "Communist Manifesto," in *Selected Writings in Sociology and Social Philosophy,* pp. 184–5.
4. Engels's references occur in his "Letter to Karl Kautsky, November 8, 1884," found in Karl Marx and Friedrich Engels, *Correspondence 1846-1895,* p. 422. Joseph Clark has also cited Engels's revisions:

> Basically, as Engels indicates, two factors have rendered so much of the old Marxian model obsolete: economic developments and working-class struggles. And Engels' friend, Eduard Bernstein, had the wit and the courage to analyze the economic trends which contradicted the Marxian model: he also supported and did honor to the working-class movement which drastically altered the conditions under which the laborer earned his daily bread. In the 80's and 90's of the last century Bernstein described economic trends which have burgeoned even more decisively since then.

Joseph Clark, "American Reality and Socialist Prospects," *New Politics,* 2 (Summer, 1963), 56.

5. Roberto Michels, *First Lectures in Political Sociology* (Minneapolis: University of Minnesota Press, 1949), pp. 80–82.
6. Seymour M. Lipset, Paul F. Lazarsfeld, Allan M. Barton, and Juan Linz, "The Psychology of Voting: An Analysis of Political Behavior," in *The Handbook of Social Psychology*, Vol. 2, Gardner Lindzey, ed. (Cambridge, Mass.: Addison-Wesley Publishing Company, Inc., 1954), pp. 1124–75.
7. John K. Galbraith, *The Affluent Society* (Boston: Houghton Mifflin Company, 1958), pp. 328–9. My interpretation of Galbraith's book thus differs somewhat from Dwight MacDonald's, to be found in "Our Invisible Poor," *The New Yorker*, January 19, 1963, p. 82.

   Not a few social scientists have discussed the economic situation of the United States in the 1950's as one of prosperity for the entire country. These analyses de-emphasized the importance of class, stressing instead the relevance of status. See the essays edited by Daniel Bell, *The New American Right* (New York: Criterion Books, 1955). Also pertinent is the analysis offered by Adolph A. Berle, Jr., in his *Power Without Prosperity, A New Development in American Political Economy* (New York: Harcourt, Brace and Co., 1952), pp. 24–6.

   Recently, several writers have challenged the assumption of imminent, pervasive prosperity. Among others, see Gabriel Kolko, *Wealth and Power in America, An Analysis of Social Class and Income Distribution* (New York: Frederick A. Praeger, 1962); Michael Harrington, *The Other America—Poverty in the United States* (New York: Macmillan Company, 1962); Conference on Economic Progress, *Poverty and Deprivation in the United States: The Plight of Two-Fifths of a Nation* (Washington: Conference on Economic Progress, 1962).

8. Economic insecurity, measured in terms of occupational skill, proves to be inversely related to working-class consciousness. Eighteen per cent of the skilled ($N = 110$), 39 per cent of the semi-skilled ($N = 251$), and 46 per cent of the unskilled ($N = 13$) workers studied were classified as militant. If one further breaks down the figures according to race, this ratio remains true for both skilled and semi-skilled, where a lack of sufficient cases does not permit comparison for the unskilled.

   Paucity of respondents also precludes detailed analysis of the impact of length of unemployment. A crude distinction between short (less than 6 months), medium (6-12), and long-term unemployment (more than one year) fails to uncover any notable differences. Marie Lazarsfeld Jahoda and Hans Zeisl, in their classical study of Marienthal, found that long-term, widespread unemployment contributed to collective lethargy, political disengagement, and presumably, a diminution of working-class militancy. However, conditions comparable to the economic malaise of Marienthal at the height of the Great Depression did not exist in Detroit when we conducted our study. See Marie Lazarsfeld Jahoda and Hans Zeisl, *Die Arbeitslosen Von Marienthal* (Leipzig: Verlag Von S. Hirzel, 1933).

9. Maurice Zeitlin made a study of Cuban workers in 1962 in which he examined the political opinions of unemployed Negro workers. Their attitude toward the Castro revolution underwent a positive change between 1959 and 1962 as a result of their experiencing the effects of the revolution. Zeitlin has viewed this experience as comparable to membership in a union, since both revolutionary movements and union organizations have the potential for creating radical political views and fostering class opinions. See Zeitlin's "Economic Insecurity and the Political Attitudes of Cuban Workers," *American Sociological Review,* 31 (February 1966), especially p. 48.

10. When the size of plants grows, so does the incidence of strikes and frequency of Communist unions. See Lipset, *Political Man,* pp. 230-32.

11. When we discuss the impact of "the union" on Negroes, what we have in mind is the C.I.O., particularly the U.A.W. It should be important, partially because on the whole the U.A.W. is not racist. Even as staunch (and solid) a critic of labor as Herbert Hill, Labor Secretary of the NAACP, has indicated the exceptionalism of the U.A.W.:

> . . . Today, as in the past, there is a profound disparity between the public image presented by the national AFL-CIO, with its professed devotion to racial equality, and the day-to-day experience of many Negro workers, in the North as well as the South, with individual unions. To be sure, there are important exceptions, particularly in the mass-production industries, where a large concentration of Negro workers actually preceded unionization. Such unions as the United

Automobile Workers, the United Packinghouse Workers, and the Rubber Workers Union have conscientiously worked to eradicate institutionalized job bias . . .

See Herbert Hill's "Labor Unions and the Negro," reprinted from *Commentary* in William Petersen and David Matza, eds., *Social Controversy* (Belmont, California: Wadsworth Publishing Company, Inc., 1963), p. 222.

12. For a discussion of block-club organization in Detroit, see Melvin Ravitz, "The Sociology of the Block Club" (unpublished paper, Department of Sociology, Wayne State University). Also pertinent is George Henderson's "The Block Club Movement Within the Detroit Tenth Police Precinct" (unpublished paper, Community Services Department, Detroit Urban League). My own participant observation of Detroit block clubs in 1961-62 indicated that they pursue a wide variety of activities. Nominally, their primary concern is neighborhood conservation; however, many sponsor political forums, work for political candidates, send representatives to city council meetings, sponsor workshops on unemployment, and/or give financial contributions to groups working for equal educational opportunity. At the time our study was made, there were hundreds of clubs organized on the block and neighborhood level within the Detroit ghetto. See Henderson, "The Block Club Movement . . . ," p. 1. Under certain conditions, block clubs contribute to a collectivistic, militant point of view. See David Street and John Leggett, "Economic Deprivation and Extremism; A Study of Unemployed Negroes," *American Journal of Sociology,* 67 (July 1961), 56–7. Also see Chapter 8 for a detailed treatment of block clubs.

13. Sometimes U.A.W. policy statements reflect concern with automation. James Stern, Staff Consultant of the U.A.W.-C.I.O. Automation Committee, has commented on the consequences of automation for blue-collar employment opportunity:

> To the extent that we have not expanded total output commensurate with the productivity gains of automation, automation will heighten the insecurity of all workers, but in particular will have an adverse effect on the lives of older workers and other disadvantaged groups.

See "Possible Effects of Automation on Older Workers," an address given at the 8th Annual Conference on Aging, University of Michigan, Ann Arbor, Michigan, June 28, 1955.

14. Thirteen of the 15 unemployed Negro unionists in this study were members of industrial unions. Most were auto workers, with the remainder predominantly in the chemical and steel unions.

15. James Q. Wilson has provided a brief but informative analysis of Negro participation in the Detroit C.I.O. See *Negro Politics* (Glencoe: The Free Press, 1960), pp. 21–48.

16. For a first-rate report on how the rank and file faced these plant problems and how their reactions differed from those of the staid leadership of the U.A.W., see Martin Glaberman, "Marxism, the Working Class and Trade Unions," *Studies on the Left*, 4 (Summer, 1964), 65–72, especially p. 68 (the page quoted).

17. Wilson Record's *The Negro and the Communist Party* (Chapel Hill: University of North Carolina Press, 1951), is a good illustration of this kind of analysis.

18. Since then, T.U.L.C. membership has declined considerably.

19. See an interview with Robert Battle III and Horace Sheffield, "Trade Union Leadership Council: Experiment in Community Action," *New University Thought*, 3 (September-October 1963), 34–41.

20. This was determined later by asking workers to identify themselves as working, middle, or lower class. The closed-ended quotation elicited the following results: working (or lower) class, N=268; middle class, N=96; don't know, N=2.

    The most prominent writer on class identification is Richard Centers. See his *Psychology of Social Classes* (Princeton: Princeton University Press, 1949). Neal Gross has presented a valuable critique of this landmark in "Social Class Identification in the Urban Community," *American Sociological Review*, 17 (1953), 393–404.

21. In order to do this, we devised five types based on a Guttman scale comparable to the one already presented in this and in the preceding chapter, and with one exception, these five types are labeled in the same manner. "Class identifiers" replace the "class verbalizers," while the measure remains valid. The Menzel coefficient of reproducibility is .75, a figure only slightly less than the one obtained (.77) when we used the class verbalizer measure. Similar coefficients may appear to suggest that the closed-ended measure of class identification is very highly correlated with our more complex measure of class consciousness (see pp. 39–42; that is, when workmen identify with the working

class, they are also located in the militant or skeptic categories, and when other workmen think of themselves as middle class, they score in the class verbalizer or class indifferent positions. If so, our measure of class consciousness is needlessly complex. However, a high correlation of this sort does not occur, although a disproportionately large number of workers who considered themselves either working or lower class also scored as militants.

22. We took this story from Alfred W. Jones's *Life, Liberty, and Property*, pp. 145, 250–51.

23. See Seymour M. Lipset, Paul Lazarsfeld *et al.*, p. 1148.

24. Karl Mannheim was one of the first to deal seriously with "The Problem of Generations," in his *Essays on the Sociology of Knowledge* (London: Routledge & Kegan Paul, Ltd., 1952), pp. 276–320.

25. Writers such as James Conant have made it clear that many Negro youths living in industrial regions in the northern United States have suffered economically, particularly since the end of the Korean War. James Conant, *Slums and Suburbs.*

26. See Seymour M. Lipset and Hans Zetterberg, "Social Mobility in Industrial Societies," to be found in Seymour M. Lipset and Reinhard Bendix, *Social Mobility in Industrial Society* (Berkeley and Los Angeles: University of California Press), pp. 69–71.

27. Bettleheim and Janowitz have observed that ethnic intolerance is more highly concentrated among those who are declassed. Bruno Bettleheim and Morris Janowitz, "Ethnic Tolerance: A Function of Social Control," in Guy E. Swanson, Theodore M. Newcomb, and Eugene L. Hartley, *Readings in Social Psychology* (New York: Henry Holt and Company, 1952), p. 596. Also see, by the same authors, *Social Change and Prejudice* (New York: The Free Press of Glencoe, 1964), pp. 29–34.

28. See Harold Wilensky and Hugh Edwards, "The Skidder," *American Sociological Review*, 24 (April 1959), pp. 215–26.

29. See "Karl Marx to S. Meyer and A. Vogt, April 8, 1870," in Karl Marx and Frederick Engels, *On Britain* (Moscow: Foreign Languages House, 1953), p. 506.

CHAPTER 6

1. Marx commented on race but he never related it theoretically to the problem of class consciousness. However, he did note that

racial differences would have a deleterious impact on the development of an independent labor movement in the United States. See Karl Marx and Frederick Engels, *The Civil War in the United States* (New York: The Citadel Press, 1961), pp. xiv, 280-81; also *On Britain*, p. 506.

2. Clark Kerr and Abraham Siegel's study contains relatively little on the advanced industrial society with its emphasis on growth of automation and subsequent reorganization of its blue-collar labor force; their research is not based upon advanced industrial towns such as contemporary Detroit. Nonetheless, their theory does have some applicability. See Kerr and Siegel.

3. For supportive evidence, see Lipset's *Political Man,* pp. 175–6, 205–7, and particularly pp. 87–8.

4. The views of the Negro workers were influenced not only by racial discrimination, marginal employment, and social isolation, but by the political activity of the Communist party and the packinghouse union. See Theodore Purcell, *The Worker Speaks His Mind on Company and Union* (Cambridge, Mass.: Harvard University Press, 1953).

5. Relevant are figures on Negro unemployment and income. At the height of the 1960-61 recession, for example, 39 per cent of the Detroit Negro labor force was reported to be unemployed; "Joblessness High for Negro in U.S.," *The New York Times,* March 5, 1961. An article written by Jose Rames presents material on the employment opportunity and income of Detroit's Negro population:

> The unemployment rate was 16.8 per cent for Negroes and 10.0 per cent for whites in 1940. It was 12 and 6 per cent, respectively, in 1950, and 17.4 and 7.1 per cent in 1960 . . .
>
> During 1959 the median income of Negro families was $4,336, while it was $7,054 for whites. Since 1949, family income for whites increased 80 per cent but Negro family income rose by only 40 per cent.

"Racial Anatomy of a City," *New University Thought,* 3 (September-October 1963), 26.

6. It should not be forgotten that our sample used certain Slavic and Central and Northwest European groups, so that in this sense it is not altogether representative, although worker selection draws from four ethnic prestige levels.

7. In 1957-58 Gerhard Lenski conducted a study of religion in

Detroit. He relied mainly upon statistical data based upon interviews of a randomly selected sample from the Detroit Metropolitan Area. Lenski computed statistics for white Jewish, Protestant, and Catholic blue-collar workers. Gerhard E. Lenski, *The Religious Factor* (Garden City, N.Y.: Doubleday and Company, Inc., 1961), p. 73.

8. S. M. Miller's distinction between "new" and "old" working class is similar to my categories "marginal" and "mainstream." In particular, his new working class is like my "marginal" category, although there are differences in emphasis: for example, he treats minority workmen as a category, while our study analyzes them as members of working-class sub-communities. Also, Miller views these blue-collar minorities as being concentrated in the service industries, where they are generally non-unionized; in our study, on the other hand, they were located disproportionately in heavy manufacturing and industrial unions. See S. M. Miller, "Poverty, Race, and Politics," found in Irving Louis Horowitz's *The New Sociology* (New York: Oxford University Press, 1964), pp. 290–312.

9. This relationship holds even when we take into account the importance of uprootedness, employment status, and a host of other considerations.

10. See "Interview with Robert Battle III and Horace Sheffield," *New University Thought*, 3 (September-October 1963), 34–41.

11. In May 1963, block clubs, churches, and many other Negro organizations (excluding the NAACP) led in the organization of a mass demonstration to protest against unemployment and the Medger Evers murder. The Detroit police estimated that 125,000 people (approximately 95 per cent of whom were Negro) marched in the parade, while 250,000 gathered in the downtown area after the march to hear Martin Luther King and prominent Negro and labor leaders. See "125,000 Walk Quietly in Record Rights Plea," *Detroit Free Press*, June 24, 1963.

12. Of course, labor unions themselves, on occasion, also discriminate on the basis of race. However, it should be noted that biased organizations (the craft unions particularly) represent a minority of unionized workers in Detroit. The overwhelming majority of workmen belonged to unions which have participated, and at times led in the fight for civil rights.

13. Ely Chinoy's study of Oldsmobile workers in Lansing, Michigan, constitutes a case in point. Based exclusively on native-born white

workers, the study strongly suggested a low level of class consciousness among most workers. See *Automobile Workers and the American Dream* (Garden City, N.Y.: Doubleday and Company, 1955).

14. These questions plus illustrative replies are in Appendix A.

15. Unfortunately, I do not have information on the total number or proportion of Poles and others unemployed in Detroit. In our sample, 11.4 per cent of workers of Slavic background were unemployed, while the figure for Germans and Britons considered together was 8.5 per cent. These figures are consistent with the model presented.

16. We computed the mean rank scores by the following procedure. First, we assigned points to each group on the basis of every respondent's ratings: 1 point was given to a group every time it was ranked as having the best chance of entering the Grosse Pointe club; 2 points to a group scored as having the second best chance of entering; 3 points, third best chance; and 4 points, least chance. Second, we divided the total score for each group by the number of respondents who actually ranked the group in question. The lower and upper limits of the scores thereby obtained were 1.0 and 4.0, respectively. As rated in turn by Negroes, Slavs, and Germans and Britons together, Negroes were rated as follows: 4.0, 3.9, 4.0; Poles scored 2.7, 2.9, 2.9; Germans, 2.0, 2.0, 1.9; English 1.3, 1.2, 1.2; "any white group" received 2.1, 2.1, 2.0.

In addition, it should be noted that we obtained a rank order distribution identical with the model ranking pattern. Ranking the four groups from best to least chance of acceptance, 45 per cent of the *entire* sample named Britons, Germans, Poles, and Negroes, in that order. There was even greater consensus on the relative standing of individual groups. Specifically, 93 per cent believed that Negroes would have the least chance, 59 per cent felt that the English would have the best chance. Forty-six per cent of the respondents ranked the Germans as second, while 57 per cent thought that Poles would have the third best chance of being accepted.

We may note at this point that the ethnic ranking and class composition of the various ethnic groups were inter-correlated. That is, those with the highest prestige also had the highest proportion of middle-class members, and so on down the line. It should be remembered, however, that no causal relationship is implied. The prestige of an ethnic group does not rest solely on its present class position; the amount of political power held by a group is one of many other factors that must be taken into consideration. And there are examples of ethnic groups that are both largely middle class and low status.

17. Among others, see Emory S. Bogardus, "Social Distance and Its Origins," *Journal of Applied Sociology*, 9 (January-February 1925), 216–26; Daniel Katz and Kenneth Braly, "Racial Stereotypes of One Hundred College Students," *Journal of Abnormal and Social Psychology*, 28 (1933), 280–92; W. Lloyd Warner *et al.*, *Democracy in Jonesville* (New York: Harper and Brothers, 1949), pp. 22, 28–9, 36, 109, 142, 146–8, 165–7; and W. Lloyd Warner and Paul S. Lunt, *The Social Life of a Modern Community* (New Haven: Yale University Press, 1945), pp. 40, 60, 64, and 71.

18. Polish-American sensitivity to its low prestige in Detroit has been analyzed by Arthur E. Wood in his *Hamtramck Then and Now* (New York: Bookman Associates, 1955), pp. 27–8, 38, 173–205.

19. When families continued to use the Polish language at home, they thereby indicated their contribution to sub-community cohesion plus the continuation of that community. A surprisingly large number of workmen and their children used Polish in this manner at the time of study. However, there were undoubtedly far fewer then than in 1945, when a school census indicated the widespread use of both Polish and English languages. See Wood, p. 36.

20. For an excellent study of the Detroit Polish community, see Peter A. Ostafin, "The Polish Community in Transition—A Study of Group Integration as a Function of Symbiosis and Common Definitions" (Unpublished Ph.D. Dissertation, University of Michigan, 1948). Also see Wood.

We also feel that Thomas and Znaniecki's remarks have relevance to the Polish-American community of Detroit:

> The fundamental process which has been going on during this period is the formation of a new Polish-American society out of the fragments separated from Polish society and embedded in American society.

See W. I. Thomas and Florian Znaniecki, *The Polish Peasant in*

Europe and America, Vol. 5 (Chicago: University of Chicago Press, 1918–20), Introduction, p. 9.

21. For the purpose of analysis, we treat Germans and Britons as one. This was made necessary by the paucity of cases in both groups; however, such collapsing of categories is partially warranted by their comparable statuses and by the extremely small differences separating the groups on questions of class consciousness.

22. An interesting topic would be the impact of industrial labor and the American left during the 1930's in Hamtramck, the center of Detroit's Polish community. Wood has alluded to their importance, pp. 60–64, 68, 81, 94, 96.

23. When focusing on generations, we can make a distinction between three types: depression, quasi-depression, and prosperity. A *depression generation* differs from other generations in that its members experienced as late adolescents, or young adults, the catastrophic consequences of economic depression. In this study, all respondents between the ages of 34 and 54 at the time of study (1960) constitute a depression generation, since they grew up during the Great Depression of the 1930's. A *quasi-depression generation* includes a category of working-class respondents who experienced prosperity as young adults but who also witnessed a prolonged period of economic depression in their later years. All workers 54 years of age and older are treated as members of a quasi-depression generation. A *prosperity generation* can be defined as those individuals who reached late adolescence or early adulthood during a period of relative economic prosperity. All respondents under 34 years of age can be treated as part of such a generation. See pp. 87–91.

Samuel Eldersveld studied the formal political power structure of Detroit in 1956-57. He concluded that ethnic background was extremely important in differentiating the attitudes of political party workers at all levels, and rank and file voters in almost all precincts. His data on both the Democratic and Republican parties support our own observations: party workers and the rank and file of English, Scotch, and German background held liberal opinions less frequently than did Poles and Negroes on such questions as socialized medicine. These differences were particularly noticeable within the Democratic party; Samuel Eldersveld, *Political Parties* (Chicago: Rand McNally and Co., 1964), pp. 24–46, 183–219, 474–91.

CHAPTER 7

1. David Street and the author have described the impact of wide-
    spread economic deprivation on Detroit Negroes during the late
    1950's; "Economic Deprivation and Extremism: A Study of Un-
    employed Negroes," *American Journal of Sociology*, 67 (July
    1961), pp. 53–7.

2. In this regard, several observers have noted:

    > The continued presence of the union's headquarters [U.A.W.]
    > and central staff in Detroit, along with the heavy concen-
    > tration of its membership here, has stimulated and facilitated
    > active involvement in local and state politics, from elections
    > for the local municipal positions to those for the highest
    > state offices. Along with the state C.I.O. organization, the
    > U.A.W. . . . [has] systematically attempted to influence the
    > selection of Democratic Party candidates, to find and run
    > candidates where Democrats have rarely or never run before,
    > and generally, they have helped to create a vigorous on-going
    > party structure in the state and have participated within
    > the party organization to push toward goals compatible with
    > the union's political objectives.

    Arthur Kornhauser, Albert J. Mayer, and Harold L. Sheppard,
    When Labor Votes (Detroit: University Books, 1956), p. 17.
    However, Daniel Katz and Samuel Eldersveld have indicated
    that the average voter is unaware of the precinct activities con-
    ducted by both major parties; "The Impact of Local Party Activ-
    ity upon the Electorate," *Public Opinion Quarterly*, 25 (Spring,
    1961), 16–20.

    This lack of cognizance does not mean that the Democratic
    party and its dominant faction, the labor union alliance, fail to
    influence the average voter. We should not forget that during an
    electoral campaign the Democratic party reaches many workmen
    who subsequently forget the contacts. Moreover, the Demo-
    cratic party may affect choice by relating to the voters through
    voluntary associations which are nominally non-political, such as
    church, nationality, and block organizations. In such instances
    of "associational linkage," voters may not be aware of the ultimate
    sources of the political activation, reinforcement, and conversion.

3. Our analysis on Democratic party organization is based largely on Samuel J. Eldersveld's *Political Parties: A Behavioral Analysis* (Chicago: Rand McNally and Company, 1964).

4. When a closed-ended measure of awareness of class position was substituted in place of our measures of class consciousness the evidence proved to be almost identical with the information presented in Table 7-1. Moreover, when we take union membership (among whites only) into account, the pattern of political preference reappears in almost identical form with our Table 7-2. The joint impact of union membership and militancy remains the same. Clearly then, the substitution does not change the findings.

5. Toward the end of the nineteenth century, Engels noted the importance of class consciousness in preparing the working class for successful participation in parliamentary politics. See Friedrich Engels, "English Fabian Socialism," in Karl Marx and Friedrich Engels, *Basic Writings on Politics and Philosophy*, p. 446. At mid-century, Marx had viewed working-class participation in constitutional politics as being a political revolution in and of itself. Somewhat earlier, of course, both Marx and Engels had specified the conditions under which working-class consciousness might contribute to revolutionary behavior. See relevant excerpts from their writings in T. B. Bottomore and Maximilien Rubel, eds., *Selected Writings in Sociology and Social Philosophy*, pp. 184–8.

6. Goetz Briefs, *The Proletariat* (New York: McGraw-Hill Book Company, 1937), p. 96.

7. Richard Centers, *The Psychology of Social Classes* (Princeton: Princeton University Press, 1949).

8. Oscar Glantz, "Class Consciousness and Political Solidarity," *American Sociological Review*, 23 (August 1958), 375–83.

9. Albert W. Jones, *Life, Liberty, and Property*, pp. 315–17.

10. Kornhauser, Mayer, and Sheppard, *When Labor Votes*, p. 43.

11. See Chapter 2, pp. 30–31.

12. Marx indicated that the bourgeoisie would lead in the construction of a new technology, the tools and techniques of capitalism, and the creation of a new division of labor. Both the new technology and division of labor would sweep away ancient prejudices and nationalisms associated with feudalism. Middle classes and working-class people would act in ways consistent with the economic demands of capitalism, itself committed to the use of the most rational production techniques. These in turn would

not allow for economically disruptive practices of the kind associated with nationalism.

In the *Communist Manifesto*, Marx notes:

> Constant revolutionizing of production, uninterrupted disturbance of all social conditions, everlasting uncertainty and agitation distinguish the bourgeois epoch from all earlier ones. All fixed, fast frozen relations, with their train of ancient and venerable prejudices and opinions, are swept away, all new formed ones become antiquated before they can ossify. All that is solid melts into the air, all that is holy is profaned, and man is at last compelled to face with sober senses, his real conditions of life, and his relations with his kind.

See Karl Marx, *Capital, The Communist Manifesto and Other Writings*, pp. 323–5.

13. Frederick L. Schuman, *The Nazi Dictatorship: A Study in Social Pathology and the Politics of Fascism* (New York: Alfred A. Knopf, 1935), pp. 52, 136–8.

14. Hans Gerth, "The Nazi Party: Its Leadership and Composition," in the *American Journal of Sociology*, 45 (January 1940), 517–41.

15. See Schuman, pp. 52, 136. The reader may wonder why I have not referred to those studies which link authoritarianism to a working-class milieu. The reason is that the poor character of the methodology devised to measure and analyze authoritarianism precludes usage of such materials. A number of critiques have made this point. Perhaps most useful in this regard is the analysis by Herbert H. Hyman and Paul B. Sheatsley, " 'The Authoritarian Personality'—A Methodological Critique," found in Richard Christie and Marie Jahoda, *Studies in the Scope and Method of "The Authoritarian Personality"* (Glencoe: The Free Press, 1954), pp. 24–50.

16. Inter-ethnic hostility was measured by recoding the questions used to measure class verbalization. It occurred when respondents expressed feelings of animosity directed toward Negroes, whites, and nationality groups. Of course, these definitions are not exact; and our measurement suffers in that we did not originally design the questions to measure anything other than class consciousness. Still, it would have been foolish to overlook our results.

CHAPTER 8

1. This analysis of Detroit block clubs and local organizations is based on observations made between September 1961 and September 1962. See Street and Leggett, "Economic Deprivation and Extremism: A Study of Unemployed Negroes," *American Journal of Sociology*, 67 (July 1961), 53–7.

2. See the abstract of Louis Wirth's "Urbanism As a Way of Life," *American Journal of Sociology*, 54 (July 1938), 1. Although Wirth did not single out the Negro ghetto as the prototype of the impersonal city, others have.

3. A detailed analysis of problems in the realm of housing is in Robert J. Mowitz and Deil S. Wright, *Profile of a Metropolis* (Detroit: Wayne State University Press, 1962), especially pp. 11–80.

4. For a discussion of neighborhood and block-club organization and activities in Detroit, see Melvin Ravitz, "The Sociology of the Block Club" (Unpublished paper, Department of Sociology, Wayne State University). Also, George Henderson's "The Block Club Movement Within the Detroit Tenth Police Precinct" (Unpublished paper, Community Services Department, Detroit Urban League). For a recent discussion of block clubs and how to organize them, see Willie Thompson and James L. Wood, *A Handbook for Block Clubs* (Berkeley: Bay Area Urban Extension Program, University of California Extension, 1967).

5. A synopsis of Cleague's recent and pessimistic views on the civil rights movement will be found in "Race Relations in 1967," *Monthly Review*, 18 (March 1967), 47–9.

6. There is considerable research on the relationship of economic insecurity to opinions about the economic order. A sampling of this material, much of it compiled during the Great Depression, includes E. A. Rundquist and R. F. Sletto, *Personality in a Depression: A Study in the Measurement of Attitudes* (Minneapolis: University of Minnesota Press, 1936) and O. M. Hall, "Attitudes and Unemployment," *Archives of Psychology*, Vol. 25, No. 165 (1934). Interesting information on political radicalism and economic dislocation can be found in E. W. Bakke, *The Unemployed Man* (New York: E. P. Dutton and Company, 1934); R. Heberle, *Social Movements* (New York: Appleton-Century-

Crofts, 1951); B. Zawdski and P. F. Lazarsfeld, "The Psychological Consequences of Unemployment," *Journal of Social Psychology*, 6 (1935), 224–51; and H. D. Lasswell and D. Blumenstock, *World Revolutionary Propaganda* (New York: Alfred A. Knopf, 1939).

7. See Appendix B for more information on these neighborhoods.

8. In the few cases in which respondents spoke of both kinds of violence, we treated the one mentioned first as the reply. Other responses included "government aid," "much loss of property," "change in parties," "can't happen," "people will accept it," "industrialists will help the people," and "bad consequences."

9. According to data compiled by the Michigan Employment Security Commission, unemployment within the Detroit Metropolitan Area was between 18 and 19 per cent in the summer of 1958. The comparative figure for 1960 was between 7.1 and 8.1 per cent of the total labor force. The percentage of unemployed in our 1960 sample was 7.7 for the total, while among Negroes the figure was 13.3 per cent.

10. When respondents in the east side neighborhood were questioned about the likelihood of a serious depression, 46 per cent of the Negroes felt that one was either imminent or already in progress.

11. In the east side neighborhood only, we asked a number of questions (dealing with the political orientation of these workers) that focused on the desirability of governmental intervention. We developed Guttman types ranging from disapproval of all governmental action, including increasing the number of war contracts given industries in depressed areas, to favoring government ownership of all industries. Political militancy was found to be directly related to expectations of violence. Moreover, unemployed or part-time employed who scored high on the government-intervention scale generally expected that a depression would lead to violent consequences. See David Street and John Leggett, "Economic Deprivation and Extremism: A Study of Unemployed Negroes," *American Journal of Sociology*, 67 (July 1961), 56.

12. Two other primary weaknesses may be mentioned. First, participation in block clubs is high only when the neighborhood or the block faces an emergency. Under non-crisis conditions a small clique takes most of the responsibility for running the club. This group generally develops a propensity to view its opinions as intrinsically more correct than those of the rank and

file, and this in-group/out-group distinction thereby serves as a basis for potential and serious division at times when the clubs are in need of solidarity—for example, when they confront realtors and merchants over business practices.

Second, block clubs suffer from a lack of co-ordination. The neighborhood councils do not always communicate information on what particular block clubs are doing on landlord-renter problems, police-community difficulties, and the like. The result is often unfortunate for the block club trying to go it alone when other clubs may have helped had they been aware of the difficulties encountered by the one unit.

EPILOGUE: FURTHER READINGS

Stanley Weir's "Forces Behind the Reuther-Meany Split," *New Politics,* 5 (Winter, 1966), 13–21.

"Corporate Imperialism for the Poor," Richard A. Cloward and Frances F. Piven, *The Nation,* 205 (October 16, 1967), 366-7.

"Galbraith Predicts Failure for Private Business Efforts to Solve the Cities' Problems," *New York Times,* October 17, 1967, p. 33.

Robert Blauner's "Whitewash over Watts," *Transaction,* Vol. 3 (March/ April 1966), 3-9, 54.

Transaction, Vol. 4 (September 1967) issue contains several articles on "Detroit: Violence on the Urban Frontier": (1) "Black Sociology," Irving Louis Horowitz, 7–8; (2) "Notes on Instant Urban Renewal," Roger Montgomery, 9–12; (3) "Breakdown of Law and Order," Tom Parmenter, 13-22; (4) "Open Letter on White Justice and the Riots," Lee Rainwater, 22-32.

Joyce Ladner discusses "What 'Black Power' Means to Negroes in Mississippi," *Transaction,* Vol. 5 (November 1967), 7–15.

The New York Times (Oct. 30, 1967) article "Ford Stays Shut Despite Accord," illustrates the press view on local plant disputes, p. 15.

Bibliography

Abrams, Mark. "Press, Polls and Votes in Britain Since the 1955 General Elections," *Public Opinion Quarterly*, 21 (1957-8), 543-7.

Alford, Robert R. *Party and Society*, Chicago: Rand McNally and Company, 1963.

Alinsky, Saul. *Reveille for Radicals*, Chicago: University of Chicago Press, 1946.

Allardt, Erik. *Patterns of Class Conflicts and Working-Class Consciousness in Finnish Politics*, Helsinki: Helsinki Institute of Sociology, 1964.

———. "Regional Imbalance and Working-Class Consciousness: An Ecological Study" (a paper presented at the International Congress of Political Science in Paris, September 1961).

———. *Social Struktur och Politisk Aktivitet*, Helsingfors: Soderstrom and Co., 1956.

———. "Traditional and Emerging Radicalism" (mimeographed paper, 1962).

Ayers, William. *The Hong Kong Strikes, 1920-26*, "Papers on China, Regional Studies Seminars," Vol. 4, Cambridge, Mass.: Harvard University Press, 1950.

———. *Shanghai Labor and the May 30th Movement*, "Papers on China, Regional Studies Seminars," Vol. 5, Cambridge, Mass.: Harvard University Press, 1950.

Bakke, E. W. *The Unemployed Man*, New York: E. P. Dutton and Company, 1934.

Barnes, Harry Elmer. *An Introduction to the History of Sociology*, Chicago: University of Chicago Press, 1958.

Battle, Robert III and Horace Sheffield. "Trade Union Leadership

Council: Experiment in Community Action," *New University Thought*, 3 (September-October 1963), 34–41.

Bauer, Otto. *Die Nationalitätenfrage und die Sozialdemokratie*, Wien, I: Brand, 1907.

Bell, Daniel. *The End of Ideology*, Glencoe: The Free Press, 1960.

————. *The New American Right*, New York: Criterion Books, 1955.

Bendix, Reinhard. "The Lower Classes and the Democratic Revolution," *Institute of Industrial Relations Reprint No. 176*, Berkeley: University of California, 1962.

Berger, Bennett. *Working-Class Suburb*, Berkeley and Los Angeles: University of California Press, 1960.

Berle, Adolph A. *Power Without Property, A New Development in American Political Economy*, New York: Harcourt, Brace and Co., 1952.

Bettleheim, Bruno and Morris Janowitz. "Ethnic Tolerance: A Function of Social Control," *Readings in Social Psychology*, Guy E. Swanson, Theodore M. Newcomb, and Eugene L. Hartley, eds., New York: Henry Holt and Company, 1952.

————. *Social Change and Prejudice*, New York: The Free Press of Glencoe, 1964.

Beynon, Erdmann D. "The Hungarian Population of Detroit," *Michigan History*, 21 (Winter, 1937), 89–103.

Bingham, June. "Reinhold Niebuhr in Detroit," *Christian Century*, 78 (March 8, 1961), 279–98.

Blauner, Robert. *Alienation and Freedom*, Chicago: University of Chicago Press, 1964.

————. "Whitewash over Watts," *Trans-Action*, 3 (March-April 1966), 3–9, 54.

Blumer, Herbert. "Collective Behavior," *Principles of Sociology*, Alfred M. Lee, ed., New York: Barnes and Noble, Inc., 1951, pp. 167–282.

Bogardus, Emory S. "Social Distance and Its Origins," *Journal of Applied Sociology*, 9 (January-February 1925), 216–26.

Bottomore, T. B. *Classes in Modern Society*, New York: Pantheon Books, 1966.

Bottomore, T. B. and Maximilien Rubel. *Selected Writings in Sociology and Social Philosophy*, London: Watts and Co., 1956.

Briefs, Goetz. *The Proletariat*, New York: McGraw-Hill Book Company, 1937.

Brooks, Robert F. *When Labor Organizes*, New Haven: Yale University Press, 1942.

Burnham, James. *The Managerial Revolution,* Bloomington: Indiana University Press, 1941.

Cammett, John M. *Antonio Gramsci and The Origins of Italian Communism,* Stanford: Stanford University Press, 1967.

Campbell, Alice Porter. "Bull Moose Movement in Michigan," *Michigan History,* 25 (Winter, 1941), 34–47.

Catlin, George B. *The Story of Detroit,* Detroit: The Detroit *News,* 1923.

Centers, Richard. "The American Class Structure, A Psychological Analysis," *Readings in Social Psychology,* Guy E. Swanson, Theodore M. Newcomb, and Eugene L. Hartley, eds., New York: Henry Holt and Co., 1952.

————. *Psychology of Social Classes,* Princeton, N.J.: Princeton University Press, 1949.

Chinoy, Ely. *Automobile Workers and the American Dream,* Garden City, N.Y.: Doubleday and Company, 1955.

Cloward, Richard A. "Are the Poor Left Out?" *The Nation,* 201 (August 2, 1965), 55–60.

Cloward, Richard A. and Richard Elman. "First Congress of the Poor," *The Nation,* 202 (February 21, 1966), 148–51.

————. "Poverty, Injustice and the Welfare State," *The Nation,* 202 (February 28, 1966), 230–35.

Cloward, Richard A. and Frances Piven. "Birth of a Movement," *The Nation,* 204 (May 8, 1967), 582–8.

————. "Corporate Imperialism for the Poor," *The Nation,* 205 (October 16, 1967), 366–7.

Cole, G. D. H. *A Short History of the British Working Class,* London: George Allen and Unwin, Ltd., 1952.

Conference on Economic Progress, *Poverty and Deprivation in the United States: The Plight of Two-Fifths of a Nation,* Washington: Conference on Economic Progress, 1962.

Cooper, Leigh G. "Influence of the French Inhabitants of Detroit Upon Its Early Political Life," *Michigan History,* 4 (January 1920), 303.

Corey, Lewis. "The Middle Class," *Class, Status and Power,* Reinhard Bendix and Seymour M. Lipset, eds., Glencoe: The Free Press, 1957.

Dancy, John C. "The Negro People in Michigan," *Michigan History,* 24 (Spring, 1940), 221.

Daugherty, Carroll R. *Labor Problems in American Industry,* Boston: Houghton Mifflin Co., 1936.

Dickie, James F. "Reminiscences of Detroit," *Michigan History*, 14 (Autumn, 1930), 579–650.

Draper, Anne. "Unions and the War in Vietnam," *New Politics*, 5 (Summer, 1966), 7–12.

Eldersveld, Samuel. *Political Parties*, Chicago: Rand McNally and Co., 1964.

Engels, Friedrich. "English Fabian Socialism," "Why There Is No Socialist Party in America," Karl Marx and Friedrich Engels, *Basic Writings on Politics and Philosophy*, Lewis S. Feuer, ed., Garden City: Doubleday and Company, Inc., 1959.

Erichsen, Hugo. "My Memories of Old Detroit," *Michigan History*, 17 (Spring, 1933), 208–10.

Faber, Seymour. "When the Recession Came to Detroit," *Dissent*, 6 (Summer, 1959), 250–54.

Fine, Sidney. "Tool and Die Makers Strike of 1933," *Michigan History*, 42 (September 1958), 310–11, 318–19.

Fischer, Ruth. *Stalin and German Communism*, Cambridge, Mass.: Harvard University Press, 1948.

Ford, Clyde. "The French Canadians of Michigan," *Michigan History*, 27 (Spring, 1943), 243–57.

Fountain, Clayton W. *Union Guy*, New York: The Viking Press, 1949.

Franklin, Leo M. "Jews in Michigan," *Michigan History*, 23 (Winter, 1939), 77–92.

Freedman, Ronald, *et al. Principles of Sociology*, New York: Henry Holt and Co., 1952.

Fuller, Earl B. "The Automobile Industry in Michigan," *Michigan History*, 12 (April 1928), 280–96.

Galbraith, John K. *The Affluent Society*, Boston: Houghton Mifflin Company, 1958.

Gay, Peter. *The Dilemma of Democratic Socialism: Eduard Bernstein's Challenge to Marx*, New York: Collier Books, 1962.

Gerth, Hans. "The Nazi Party: Its Leadership and Composition," *American Journal of Sociology*, 45 (January 1940), 517–41.

Glaberman, Martin. "Marxism, the Working Class and Trade Unions," *Studies on the Left*, 4 (Summer, 1964), 65–72.

Glantz, Oscar. "Class Consciousness and Political Solidarity," *American Sociological Review*, 23 (1958), 375–83.

Glazer, Sidney. "The Beginnings of the Economic Revolution in Michigan," *Michigan History*, 34 (September 1950), 193–202.

————. "The Michigan Labor Movement," *Michigan History*, 29 (Spring, 1945), 73–8.

Goldschmidt, Walter. *As You Sow*, Glencoe: The Free Press, 1947.

Gross, Neal. "Social Class Identification in the Urban Community," *American Sociological Review*, 18 (1953), 398–404.

Haber, William, Eugene C. McKean, and Harold C. Taylor. *The Michigan Economy, Its Potential and Its Problems*, Kalamazoo: The W. E. Upjohn Institute for Employment Research, 1959.

Haer, John L. "An Empirical Study of Social Class Awareness," *Social Forces*, 36 (1957), 117–21.

Hall, O. M. "Attitudes and Unemployment," *Archives of Psychology*, Vol. 25, No. 165 (1934).

Hammond, Barbara and J. L. *The Town Labourer, 1760–1832*, Vol. 1 & 2, London: B. Longmans, Green and Co., 1949.

Handlin, Oscar. *The Uprooted*, Boston: Little, Brown and Co., 1952.

Harrington, Michael. *The Other America—Poverty in the United States*, New York: Macmillan Company, 1962.

Heberle, R. *Social Movements*, New York: Appleton-Century-Crofts, 1951.

Heinmann, Eduard. *History of Economic Doctrines*, New York: Oxford University Press, 1964.

Henderson, George. "The Block Club Movement Within the Detroit Tenth Police Precinct" (unpublished paper, Community Services Department, Detroit Urban League).

Hill, Herbert. "Labor Unions and the Negro," *Social Controversy*, William Petersen and David Matza, eds., Belmont, Calif.: Wadsworth Publishing Co., Inc., 1963, pp. 221–33.

Horowitz, Irving Louis. "Introduction: The Sociology of Ludwig Gumplowicz," in Ludwig Gumplowicz, *Outlines in Sociology*, New York: Paine Whitman Publishers, 1963.

————. *Three Worlds of Development*, New York: Oxford University Press, 1966.

————. "Comment . . . Black Sociology," *Trans-Action*, 4 (September 1967), 7–8.

Hoult, Thomas F. and Albert J. Mayer. *The Population Revolution in Detroit*, Detroit: Institute for Regional and Urban Studies, 1963.

Howe, Irving and Lewis Coser. *The American Communist Party*, Boston: Boston Press, 1957.

Hyman, Herbert H. and Paul B. Sheatsley. "'The Authoritarian Personality'—A Methodological Critique," *Studies in the Scope and Method of "The Authoritarian Personality,"* Richard Christie and Marie Jahoda, eds., Glencoe: The Free Press, 1954.

Isaacs, Harold. *The Tragedy of the Chinese Revolution,* Stanford, Calif.: Stanford University Press, 1951.

Jacobs, Paul. *The State of the Unions,* New York: Atheneum, 1963.

Jahoda, Marie Lazarsfeld and Hans Zeisl. *Die Arbeitslosen Von Marienthal,* Leipzig: Verlag Von S. Hirzel, 1933.

Janowitz, Morris. "Black Legions on the March," *America in Crisis,* Daniel Aaron, ed., New York: Alfred A. Knopf, 1952.

Jones, Alfred W. *Life, Liberty and Property,* Philadelphia: J. B. Lippincott Co., 1941.

Katz, Daniel and Kenneth Braly. "Racial Stereotypes of One Hundred College Students," *Journal of Abnormal and Social Psychology,* 28 (1933), 280–92.

Katz, Daniel and Samuel Eldersveld. "The Impact of Local Party Activity Upon the Electorate," *Public Opinion Quarterly,* 25 (Spring, 1961), 16–20.

Kerr, Clark and Abraham Siegel. "The Inter-Industry Propensity to Strike—an International Comparison," *Industrial Conflict,* Arthur Kornhauser, Robert Dubin, and Arthur M. Ross, eds., New York: McGraw-Hill Book Co., 1954.

Kolko, Gabriel. *Wealth and Power in America, An Analysis of Social Class and Income Distribution,* New York: Frederick A. Praeger, 1962.

Kornhauser, Arthur, Albert J. Mayer, and Harold L. Sheppard. *When Labor Votes,* New York: University Books, 1956.

Labor Policies of Employers' Associations in Violation of Free Speech and Rights of Labor, Report of the Committee on Education and Labor, No. 6, 76th Congress, 1st Session, Washington, D.C., 1939, Parts 4–8.

Landecker, Werner S. "Stratification in Urban Society," *Principles of Sociology,* Ronald Freedman *et al.,* New York: Henry Holt and Company, 1952, pp. 449–88.

Lasswell, Harold D. and Dorothy Blumenstock. *World Revolutionary Propaganda,* New York: Alfred A. Knopf, 1939.

Lee, Alfred McClung and Norman D. Humphrey. *Race Riot,* New York: The Dryden Press, 1943.

Lenin, Vladimir I. "What Is To Be Done," *Selected Works,* Vol. 2, New York: International Publishers, 1943.

Lens, Sidney. *The Crisis of American Labor,* New York: The Sagamore Press, 1959.

Lenski, Gerhard E. "American Social Classes, Statistical Strata or Social Groups," *American Journal of Sociology*, 58 (1952), 139–49.

———. *Power and Privilege*, New York: McGraw-Hill Book Co., 1966.

———. *The Religious Factor*, New York: Doubleday and Company, 1961.

Lipset, Seymour M. "Must Tories Always Triumph?" *Socialist Commentary* (November 1960).

———. *Political Man*, Garden City: Doubleday and Company, Inc., 1960.

Lipset, Seymour M., Paul F. Lazarsfeld, Allan M. Barton, and Juan Linz. "The Psychology of Voting: An Analysis of Political Behavior," *The Handbook of Social Psychology*, Vol. 2, Gardner Lindzey, ed., Cambridge, Mass.: Addison-Wesley Publishing Company, Inc., 1954, pp. 1124–75.

Lipset, Seymour M. and Hans Zetterberg. "Social Mobility in Industrial Societies," *Social Mobility in Industrial Society*, Seymour Lipset and Reinhard Bendix, eds., Berkeley and Los Angeles: University of California Press, 1959.

Manis, Jerome G. and Bernard N. Meltzer. "Attitudes of Textile Workers to Class Structure," *American Journal of Sociology*, 60 (July 1954), 30–54.

Mannheim, Karl. "The Problem of Generations," *Essays on the Sociology of Knowledge*, London: Routledge & Kegan Paul, Ltd., 1952.

Marquardt, Frank. "Anxiety Comes to the Auto Capital," *Dissent*, 1 (Summer, 1954), 258–62.

———. "The Auto Worker," *Dissent*, 4 (Summer, 1957), 382–3.

———. "The 'Guaranteed Annual Wage,'" *Dissent*, 2 (Autumn, 1955), 297–8.

Marx, Karl. "The Communist Manifesto," *Capital, The Communist Manifesto, and Other Writings*, Max Eastman, ed., New York: The Modern Library, 1932.

———. "The Eighteenth Brumaire of Louis Bonaparte," *Selected Writings in Sociology and Social Philosophy*, T. B. Bottomore and M. Rubel, eds., London: Watts and Co., 1956.

———. *The German Ideology*, New York: International Publishers, 1947.

———. "Wage, Labor, and Capital," *Selected Works*, Vol. 1, New York: International Publishers, 1933.

Marx, Karl and Frederick Engels. *The Civil War in the United States,* New York: The Citadel Press, 1960.

―――. "Karl Marx to S. Meyer and A. Vogt, April 8, 1870," *On Britain,* Moscow: Foreign Languages House, 1953.

―――. "Letter to Karl Kautsky, November 8, 1884," *Correspondence 1846-1895,* New York: International Publishers, 1946.

Meyer, Alfred G. *Marxism,* Cambridge, Mass.: Harvard University Press, 1954.

Michels, Roberto. *First Lectures in Political Sociology,* Minneapolis: University of Minnesota Press, 1949.

Miljeric, June N. "The Yugoslav People," *Michigan History,* 25 (Autumn, 1941), 358–68.

Miller, Delbert C. and William H. Form. *Industrial Sociology,* New York: Harper and Row, 1964.

Miller, S. M. "Poverty, Race and Politics," *The New Sociology,* Irving Louis Horowitz, ed., New York: Oxford University Press, 1964.

Miller, S. M. and Frank Reissman. "Working-Class Authoritarianism: A Critique of Lipset," with Seymour Lipset's "Reply," *British Journal of Sociology,* 12 (September 1961), 263–81.

Mills, C. Wright. *New Men of Power,* New York: Harcourt, Brace and Co., 1948.

―――. *Power, Politics and People,* New York: Oxford University Press, 1963.

―――. *White Collar,* New York: Oxford University Press, 1951.

Mitrany, David. *Marx Against the Peasant,* Chapel Hill: University of North Carolina Press, 1951.

Montgomery, Roger. "Notes on Instant Urban Renewal," *Trans-Action,* 4 (September 1967), 9–12.

Mowitz, Robert J. and Deil S. Wright. *Profile of a Metropolis,* Detroit: Wayne State University Press, 1962.

Neibuhr, Reinhold. *Leaves from the Notebook of a Tamed Cynic,* Hamden, Connecticut: The Shoestring Press, 1956.

Nevins, Allen. *Ford: The Times, The Man, The Company,* New York: Charles Scribner's Sons, 1954.

Ostafin, Peter A. "The Polish Community in Transition—A Study of Group Integration as a Function of Symbiosis and Common Definitions" (unpublished Ph.D. dissertation, University of Michigan, 1948).

Parker, Michael. "Watts: The Liberal Response," *New Politics,* 5 (Summer, 1965), 41–9.

Parmenter, Tom. "Breakdown of Law and Order," *Trans-Action*, 4 (September 1967), 13–22.

Peck, Sidney. *The Rank and File Leader*, New Haven: College and University Press, 1963.

Perlman, Selig. *A History of Trade Unionism in the United States*, New York: Macmillan Co., 1923.

Pope, Liston. *Millhands and Preachers*, New Haven: Yale University Press, 1941.

Potter, William W. "Fifty Years of Michigan Progress," *Michigan History*, 8 (October 1924), 431–41.

Powell, Elwin H. "Reform, Revolution, and Reaction: A Case of Organized Conflict," *The New Sociology*, Irving Louis Horo-

Preis, Art. *Labor's Giant Step*, New York: Pioneer Publishers, 1964. witz, ed., New York: Oxford University Press, 1964.

Purcell, Theodore. *The Worker Speaks His Mind on Company and Union*, Cambridge, Mass.: Harvard University Press, 1953.

Rainwater, Lee. "Open Letter on White Justice and the Riots," *Trans-Action*, 4 (September 1967), 22–32.

Rankin, Lois. "Detroit Nationality Groups," *Michigan History*, 23 (Spring, 1939), 129–84.

Ravitz, Melvin. "The Sociology of the Block Club" (unpublished paper, Department of Sociology, Wayne State University).

Record, Wilson. *The Negro and the Communist Party*, Chapel Hill: University of North Carolina Press, 1951.

Reissman, Frank. "The Myth of Saul Alinsky," *Dissent*, 14 (July-August 1967), 469–78.

Robinson, Edgar E. *The Presidential Vote, 1896-1932*, Stanford, Calif.: Stanford University Press, 1947.

Rosenberg, Morris. "Perceptual Obstacles to Class Consciousness," *Social Forces*, 32 (October 1953), 22–7.

Rundquist, E. A. and R. F. Sletto. *Personality in a Depression: A Study in the Measurement of Attitudes*, Minneapolis: University of Minnesota Press, 1936.

Sahlins, Marshall D. and Elman R. Service. *Evolution and Culture*, Ann Arbor: University of Michigan Press, 1960.

Sarasohn, Stephan B. and Vera H. *Political Party Patterns in Michigan*, Detroit: Wayne State University Press, 1957.

Schuman, Frederick L. *The Nazi Dictatorship: A Study in Social Pathology and the Politics of Fascism*, New York: Alfred A. Knopf, 1935.

Schumpeter, Joseph A. *Social Class and Imperialism, Two Essays,* New York: Meridian Books, 1955.

Schwertzer, Arthur. *Big Business in the Third Reich,* Bloomington: Indiana University Press, 1964.

Sheppard, Harold L., Louis A. Ferman, and Seymour Faber. *Too Old to Work—Too Young to Retire: A Case Study of a Permanent Plant Shutdown,* Senate Special Committee on Unemployment Problems, 86th Congress, 1st Session, Washington, D.C., 1960.

Silberman, Charles H. *Crisis in Black and White,* New York: Random House, 1964.

Starring, Charles R. "Hazen S. Pingree: Another Forgotten Eagle," *Michigan History,* 32 (June 1948), 129–50.

Stockton, William. "Fifty Years of Industrial Progress in Detroit," *Michigan History,* 10 (October 1926), 609–10.

Stouffer, Samuel A., Louis Guttman, Edward A. Suchman, Paul F. Lazarsfeld, Shirley A. Star, and John A. Clausen. *Measurement and Prediction,* Studies in Social Psychology in World War II, Princeton: Princeton University Press, 1950.

Sturmthal, Adolf. *Workers Councils,* Cambridge, Mass.: Harvard University Press, 1964.

Sward, Keith T. *The Legend of Henry Ford,* New York: Rinehart, 1948.

Thompson, E. P. *The Making of the English Working Class,* New York: Pantheon Books, 1963.

Thompson, Willie and James L. Wood. *A Handbook for Block Clubs,* Berkeley: Bay Area Urban Extension Program, University of California Extension, 1967.

Touraine, Alain. *La Conscience ouvrière,* Paris: Le Seuil, 1966.

Trotsky, Leon. *History of the Russian Revolution,* New York: Doubleday and Company, Inc., 1959.

Ulam, Adam. *The Unfinished Revolution,* Cambridge, Mass.: Harvard University Press, 1960.

Warner, W. Lloyd, *et al. Democracy in Jonesville,* New York: Harper and Brothers, 1949.

Warner, W. Lloyd and Paul Stunt. *The Social Life of a Modern Community,* New Haven: Yale University Press, 1945.

Weir, Stanley. "Forces Behind the Reuther-Meany Split," *New Politics,* 5 (Winter, 1966), 13–21.

Widick, B. J. *Labor Today,* Boston: Houghton Mifflin, 1964.

———. "The UAW: Limitations of Unionism," *Dissent,* 6 (Autumn, 1959), 446–54.

Wilensky, Harold. "Class, Class Consciousness and American Workers," *Institute of Industrial Relations Reprint No. 283,* Berkeley: University of California, 1966.

———. *Intellectuals in Labor Unions,* Glencoe: The Free Press, 1956.

Wilensky, Harold and Hugh Edwards. "The Skidder," *American Sociological Review,* 24 (April 1959), 215–26.

Wilensky, Harold and Charles Lebeaux. *Industrial Society and Social Welfare,* New York: The Free Press of Glencoe, 1965.

Williams, Walter. "Cleveland's Crisis Ghetto," *Trans-Action,* 4 (September 1967), 33–42.

Wilson, James Q. *Negro Politics,* Glencoe: The Free Press, 1960.

Wittfogel, Karl. *Oriental Despotism,* New Haven: Yale University Press, 1957.

Wood, Arthur E. *Hamtramck Then and Now,* New York: Bookman Associates, 1955.

Zawdski, B. and P. F. Lazarsfeld. "The Psychological Consequences of Unemployment," *Journal of Social Psychology,* 6 (1935), 224–51.

Zeitlin, Maurice. "Economic Insecurity and the Political Attitudes of Cuban Workers," *American Sociological Review,* 31 (February 1966), 35–42.

Name Index

Aaron, Daniel, 203
Abrams, Mark, 26, 190, 194
Allardt, Eric, 74, 210
Apostle, Richard, 206
Ayers, William, 210

Bagwell, Paul D., 120
Bakke, E. W., 225
Barnes, Harry E., 197
Baronas, Albert, 206
Barton, Allan M., 78, 88, 212
Battle, Robert, III, 215
Bauer, Otto, 32–4, 197
Bell, Daniel, 212
Bendix, Reinhard, 197, 216
Berger, Bennett, 205
Berle, Adolph A., 212
Bernstein, Eduard, 211
Bettleheim, Bruno, 216
Beynon, Erdmann D., 202
Bingham, June, 202
Blalock, Hubert M., 181, 182, 191–2
Blauner, Robert, 154
Blumenstock, Dorothy, 226
Blumer, Herbert, 206
Bogardus, Emory S., 220
Bottomore, T. B., 193, 223
Braly, Kenneth, 220
Briefs, Goetz, 124, 223
Brooks, Robert F., 192
Browder, Earl, 25

Bryan, William Jennings, 45

Campbell, Alice P., 201
Catlin, George B., 199
Centers, Richard, 26–7, 124, 194, 215, 223
Chavez, Cesar, 145
Chinoy, Ely, 218–19
Christie, Richard, 224
Clark, Joseph, 211
Cleague, Reverend Albert, 138, 225
Cloward, Richard, 154
Cole, G. D. H., 70, 71, 208
Conant, James, 216
Cooper, Leigh G., 200
Corey, Lewis, 36, 38, 197
Coser, Lewis, 194, 197, 203
Coughlin, Father Charles E., 52

Dancy, John C., 203
Daugherty, Carroll R., 192
Debs, Eugene V., 45
Dickie, James F., 200
Driscoll, David, 206
Dubin, Robert, 190

Eastman, Max, 192
Edwards, Hugh, 94, 216
Eisenhower, Dwight D., 54
Eldersveld, Samuel, 206, 221, 222–3
Engels, Friedrich, 31, 32, 69, 70, 71, 73, 77–8, 125, 196, 197, 208,

Subject Index

affluence, viii, 18–19, 30–31, 78
affluent society, 78–9
agrarian culture, 63
agrarian region, 7, 10, 11, 17, 62, 63, 65, 66, 73, 74, 146; definition of, 10–11
agrarian sub-culture, 29
agrarian-industrial countries, 69
agrarian-industrial mobility: defined, 10; as source of working-class consciousness, 9 ff.
agrarian-industrial society, 10
Agricultural Farm Workers Organizing Committee, 145
agricultural workers, 66, 145–8
Akron sit-down strikes, 6, 16, 24, 25, 74
Allen Park, Michigan, 54
America First, 51
American labor, character of, 20, 21, 24, 25
American Motors Corporation, 56
anarcho-syndicalism, 72
Anglo-Saxons, in Detroit: and Depression generation, 116–17; employment status, 107; ethnic disintegration, 114; and inter-ethnic prejudice, 219–20; as mainstream working class, 99 ff.,

114; status rank, 109; in survey sample, 174–80
antagonistic relations, at workplace, 20
anti-capitalism, 52, 78, 126
anti-Semitism, 52, 126
anti-Semitic organizations, 51
Appalachia, 11, 63
Appalachians, 73
aristocracy, and industrialization, 207
Austria, 126
Austro-Hungarian Empire, 32
authoritarianism, 224
automation, 7, 9, 55, 60, 77, 138, 146, 147, 149, 214; and unions, 57, 59
automobile firms, 55–6
automotive revolution, 44
auto workers, 24, 55

backward countryside, 71
bargaining, 22, 97, 149
Belgium, 124
Berlin, 126
Big 3 auto companies, 149
Birmingham, England, 16
Black Legion, 51
Black Power, 154
black underdog, 153

243